To
Sir David Attenborough,
who has been my inspiration

AN EXPLORER'S NOTEBOOK

OTHER BOOKS BY TIM FLANNERY

The Weather Makers

Mammals of New Guinea

Tree Kangaroos: A Curious Natural History
with R. Martin, P. Schouten and A. Szalzay

*Possums of the World: A Monograph of the
Phalangeroidea* with P. Schouten

Mammals of the South West Pacific and Moluccan Islands

Watkin Trench 1788 (ed.)

The Life and Adventures of John Nicol, Mariner (ed.)

Throwim Way Leg

The Birth of Sydney

*Terra Australis: Matthew Flinders' Great Adventures in the
Circumnavigation of Australia* (ed.)

The Eternal Frontier

The Explorers

A Gap in Nature with P. Schouten

Astonishing Animals with P. Schouten

Chasing Kangaroos

The Future Eaters

Now or Never

Here on Earth

Among the Islands

TIM FLANNERY

AN EXPLORER'S NOTEBOOK

ESSAYS ON LIFE, HISTORY & CLIMATE

Atlantic Monthly Press

New York

All photographs used in this book are from the author's collection.
Drawing on page 9 by Peter Schouten.
Grateful thanks to the State Library of Victoria for assistance with the John Audubon image on page 206.

"Getting to Know Them" first appeared in the *New York Review of Books*, April 2010. "A Heroine in Defense of Nature" first appeared in the *New York Review of Books*, November 2012. "After the Future" is excerpted from "After the Future: Australia's New Extinction Crisis," *Quarterly Essay*, issue 48, November 2012.

First published in Australia in 2007 by The Text Publishing Company.

Printed in the United States of America

ISBN 978-0-8021-2231-5
eBook ISBN: 978-0-8021-9279-0

Atlantic Monthly Press
an imprint of Grove/Atlantic, Inc.
154 West 14th Street
New York, NY 10011

Distributed by Publishers Group West

www.groveatlantic.com

14 15 16 17   10 9 8 7 6 5 4 3 2 1

Contents

PART THREE
Climate: 2006–2007

Introduction

Publishing a collection of my essays that spans more than twenty years evokes mixed feelings. Excavating the earliest ones from the archives and rereading them felt rather like discovering a photograph of a much younger me engaged in what was then a passionate pursuit, but which today is the stuff of fond memories and objective interest. At times I was pleasantly surprised by my passion and articulateness, but more often I felt embarrassed by the naivety, impatience and assumed self-assuredness of that young man. Words have a way of trapping you—fossilising you—at a point in time, but thankfully new words can reverse that process.

The earliest pieces were written by a young researcher fascinated with kangaroos, fossils and Australia's past. Then there are several longer essays written by a biologist exploring the rainforests of Melanesia, hoping to discover new mammals and understand the forests' ecological complexity. And finally there's a recent essay by a climate change campaigner trying to come to terms with how the climate problem is transforming the world and our societies.

I would argue that there are natural links between these three superficially different career phases. Exploring Australia's fossil record and the evolution of kangaroos led me to realise that rainforests were the ancestral habitat of much of Australia's flora and fauna. If I was ever to understand the continent's fossil record,

I felt that I'd need to study living rainforests. And where better than New Guinea, where various mammal lineages known only as fossils in Australia continue to survive? Doing this led me to an acute awareness of the power of climate to influence life on Earth, and from there I felt a need to understand contemporary climate change.

But there is another thread running through these explorations in time and space: a strong desire to understand why things are as they are has always motivated me. Why do kangaroos—alone among large mammals—hop, and why have they been so successful in Australia? How many kinds of tree kangaroo are there, and are any endangered? Why do we love as we do? Asking questions such as these is something I am compelled to do. Indeed, my curiosity has been my scientific north star and, while it may encompass some free-thought associations, it has guided me throughout a fulfilling career in science.

A large section of this book comprises reviews I've written of other people's work. Originally published in the *New York Review of Books* and *The Times Literary Supplement*, these exercises in writing have been especially important to my development. Book reviewing is a privilege, and to be able to pen a leisurely review of 4000 words which permits a broad exploration of a topic, is a rare privilege indeed. It forces one to master at a deep level what is being said by the author, and to try to penetrate how a book has been constructed. While a reviewer is expected to convey his or her views, this has always remained secondary. At the heart of good reviewing, I feel, is simple *explication de texte*.

Climate change has become such a central preoccupation for me that I've penned an essay for this book, reflecting on how our human response to the problem has evolved over the past two years. Because of my wide travels and engagement with so many different people over this time, I've been fortunate enough to see how our politics and science have evolved. Indeed, the developments have been so profound that I believe a true revolution in public understanding of the issue has occurred, and with it a new willingness to tackle the problem.

PART ONE

In the Field
1985–2002

Beginnings

FROM *Country: A Continent, a Scientist & a Kangaroo*, 2004

In late November 1975, I temporarily set aside work at the museum and set out to see my country. My friend Bill and I left Melbourne with a few dollars in our pockets, intent on circumnavigating the continent at the height of summer.

I had decided to use the trip to collect specimens of comparative anatomy. To this end, and blissfully unaware of the need for a permit even to touch a native animal killed on the roadside, my bike was equipped with a small strap-on esky behind the pillion seat, inside of which rattled a large and gruesome-looking defleshing knife. I had thought far enough ahead to decide that I would donate any specimens collected to the museum, but more immediate issues had evaded consideration.

We headed west for Adelaide and then Perth, and it was only when we stopped, roadside, beside my first intended specimen—a splendid male western grey as large as myself—and set to work with my knife, that it occurred to me that other travellers in the South Australian outback might find such activities unsettling. Almost as soon as the thought formed in my mind the rumble of an approaching car was heard and, suddenly embarrassed at the spectacle I presented, I walked briskly away from the prone roo, whistling into the air and trying to hide the 50-centimetre-long knife behind my back.

Ever tolerant, Bill agreed that we should camp nearby so I could perform the gruesome deed under the cover of darkness. After eating Irish stew from our billy I set out, parking my bike in front of the carcass with the headlight on so that I could see what I was doing. The job was made unduly difficult because I had neglected to sharpen my sabre, and after a long, bloodied struggle it became evident that to retrieve the all-important skull I would have to use the weight of the carcass to separate the neck muscles. Wet with blood and lurching under the full weight of the dead marsupial, I was so preoccupied that I didn't hear the approaching rumble until it was too late. As the car accelerated past I glimpsed the family inside, horror-struck, mouths agape, staring at the frenzied bikie who was waltzing drunkenly with a disembowelled kangaroo on a lonely country road. As they disappeared into the distance I finally detached the head, after which I impinged on Bill's good humour yet again by boiling it, to remove the flesh, in our all-purpose billy.

Although our route kept us close to the coast, the green fringe of the continent soon gave way to the muted colours of the interior. It is surprising how narrow that life-giving fringe is. Nowhere in Australia is far from the outback, and every centimetre of the country is touched at some time or other by its winds, dust and flies. The flat dry inland was an utterly unfamiliar landscape, and one for which we were ill-prepared, for the Guzzis were possibly the worst bikes to take on such a trip. Mine did not even have air filters, instead sporting elegant bell-mouths on its carburettors. But we didn't care. We were nineteen, and we were free.

On the Nullarbor, nothing among the low blue-tinged bushes stretching to the horizon stood higher than my knees. The sun baked our skin and the mirage ate up the distance, creating a sense of going nowhere. For hour after hour there was nothing but a road and a line of power poles stretching in both directions—a scar through the blue-green of the saltbush—with no sign of life.

But life there was, for the locusts were swarming. The first we came across were tiny and struck our legs like bullets—painful even beneath leather boots. The next swarm, still wingless, was larger and could leap a little higher, but their bodies were softer. The lot after that had sprouted wings, and they struck anywhere. Driving into a locust cloud at 120 kilometres per hour was like driving into a living hailstorm. Any exposed skin was soon stinging with pain, and we struggled to see the highway ahead through visors smeared with the white and yellow fluid of squashed insects.

Then there was a sign: Head of the Bight. We followed the dirt track, fatigued as the heat and the stifling air caught up with us. We got off our bikes and walked a few metres to where the endless plain suddenly ceased, as if sliced by a sabre far sharper than my own.

After days of unvarying flatness the terror of the crumbling vertical cliff at our feet was compounded by the Southern Ocean, which raged with such force at its base that I could feel the shock of the waves through my boots. Its booms made me stumble involuntarily backwards to the heat, flatness and still air of the inland.

As we rode on we discovered other living things in that seemingly desolate landscape: an emu with a stately stride, a red kangaroo lying in the shade of an insignificant bush. Close to the Western Australian border, mounds began to appear. They marked the burrows of southern hairy-nosed wombats, and some of them were large enough to crawl down. I squeezed head-first into one, vainly hoping to spot a wombat, and was surprised at how cool it was inside. Another chance to venture further underground soon arose. Cocklebiddy Cave is a huge cavern lying beneath the Nullarbor Plain a little to the north of the road. We parked our bikes before clambering down to a yawning pit. It was an awesome space, cool and gloomy as a cathedral, but what fascinated me most was the scattering of small bones, mostly of native mice and rats, which had become extinct on the Nullarbor only thirty or forty years earlier.

We paused just east of Kalgoorlie to admire the knotted, greasy trunks of the gimlet gums, and strode over the thin crust of dried moss and lichen, which along with the last flowers of springtime suggested that this could sometimes be a gentle land. But now it was flat and dusty, the mallee a maze of uniformity where you could easily get lost. Among the knotted trunks we saw lizards and birds, and more of that subtle beauty that is so characteristically Australian—a warty grey mallee-root, a gum tree shedding its old bark in flakes and fine strips. Then, in a small clearing, we stumbled upon an arrangement of mouldering sticks on the ground, and some sturdier branches still standing. It was the remains of an ancient gunyah, though how long the bough shelter had lain decaying there we could not tell, nor could we fathom why an Aborigine had chosen that obscure place to rest. Certainly it was of a size to allow one person only in its shade.

Over the years the vision of that gunyah has frequently returned to me, and I've imagined a solitary Aboriginal hunter returning to it with a catch of rabbit-sized marsupials, to spend the night in comfort. For someone who had never met an Aborigine, and who had spent their life amid the European grandeur of Melbourne, that gunyah came as a deep shock, for it put my society in context and made the Aboriginal occupation of Australia a palpable, recent reality.

Australia's Oldest Marsupial?

Australian Natural History, SPRING 1985

Reconstructing fossil animals is a great paleontological pastime. For many years adults and children alike have marvelled at the insights that reconstructions provide about the life of past epochs. There is, however, much misunderstanding about how such reconstructions are made. Indeed some creationists have been quick to exploit this misunderstanding and cite such works as attempts by scientists to mislead the public. The reconstruction presented here (drawn by Peter Schouten) is the result of considerable research and the story behind it illustrates how scientific reconstructions are made.

The most important thing to realise about this drawing is that it is a hypothesis; it is based as much on the inferred relationships of the fossil animal as it is on the actual fossil jaw fragment, containing three teeth, found at Lightning Ridge.

The group of paleontologists currently working on the Lightning Ridge mammal jaw agree that it represents a monotreme and that it probably belongs to a group of animals ancestral to the only living monotremes—the platypus and echidnas. This is the single most important piece of information used in guiding our reconstruction. Its importance lies in the fact that it indicates, in a very real way, that the Lightning Ridge animal is not extinct—it

has simply changed. The living echidnas and platypus are the descendants of the group to which the Lightning Ridge fossil belonged. Thus its genetic material has been handed down, generation after generation for over 120 million years.

But how do we determine which features of the platypus and echidnas were present in their common ancestor (represented by the Lightning Ridge fossil) and which have developed since?

Some features of monotremes are unique among mammals and were presumably present in their common ancestor. These include the presence of a skin-covered bill, rich in nerve endings, and the presence of a spur on the hind foot. These structures are present in both the platypus and echidnas (although the bill is specialised in both forms). If they were *not* present in the common ancestor of both families, then we must assume that these otherwise unique structures were independently developed in both the platypus and echidnas. But this is highly unlikely and it is much more probable that these features were present in the ancestral monotreme.

This kind of deductive reasoning can be used to determine the probable nature of many aspects of our fossil beast. We have, for instance, used such information to reconstruct the snout, eye, ear, tail, stance and limbs of the Lightning Ridge mammal.

Of course there are aspects of the fossil mammal's form that we cannot know. For instance, did it possess horns? It is possible that it did, but because all its descendants lack such structures we have no evidence for their existence and thus have not included them. And because we have not included features (such as horns) for which we have no data, this reconstruction is a conservative estimate of what the animal might have looked like. It includes only the features likely to have been present in the ancestral monotreme.

And what about the one piece of hard evidence that we

have—the jaw fragment? All of our information about the animal's relationships is of course derived from this specimen, and it also tells us the animal's approximate size, a little about the shape of the snout and something of its diet. All of this information (except that relating to diet) is included in the reconstruction.

The reconstruction, therefore, represents a visual summary of the paleontologists' knowledge of the animal's relationships. The fossil jaw itself provides only a small piece of direct data used in the drawing. It is what the jaw tells us about the kind of animal that possessed it (in this case a primitive monotreme) that is important. Only with the discovery of more complete fossils can we rigorously test this hypothesis. It is clear, however, that alternative hypotheses could lead to different reconstructions.

Journey to the Stars

Australian Natural History, SPRING 1987

In April 1987 a joint expedition from the Australian Museum and the Papua New Guinea Division of Wildlife filled in one of the few remaining 'blank spots' in our knowledge of the fauna of New Guinea. The expedition, consisting of myself, Hal Cogger and Lester Seri, travelled to the Star Mountains in far western Papua New Guinea with the purpose of surveying the mammals, reptiles and birds of this region, which until then had remained largely unknown.

Since they were first named in 1910, the Star Mountains have fascinated explorers and naturalists alike. But until 1965 they remained as inaccessible as the celestial bodies that are their namesakes, and it is ironic that humanity had well and truly entered the space age before the jagged peaks of the 'Stars' (Scorpion, Capella and the Antares) had been visited. And it was not for lack of trying that they remained unexplored. The renowned 1936–37 Archbold Expedition from the American Museum of Natural History made a determined attempt to ascend the Stars and nearby ranges, but the loss of their aircraft meant that they could push no further than the foothills. The 1965 British Climbing Expedition that finally conquered Capella and Scorpion took six months and many aerial resupply drops before they were successful. Twenty-two years would elapse between the first ascent and our visit, and yet during this time the Stars' vertebrate fauna would remain unseen and unknown.

Our opportunity to visit the Star Mountains came through the commitment of the Ok Tedi Mining Company Ltd (OTML). The company has created one of the world's largest gold and copper mines at Mount Fubilan in the southern foothills of the Star Mountains. The terrain is unbelievably difficult to negotiate, with 339 rainy days per year and frequent landslides. Because of the size of their project, and the unique environment within which it is situated, OTML has gone to considerable lengths to ensure that no long-term environmental damage will ensue. Our expedition would be an expensive one, and was in a region in which the mine would have only a minor impact. OTML, however, could see the advantage of having baseline data from the area, and thus fully supported our proposal.

Even with the help of OTML, it is not easy to reach the Stars. To walk from the mine site would take over a week. A round trip by helicopter takes forty-five minutes, but it has its own difficulties and dangers. We chose to use the helicopter, but this left us with many problems to resolve. We had never seen our proposed landing site on Mount Capella, and didn't know if it was suitable for landing or had drinking water nearby. We didn't know about local weather conditions (which we later found to be treacherous) and the helicopter would be operating near its altitudinal limit. It was clearly essential to carry out an extensive reconnaissance of the area, both to test the helicopter at high altitudes and to inspect the terrain and weather.

We discovered that the maximum load the chopper could safely carry was 160 kilograms, and that the weather was so changeable that flying could be called off at any moment. Thus equipment for each load had to be chosen carefully. It was decided that I should travel up first. More than half the load would be taken up by my bodyweight alone. With the remaining seventy-five kilograms, I had to include clothes, personal equipment, a tent and enough food to last for a week or more in case the weather closed in and left me stranded.

Stepping out of the helicopter onto the herbfield that was our chosen campsite was like entering another world. Twenty-five minutes before, I had been standing in the noisy, crowded mining town of Tabubil. The herbfield where I now found myself, called Dokfuma, was silent and freezing. Mist was still hanging over much of the tiny valley, but through it I could glimpse the mossy, gnarled southern pines that ringed the area. A tiny frog called from a moss mound, and nearby I could hear the distinctive beating of wings. These belonged to the majestic MacGregor's bird of paradise (*Macgregoria pulchra*), which remained hidden in the mist.

For a short time I felt like the loneliest person on earth, standing in a dank and almost silent valley, in a spot where perhaps no human had stood before. As the faint sound of the returning helicopter grew louder, I was reminded that there was work to be done. Our time was limited; and before long a camp had to be set up, equipment sorted and made serviceable, and traps put down. I quickly remembered that Dokfuma is at 3200 metres above sea level, as the smallest exertion left me gasping for breath and feeling altitude sick.

Over the week we spent at Dokfuma, we slowly became familiar with its topography and plant and animal life. The mixed vegetation of the small valley is a testament to the intermediate position of New Guinea. Many of the trees were southern pines, with *Dacrycarpus* (similar to the Huon pines of Tasmania), *Phyllocladus* (celery-top pine) and *Papuacedrus* (native cedar) species being the most common. The nearest relatives of these trees are today found in Tasmania, New Zealand and South America and they are evidence of Gondwanan connections. Yet among these relics grew some surprising newcomers: a beautiful red-flowered *Rhododendron* of Asian origin, epiphytic orchids of the genus *Dendrodium*, and a small umbrella tree (*Schefflera* sp.) that attracted flocks of small green parrots.

Each day the camp was enlivened by visits from MacGregor's bird of paradise, which is the least known member of its family. This striking crow-sized bird fearlessly approached our camp and after observing us would fly—or more often glide—off with the characteristically loud 'whoosh' made by its wing feathers. As it hopped about among the branches of its favourite food tree (*Dacrycarpus*), its extraordinary orange eye-wattles would wobble comically. MacGregor's bird of paradise is only found on the highest peaks of the Snow, Star and Owen Stanley mountains, and its fearlessness, large size and restricted distribution make it vulnerable to any kind of habitat disturbance or exploitation. Other birds that were constant camp visitors included the Snow Mountains mannikin (*Lonchura montana*), alpine pipit (*Anthus gutteralis*) and grey-headed thrush (*Turdus poliocephalus*). Droppings of the dwarf cassowary (*Casuarius bennetti*) were also seen in a small glade.

The tiny frog that I had heard on my first morning turned out to be one of the most interesting finds of the expedition. On some of the other high peaks of New Guinea, only one species of frog (family Microhylidae) is present. At Dokfuma, two microhylid species occur. Each has its distinct call and habits, one preferring clear ground among the ferns and herbs, the other preferring the forest edge or moss mounds. Both species appear to be undescribed, while the only reptile that we found in the area, a small black skink, is related to a form that occurs on a number of high peaks in the New Guinean cordillera.

The mammal fauna of Dokfuma was harder to find, but also had its share of surprises. On our first afternoon after setting up camp, the three local men that accompanied us had gone hunting with a dog. In the distance we could hear the uncanny howling so typical of New Guinean dogs when they've located an animal, and so we awaited their return with interest. Griem, our most active and diminutive hunter, arrived first with a large *billum* (string bag) slung across his chest.

'D'bol!' he ejaculated, as he opened the *billum* to reveal a large brown tree kangaroo. I became increasingly excited as I examined the animal, for it looked unlike any tree kangaroo I had seen before. While clearly related to Doria's tree kangaroo (*Dendrolagus dorianus*), which is common in eastern New Guinea, it differed in a number of ways. Had we discovered a race of tree kangaroos unique to the Star Mountains? Only time and a thorough study, now underway, will resolve that question.[*]

In my excitement at examining the animal, I had quite overlooked a second man, Serapiap, who was carrying a small brown ball of fur. It turned out to be a nearly independent young tree kangaroo. 'Capella', as he was soon named, became our constant companion and camp mascot.

On some still mornings the eerie chorused howling of New Guinean wild dogs drifted in across the misty valley. Signs of their presence in the form of well-worn trails and droppings were abundant, yet we never sighted one of these shy animals.

---

[*] The distinct tree kangaroo was subsequently named *Dendrolagus dorianus stellarum*.

Shortly after dark, Dokfuma's most abundant mammal inhabitants became active. The rats of the alpine herbfields come in many shapes and sizes. We found three different kinds. The most common is a species of *Rattus*, and not very different to look at from the bush rats found in Australia. It is, however, only half the size of these and clothed in long luxuriant fur. It may well be unique to the Star Mountains and is possibly an unnamed species. Only slightly less common than this animal is a mosaic-tailed rat. This handsome beast may also be an undescribed species, as it doesn't resemble closely any mosaic-tailed rat that I have seen from elsewhere in New Guinea. A baby mosaic-tailed rat was found in a moss nest in a small tree around the herbfield margin. Towards the end of our stay we found the third rodent species. It was a tree mouse (*Pogonomelomys ruemmleri*) that is known from other high mountain peaks in New Guinea. It is a curious little animal with a short face and large eyes, and a prehensile tail with a grasping tip for climbing about in low bushes and trees.

Only two additional mammal species were obtained during our stay. One was a tiny marsupial, the long-tailed pygmy possum (*Cercartetus caudatus*), which is common in New Guinea's high mountains. The other was a tiny bent-winged bat (*Miniopterus macrocneme*), which was attracted to our camp at night by the innumerable moths that flocked to our kerosene lamp. Very few bats occur high in New Guinea's mountains, so it was surprising to be visited nightly by these tiny insectivores.

As the time drew near to leave Dokfuma, we again began to wonder if our departure would be delayed by bad weather. But the morning of the appointed day broke clear and sunny, and our evacuation was effected without incident. By the time the last of us had arrived back in the hot and humid mining town of Tabubil, it was easy to believe that Dokfuma had been a dream. Dokfuma is such a different place, an 'island' of alpine plants and freezing peaks in a sea of tropical verdure. For the zoologists of the expedition, our journey to this unique environment had been as exciting as travelling to the heavenly stars themselves.

Skinning a possum on Woodlark Island, Papua New Guinea, 1987.
These creatures are caught by the local people as food, and I paid those
who would bring me their catch to skin and sample.

Prickled, Not Pricked

Australian National History, AUTUMN 1989

When Europeans first encountered Australia's monotremes—the platypus and short-beaked echidna—they were indeed baffled. However, we were, and in many respects still are, not the only people to be beguiled by these extraordinary egg-laying mammals. New Guinea's own monotreme, the long-beaked echidna (*Zaglossus bruijni*), poses a prickly problem for village naturalists.

In contrast to the other mammals they are familiar with, both male and female echidnas lack any sign of external genitalia. Young are hardly ever seen and the long-beaked echidna's means of reproduction remains a mystery to nearly all. Tavade hunters from Central Province believe that the long-beaked echidna reproduces by plunging a long, tube-like organ into the ground and bleeding through it. The young forms from a clot of blood, and the parent returns periodically to feed it urine and more blood, produced from the same extraordinary organ. The young digs its way out of the subterranean chamber only when nearly full-grown. Although seemingly farfetched, this account may be based on actual observations. Male long-beaked echidnas have a large and bizarre penis (it has four lobes at the end), which is usually retracted completely into the body. Perhaps some Tavade hunter was lucky enough to observe a male echidna rampant, so to speak, and deduced the rest.

The people of Hatam in the Arfak Mountains of far western Irian Jaya also seem to have got only half of the picture. They believe that the long-beaked echidna hatches from an egg laid by the black-billed sicklebill (*Drepanornis albertisii*), a bird of paradise whose beak bears an uncanny resemblance to the echidna's bill. The egg that hatches the echidna is one that has fallen from the nest onto the ground. There, its contents undergo the necessary metamorphosis. Although the Hatam people have discovered that echidnas do indeed hatch from eggs, the rest of the animal's reproductive cycle remains a mystery to them and is subject to fanciful interpretation.

Perhaps the strangest echidna story belongs to the Etolo people of the Southern Highlands Province, for they believe that echidnas do not reproduce at all! The Etolo distinguish four or five kinds of echidnas which they name after game animals such as 'tree-kangaroo echidna' or 'cuscus echidna', and claim that very old animals actually transform into echidnas: the animal's head is slowly resorbed into the echidna's rear end, its tail shortens and stiffens to become the echidna's bill, and then the spines develop. Even this extraordinary transformation sequence may be based upon some observation of wildlife. The Etolo have doubtless seen insects undertake equally remarkable transformations, and an echidna's feet *do* seem to face slightly backwards, perhaps suggesting some previous reversal in direction!

All these cogitations remind me of a tenth-century English riddle. In translation, it goes something like this:

I'm a strange creature, for I
satisfy women,
a service to the neighbours! No-
one suffers
at my hands except for my
slayer.
I grow very tall, erect in a bed,
I'm hairy underneath. From
time to time
a beautiful girl, the brave
daughter
of some churl dares to hold me,
grips my russet skin, robs me of
my head
and puts me in the pantry. At
once that girl
with plaited hair who has
confined me
remembers our meeting. Her
eye moistens.
What am I?

The riddle works because our imagination is pricked by a phantom. Indeed, it looms so large that other explanations are overlooked. Perhaps the long-beaked echidna, with its multitude of prickles yet seemingly 'unpricked', has played a similar trick in the minds of many Melanesians. Oh how straightforward and boring life would be if echidnas had external genitals like the rest of us, and we could see straight away that the answer to the riddle was an onion!

Emperor, King and Little Pig:
The Three Rats of Guadalcanal

Australian Natural History, AUTUMN 1991

This is the story of three rats, two apes and an island. The three rats and the island are named in the title; the two apes are myself and an English naturalist, Charles Morris Woodford.

After chasing rats through the undergrowth for three years Woodford was made colonial administrator of the Solomon Islands. But that was in 1888, and in those days few Britons, except for eccentric biologists, had ventured to the Solomons. The rat-catcher/administrator left us an account of his days as a biologist entitled *A naturalist among the head hunters, being an account of 3 visits to the Solomon Islands in the years 1886, 1887 and 1888.* Like myself, he wished to climb the high mountains of Guadalcanal. His first attempt to contact the mountain people failed when his messenger went missing, presumed eaten. His second eventuated only after some intimidation and bribery, but failed to reach the summit when the village that was his objective at the foot of the mountain ceased to exist, twenty of its twenty-nine inhabitants being killed by neighbouring tribes within a week of his arrival. Although not quite as hair-raising, my trip to the mountains did have its moments.

Although Woodford was restricted to the lowlands, he made marvellous collections. Like most nineteenth-century naturalists, he was more interested in the gaudy butterflies and birds of the tropics than rats. Nonetheless, he did send a few examples of the more humble murids back to the British Museum for study. The natives of the coastal village of Aola, where he stayed, had presumably caught these.

Fortunately, Mr Michael Thomas, then Curator of Mammals, had more than a passing interest in rats, and—unusual in a nineteenth-century scientist—a sense of humour. In 1888 he named the rats *Mus imperator*, the second in size *Mus rex* and, in 1904, the smallest and fattest *Uromys porculus*. These scientific names translate from Latin as Emperor Rat, King Rat and Little Pig Rat. Thomas subsequently transferred them all to the genus *Uromys*, which includes the large mosaic-tailed rats of the rainforest of Australia and New Guinea. He noted that: 'It is in their relation to each other that their chief interest lies, for they seem to be the slightly modified descendants of one single species that has been isolated for some considerable time.'

Time has proved Thomas to be correct in this but the situation is even more curious than he suspected: not only are the three species close relatives but they are not related to any other Solomon Islands rodents, and are closest to species from New Guinea and Australia. Many islands in between hold no such rats and just how three species came to coexist on this one island is still a mystery.

Very little is known about the biology of the three rat species. The emperor rat is large and grey, and is known from three individuals. It is over sixty centimetres long, a third of which is tail. The king, known from perhaps half a dozen specimens, is also grey and about the same total length, but with the tail comprising more than one half of this. The little pig, known from a single animal, is not much larger than a brown rat (*Rattus norvegicus*), but is a beautiful brownish-red colour, is rather rotund and has a ridiculously short tail.

Woodford reported that the emperor rat was entirely terrestrial, as its relatively short tail and great bulk might suggest; the king rat he thought was tree-dwelling; but he recorded nothing of the habits of the little pig, although its shape suggests that it too might be ground-dwelling.

Shortly after emperor, king and little pig were announced to the world they were forgotten. One hundred years later I picked up a copy of Thomas's work and became enchanted by these strange animals. They interested me from a biological perspective for a number of reasons. First, they represent the furthest extension of non-flying native mammals into the Pacific Ocean; all land mammals (except bats) found on islands further east have been introduced by people. Second, they are the only land mammals endemic to Guadalcanal. Therefore, the role they have to play in the forest and their interactions with each other may be easier to understand and may teach us much about more complex environments. Third, the three species seem to have arisen from a single ancestor. By studying them I might be able to learn about patterns of speciation in rats. And fourth, they were so mysterious—and I love large murids!

To my surprise I found that not one scrap of information had come forth on any of the rats since Thomas's description. In Australia, if fifty years elapse without a sighting, a species is considered extinct. This, however, seemed to be an unfair test to apply to the Guadalcanal rats, as I was fairly certain that no one had looked for them over the intervening century. The National

Geographic Society awarded me a small grant to investigate the problem and I was soon on my way to Guadalcanal, where I was to spend the early part of the festive season of 1987 in nocturnal wanderings along steep and slippery jungle slopes looking for the lost emperor, king and little pig.

The place I had chosen for the search was the Poha River valley, just west of the Solomon Islands' capital Honiara. Archaeological research by David Roe of the Australian National University had revealed that in the last few thousand years at least two of the three rat species had inhabited the valley.

I knew that some kind of rat still inhabited the area as I found, in parts of the rainforest, piles of nutshells from the Ngali tree (*Canarium indicum*) that had clearly been opened by a largish rodent. But what kind? Local people rarely encounter forest rats and so were of limited help. Intensive trapping also yielded no result, and the chance to gain detailed information seemed to be slipping away. Only one technique remained: spotlighting night after night in the hope that I might see one.

As luck would have it, I had a success of sorts on my very first night. I set out from my base camp after dark with two local assistants and had barely gone fifty metres when I saw, by the side of the path, a reed moving in a peculiar manner. Soon a kitten-sized red creature emerged and sniffed curiously in our direction. I was entirely taken by surprise and was loath to shoot the animal if there was a possibility of capturing it alive.

I signalled for one of my assistants to move in behind it while I kept the spotlight trained on its eyes. Instead, he casually reached forward and instantly the creature vanished into the dense canes. Looking confused, the assistant later explained that he had never before seen anything like the animal and on first sight had thought that it must have been a baby possum (*Phalanger orientalis*), which also has red fur but moves quite slowly and is easy to catch by hand.

I didn't see anything like the animal again after a further month of searching. To this day I don't know what it was. It was definitely a native rat somewhat resembling the little pig but it was climbing a reed and seemed to use its tail to grip with. The only little pig known has a very short tail and doesn't look as if it could climb well. I tend to think that it was a fourth species of a rat, one as yet unknown to science. At least the episode taught me how exasperatingly difficult it can be to gather information on rainforest animals.

After further work in the Poha River valley I discovered that the king rat still inhabited the area: I found a single specimen in the same patch of forest where I made the sighting of the unknown rat. Late one night, high overhead in a huge forest tree, I saw a slight movement. I took a shot up into the canopy, with only the faintest hope that it might be anything but a possum (a creature introduced to the Solomons and greatly relished as food).

To my delight a very aged and silvery rat fell from the canopy ahead of us. It was such an old male that its teeth were worn down to the gums and it was clearly having trouble finding enough nourishment. Although it might seem counterproductive to shoot in such circumstances, the extreme difficulty of gathering information in any other way had left me with no option. At least I had the first firm evidence in a century that the king rat lived and we could gain some idea of genetic relationships and diet from detailed studies of the body.

I took the rat back to the village where the elders were surprised and identified it as the animal they knew as *siru* in their Nginia language. Many of the locals had never encountered it before, and our conversation, which continued late into the night, acted as a sort of cultural revival, the old men telling the younger villagers and me long-ago stories about the rat that was fast becoming myth.

Following my return to Australia the interest that my work kindled in the Guadalcanal rats continued. After much trouble, a veterinarian working in Honiara obtained two live king rats caught by local people in a high mountain area called Gold Ridge. The female soon died but the young male still survives and is being kept as a pet by a wildlife photographer in the Solomon Islands' capital.

During my work in the Poha River area, the old men had told me they had last seen the huge, ground-dwelling species (the emperor rat?) about thirty years ago, high in the mountains at the head of the Poha River. This, coupled with the find at Gold Ridge, made me determined to return to Guadalcanal and explore the mountain forests.

I had the opportunity to do just that in May 1990. The initial negotiations with landowners for permission to enter the Gold Ridge area were done by staff of the Solomon Islands Ministry of Natural Resources. Permission was granted but we had to abide by some taboos, the worst of which was a total prohibition upon cutting any uncooked animal on the mountain! This meant that we could not take tissue samples for biochemical analysis and could not even skin any rats, possums, birds or flying foxes before they went into the cooking fire! I could see myself doing a half-day's run down the mountain, scalpel in hand, if any vital specimen were found. Even if my fitness failed, I might at least gain some ecological information on the rats through observations.

On the afternoon of my arrival at Gold Ridge there was an air of tension at the mining camp. Many people had moved from the bush to be near the camp and road, and a quickly growing 'shanty town' was evident. Relations between the local residents and the mining company seemed strained, and some ill will was clearly spilling over onto us. The next morning, just before we were to leave, an additional demand was put to us. We were to pay $2000 to a local landowner in order to cross the land between the mountain and the mining camp. The owners of the mountain were still willing for us to complete our expedition, but disputes originating elsewhere had led to an unfavourable reaction in some quarters and we reluctantly decided to try to reach the summit by another route. The only other way to do this was by ascending the south face via the 'Weather Coast' of southern Guadalcanal, so called because of the appalling weather conditions that prevail there, with many areas receiving in excess of 8000 millimetres of rain per annum.

Fortunately we met Peter, a young man at Gold Ridge whose village was on the opposite side of the mountain. He convinced us that if we could just get to his village of Valearanisi our problems would be over. Thus we set out that day to get as far around the island as we could by car and then to hire a canoe to complete our journey to the Weather Coast. On the way, Peter entertained us with tales of friendly people and an abundance of giant rats. He even told us of one man known as Hue Hue (the local language name of the largest rat species), who had gained this appellation on account of the prodigious numbers of the species he had caught. Problems began again at Lambi where the road terminates, when it became clear that no one was willing to risk a journey to the Weather Coast that season.

I travelled by small canoe through high seas and rain, from coastal village to coastal village, searching for someone willing to take us, but without success. I arrived back at the safe harbour of Lambi after dark, depressed and sodden. That night I determined that we had wasted enough time and that we might as well use a twentieth-century luxury unavailable to Woodford: the helicopter based at Henderson Field.

We set off for Henderson before dawn on a market truck. The helicopter pilot estimated that it would cost us around US$1100 for the trip and this seemed a reasonable price to pay for reaching our Shangri-la. In fact, the chopper was to cost twice as much—that information on rats was looking terribly expensive—and Valearanisi to be less than paradise on earth for emperor, king and little pig.

Our arrival at Valearanisi was not unexpected, for we had got a message through on public radio that we were coming and a welcoming committee had gathered. The local people were hospitable and friendly but, once again, previous dealings with mining companies were to prove a bane.

The village headman explained that a $500 entry fee was expected from any strangers entering their land, as the mining companies happily paid that much and more. I was further surprised to discover a comprehensive employment agreement being proposed, covering night rates, time-and-a-half on Saturday, Sunday off, and a living-away-from-home allowance—benefits to which I myself was not entitled when in the field. Where a century before Woodford had encountered headhunters, I found sophisticated industrial relations advocates who would make the Australian Council of Trade Unions proud! I stress, however, that such concern for financial detail is unusual in the Solomon Islands and even here people were enthusiastic to learn about their natural environment with us. I suppose that if I had to deal with mining companies on a regular basis I would learn to be just as careful about contracts and matters financial.

We started our ascent of the mountain that afternoon. After two days of agonised walking, often through rain on slippery mud trails, we reached the mossy forest above 900 metres that we hoped would be a rat refuge and everything seemed worthwhile again. We made camp in the only level spot we could find; a small gully that was so muddy it soon resembled the trenches at Verdun. I set out the box traps and the following morning saw that several had gone off. Upon peeking into the first my heart began to soar, for in the corner crouching was a dark ratty shape. No less than three traps held rats and it seemed that victory was at hand!

Imagine my disappointment when I had a good look and found I had trapped three Pacific rats (*Rattus exulans*), a prehistorically introduced species that elsewhere in the Pacific has caused local extinctions. These rats were very dark and large compared to others I had seen, and had clearly undergone some local adaptation to the extreme conditions over the few thousand years they had inhabited the area. The mossy forests were full of these peculiar rats. And feeding upon them were the largest feral cats that I have seen. Together with the abundant feral pigs, these introduced animals had totally devastated the mossy forest. Far from being a refuge, the forest was all but devoid of native life on the ground.

I persisted in spotlighting for several nights, often in chilling rain over near-vertical slippery slopes, but only succeeded in nearly shooting myself after a seven-metre tumble. No native rats were to be seen and detailed questioning of the local people revealed that the large rats were very rare, if not already extinct, in the region. Needless to say, Hue Hue was conspicuous by his absence, his namesake not having been seen in over thirty years.

One lives and learns, I suppose, and the result of field work is not always as anticipated. I am sure that Woodford counted his rats as among the least interesting of his biological discoveries, yet I consider them among the most fascinating. And what had we achieved at the end of one of the most difficult expeditions I have undertaken? High on the mountain we had discovered a new and spectacular kind of monkey-faced bat (genus *Pteralopex*). We only located a single specimen but its bright red eyes and black-and-white wings make it among the most distinctive of the bats I have seen. We had also gathered information that is invaluable for the environmental management of Guadalcanal. Many had assumed that the mountains would act as a wildlife refuge even if the entire lowlands were logged and altered (and this process is already well advanced). This is clearly not the case and it would be valuable if management plans could be put in place that reserve some lowland forest before it is all either logged or turned to gardens.

I doubt that I'll be rewarded with a political appointment like Woodford was. Still, I think the effort of undertaking such work is worth it. It would be a pity should the emperor, king, little pig and perhaps their unknown cousin slip into oblivion without anyone raising a helping hand. Then again, it might even be too late for the emperor and little pig. Generally, ground-dwelling species in the Solomon Islands seem to have suffered worst, perhaps as the result of the introduction of cats and dogs. Yet Guadalcanal is a big place and I'm not yet willing to give up. There are still some extensive mountain blocks that remain unexplored. And perhaps the kingdom of the rats survives there.

In 1988 the Kwaio people of Malaita in the Solomon Islands were still leading almost entirely traditional lives. Mike McCoy (who took this photograph) arranged for us to conduct a faunal survey there. Here I'm surrounded by young mothers and children.

The Fall and Rise of Bulmer's Fruit Bat (with Lester Seri)

Australian Natural History, AUTUMN 1993

Darkness had descended, and clouds of mosquitoes surrounded us, crawling into our ears, nose and eyes. We were unable to slap them for fear of disturbing the bats. Then at last we heard their distinctive 'pok pok pok' wingbeat as they left the roost. The noise of one bat after another colliding with the net high above our heads sounded encouraging until we realised they were bouncing off again. The net had been set too tight, and we would have to climb high into the canopy of trees above the cave to loosen it. And it had to be done quickly. In ten minutes the skies would be empty of bats.

The previous three hours had been pure terror. In order to set the net we had to climb two large trees that overhung the rim of this enormous cave, which plunges down vertically for several hundred metres. It was a fifteen-metre climb to the canopy, and we had first to cut a clearing for the net with bush knives. Then we each had to manipulate a seven-metre pole, with mist net attached, into place, and fasten it to the trees. All the while the light was fading, and the vines I had used to ascend were becoming smooth with wear. The thought of climbing the tree again filled me with dismay; then I realised from the sounds overhead that Lester was already halfway up his tree.

The climb seemed easier in the darkness for I could not see the yawning chasm below, nor could I see the tree sway as I reached the thinner branches of the crown. Almost immediately upon loosening the net a bat struck and became firmly entangled. I held onto the tree with a crooked elbow, stuck the torch in the fork of a branch, and began to haul in the net. The bat was understandably furious, attempting to bite everything around it, and was much larger than I had expected. When I reached it I realised I'd have to cut the net, and carry down the section containing the violently struggling bat.

Net-cutting done, I began my descent in darkness, for in the struggle to pull in the net my torch had fallen. Suddenly I began to feel my centre of gravity shift, and I realised I was supporting myself on the mist-net pole that I had tied loosely to the tree. I grabbed wildly for further support and caught a liana. I climbed down the last few metres shaking, the furious fruit bat struggling to be free.

Lester was waiting with a calico bag. Carefully he placed the bat inside, then took up his torch and peered in. We looked in amazement at the indignant face of this bat that was once thought to have become extinct at the end of the last ice age, 10,000 years ago. We hugged each other with joy—after eight years field work together in rugged western Papua New Guinea we had rediscovered Bulmer's fruit bat.

These are my thoughts recorded on the evening of 3 May 1992. It documents the end of a long search for one of New Guinea's most intriguing mammals: *Aproteles bulmerae*, commonly known as Bulmer's fruit bat, a species *twice* thought to be extinct.

The story of Bulmer's fruit bat began in the early 1970s when James Menzies of the University of Papua New Guinea tried to identify the fossilised bones of some bats found in a rock shelter in Chimbu Province, Papua New Guinea. He found that many of the bones, particularly those from the upper (more recent) layers, were those of the bare-backed fruit bat (*Dobsonia moluccensis*), which is the common large fruit bat of the mountains of New Guinea today. In the lower levels of the site (those dated to 10,000 to 12,000 years old), however, he found abundant remains of a second species. It was somewhat larger than the bare-backed fruit bat, and its teeth were very different. Surprisingly it lacked incisor teeth—a very unusual feature among fruit bats. Realising that he had found an undescribed species, Menzies named it *Aproteles*, meaning 'incomplete at the front' referring to its lack of incisor teeth, and *bulmerae*, for the archaeologist Susan Bulmer who had excavated the bones.

Menzies noted that, although remains of Bulmer's fruit bat were very common in layers dating to 10,000 years ago and older, it was not present in more recent levels. Considering that it had never been found as a living animal, Menzies quite reasonably deduced that it was now extinct, and had been so for around 10,000 years.

There matters lay until the anthropologist David Hyndman (University of Queensland) began working with the Wopkaimin people in far western Papua New Guinea in the mid-1970s. Hyndman was interested in Wopkaimin hunting methods and so one day accompanied a group of hunters to a large cave at Luplupwintem to obtain fruit bats. With the aid of store-bought ropes they entered the cave and, using a shotgun, killed between 200 and 300 bats. Hyndman was unsure of the identity of the species they had caught, so he kept two skulls and even made up a study skin (a dried skin stuffed with cotton wool) to send to Jim Menzies for identification. Unfortunately the skin was lost before it reached the university, but the skulls arrived and, to Menzies' great surprise, they were from Bulmer's fruit bats.

In 1980 Hyndman and Menzies published their findings but reported that, although the cave sheltered 'a great number' of bats in 1975 when Hyndman first entered it, when he returned in 1977 only two bats were roosting there. Evidently the colony had been exterminated by hunters. In 1985 Menzies returned to the site, only to find it entirely deserted, and inquiries by us in 1987 led to a similar conclusion. Between 1984 and 1990 we carried out an extensive mammal survey of the region, visiting almost every major cave we heard about, but found no signs of the bat. By 1990 it was thought again that Bulmer's fruit bat was extinct. Indeed it had the dubious honour of being considered the only New Guinean mammal to have become extinct in recent times.

In 1991 a most unexpected turn of events led to new hopes that the bat had survived the massacres of the mid-1970s. The Mammal Section of the Australian Museum was granted funds to deal with a backlog of nearly 2000 unregistered specimens that had built up over the years. Alexandra Szalay was employed to carry out this work, and on 6 June 1992 she brought a dusty cardboard box containing several fruit bat skulls to me for identification. One seemed unusual, for its shape was different and it lacked incisor teeth. For a moment we mused about the accident that might have deprived a common fruit bat of its front teeth, but then I remembered the meaning of *Aproteles*. Astonished, I rushed for Hyndman and Menzies's paper. It took only a moment to determine that the skull was a third modern specimen of Bulmer's fruit bat. But when and where had it been collected? The number it bore, '24/85', seemed to reveal no clues.

Thankfully Alexandra was by now familiar with all of the various numbering systems used by the Mammal Section through the years. She recognised the number as one assigned to the specimen during preparation. Examination of the preparation book for 1985 revealed that there had also been a skin, collected by Steve Van Dyck (Queensland Museum) at Ofektaman in the Telefomin Valley in February 1984. It had been identified as *Dobsonia moluccensis* (the bare-backed fruit bat), and lodged in the collection. Examination of the skin soon revealed that, although superficially similar to that of the bare-backed fruit bat, there were some significant differences. These included an extra claw on each wing, brown claws instead of white, and fur that was browner and much finer.

X-ray photography of the skin revealed even more important details. The ends of the bones of the wings were all unfused. This meant that the animal was young, probably less than a year old. As it had been collected in February 1984, it must have been born in the first part of 1983. At least *some* Bulmer's fruit bats must have survived the 1970s. But where were they roosting, and how many were left?

Unfortunately the specimen was accompanied by only meagre data and a very general location. Steve Van Dyck was contacted and a critical piece of information was recovered from his diary. The bat had been sold to him by a hunter named Woflayo. Since Steve did not speak Telefol (Woflayo's language), and Woflayo had no English, this accounted for the paucity of information accompanying the specimen.

We now felt that we had enough clues to justify an expedition to the area to begin a new search for the bat. As is usual, however, we entirely lacked the necessary funds. Fortunately, Ok Tedi Mining

Ltd offered to finance the research. Our first objective was to re-examine the cave visited by Hyndman in the 1970s. Neither of us had seen the location before, and we both felt we could learn a lot by examining the old roost site, even if it had long been abandoned. The cave is perched on the edge of a limestone plateau that ends abruptly at the Hindenberg Wall, a huge limestone escarpment over a kilometre high. The only practical way for us and our equipment to reach the site was by helicopter. From Ok Tedi, the ride took just twenty minutes, during which we enjoyed the breathtaking scenery.

The helicopter could not land at the cave because of dense forest, so our small party was dropped into a grassland two or three minutes flight time to the north (a difficult three-hour walk away). The opening to the cave was a 400-metre-deep conical shaft, 200 metres wide at the top.

Way below in the gloom a cathedral-like cavern opened up. Sounds, reminiscent of the cries of parakeets, but quite different from those of any bat we had ever heard, emanated from the hole. Then, quite suddenly, a dark shape swooped from the cavern into the gloom of the main shaft. It was a large fruit bat.

We considered for some hours how we should proceed. The cave was clearly inaccessible to us, so we could not carry out a detailed study. The most pressing question was to establish the identity of the bats roosting in the cave. Were they the common bare-backed fruit bat, or the superficially similar Bulmer's fruit bat? The only way to be sure was to get a bat in hand.

That evening as the light faded, a few bats began to emerge from the cavern and circle in the gloom of the shaft. They uttered a continuous bird-like call as if signalling to those still inside. Before last light the entire colony had emerged and flown over the lowest part of the shaft opening. Lester counted 137 bats. As we walked three hours back to our campsite in the dark and rain, it was clear that if we were to examine a specimen we would have to hoist a mist net above the canopy that grew on the edge of the opening. Over the next two days we examined the area and planned our netting.

Bulmer's fruit bat is a large, blackish-coloured animal with a wingspan of over one metre. Its wings meet in the middle of the back, making the back appear naked and giving the bat extreme manoeuvrability in flight. It is the largest bat species to roost in caves, and because it must rely on sight in its dimly lit environment, it is one of the few bats that can hover. Indeed, it can even fly backwards!

We are only now beginning to investigate the natural history of Bulmer's fruit bat, but already we think we understand the reason for its precipitous decline. Its main problems seem to stem from the fact that it is a large bat and thus a prime target for hunters. It also has quite specific roost requirements, and thus is very sensitive to human interference. Although we never entered the cave at Luplupwintem, the bats were clearly aware of our presence, for over the three nights that we observed them they delayed their departure by almost an hour. Human disturbance appears to be a real threat to Bulmer's fruit bat, and we suspect that its extinction in other parts of New Guinea 10,000 years ago was due to a human population increase associated with the development of agriculture at that time. Its survival in Luplupwintem is doubtless due to the unique topography of the cave, for it is large enough to accommodate a colony of thousands and is an almost invulnerable refuge.

By talking to Wopkaimin hunters we were able to reconstruct the events that led to its near extinction at Luplupwintem, its last stronghold. The 1970s were a time of enormous cultural upheaval for the Wopkaimin. Traditionally they had lived in small, isolated family groups dependent upon gardens cut out of the sodden rainforest of the southern Star Mountains. The Wopkaimin who live in Bultem Village (the village nearest the cave) were entirely forbidden by taboo to disturb the bats, although they occasionally allowed other Wopkaimin to enter the roost. On these occasions one of the region's bravest men might descend on a long rattan rope carried to the entrance by many helpers. With bow and arrow he might secure two or three bats from the cathedral-like roof above before returning to the surface.

But then outsiders began to arrive. Geologists and others began planning for the Ok Tedi mine, and the Papua New Guinean administration began to assert itself. New technologies such as nylon rope and shotguns had arrived in the Star Mountains, and local hunters were acquiring the purchasing power to obtain them.

This technological change was accompanied by a breakdown in traditional lifestyles. The attention of the Wopkaimin was naturally focused on matters to do with the mine and government, and traditional obligations often went unattended. When hunters from the neighbouring Tifalmin area entered the cave three times between 1975 and 1977, killing thousands of bats, the Wopkaimin were too preoccupied with these other matters to retaliate for this breach of tradition and theft of resources. Indeed, Wopkaimin hunters themselves entered the cave and, with shotguns, killed hundreds of bats. By 1977 only a tiny remnant population remained.

We do not know what happened to that remnant. It is possible that a few bats always roosted in the cave but remained undetected; but it is also possible that the remnant colony fled and, for a decade or more, roosted in less suitable sites. The animal shot by Woflayo and sold to Steve Van Dyck in 1984 does not shed much light on this problem. It was killed while feeding in a fig tree just outside the village of Tama, some thirty kilometres north-east of Luplupwintem. A bat as large as Bulmer's fruit bat could easily cover that distance in a night, but it is just as likely that it had come from closer by. What it does reveal, however, is that the bat is vulnerable to predation not only in its cave, but also away from the roost. If enough bats are killed while foraging, then protection of the roost alone will be inadequate to conserve the tiny remnant population.

Fortunately, Lester will be undertaking a long-term study of Bulmer's fruit bat. This study, funded by Ok Tedi Mining Ltd, will clarify much about the species. We hope to learn, for example, what it feeds upon and where it finds its food, and if any rainforest plants are dependent upon it for pollination or seed dispersal. We need to know when it breeds and how often, and what is special about its roost at Luplupwintem. If successful, the rise of Bulmer's fruit bat should continue. But these are perilous times, for we will be trying to preserve a tiny remnant of an ice age species in an environment of turbulent social and environmental change. Only with understanding and goodwill can we succeed.

Eating tuna, Solomon Islands, 1988. When local foods were in short supply, I fell back on tinned fish as a staple—it became a sickeningly monotonous diet.

The Case of the Missing Meat Eaters: Why Are Australia's Carnivores Such Cold-blooded Killers?

Natural History, JUNE 1993

During ice ages, when sea level is low, Australia, Tasmania, New Guinea and their smaller neighbours coalesce into a single great island. Dubbed Meganesia by scientists, this landmass covers an area of almost 4 million square miles and is a single geological entity, carried across the Southern Hemisphere by plate tectonics. Meganesian plants and animals thus share a common biological heritage, and even when the sea carves their great island homeland into discrete pieces, the flora and fauna retain their affinities. In addition to an abundance of marsupial mammals and a dearth of placental mammals, one of Meganesia's most striking features is its extraordinary lack of large mammalian carnivores.

This unusual situation is perhaps best illustrated by going back some 60,000 years, before the arrival of humans in Australia. At that time, Meganesia was home to approximately sixty species of mammals that weighed more than nine kilograms. Of these, not more than three were meat eaters, and all are now extinct. Only two other warm-blooded carnivores weighed more than 4.5 kilograms, and they still survive: the Tasmanian devil and the spotted-tailed quoll. Each of these species fills, or filled, a somewhat different ecological niche.

The Tasmanian devil, a scavenger and bone-cruncher that takes whatever prey comes its way, is perhaps best described as a miniature marsupial hyena. Also a marsupial, the spotted-tailed quoll is weasel-like or civet-like in both appearance and in its stealthy behaviour. The now-extinct thylacine (which survived in Tasmania until 1936) was roughly the size and shape of a wolf and was Meganesia's only dog-like marsupial carnivore. The marsupial lion, also extinct, was one of the few carnivores to have arisen from herbivorous ancestors and had large, slicing premolars. Some nineteenth-century scientists speculated that this animal was a vegetarian that fed mainly on melons. But the discovery of a well-preserved fossil paw revealed that it was equipped with a big hooded claw, and the marsupial lion is now believed to have been an adept predator. Despite its common name, it was closer in size to a leopard than a lion and may have been the marsupial equivalent of the medium-sized cats on other continents.

The marsupial giant rat kangaroo weighed a hefty forty kilograms and stood over a metre tall but had teeth similar to those of much smaller insectivores. This beast lived throughout eastern Australia—in woodland, grassy steppe-land and savannah—during the last ice age. Its ecology, however, is enigmatic. It may well have been an omnivore, eating plants, scavenging carcasses, and opportunistically preying on bird eggs and small vertebrates. If such an interpretation of its diet and habits is correct, this primitive kangaroo may have filled a niche similar to that of some small bears.

In the entire Australasian region, therefore, the broad carnivore niches were filled by just one mammal species each—dog-like, cat-like, civet-like, scavenging, and, possibly, bear-like animals. In contrast, even today the United States (the lower forty-eight states of which are roughly the size of Australia) is inhabited by three bear species, five kinds of dogs, six kinds of cats, six species of weasels and their relatives, as well as raccoons, ringtails and coatis. And the region's abundance of carnivores pales when compared with its fauna during the Pleistocene, when dire wolves, various bears, jaguars, cheetahs, lions and sabretooths also roamed the continent. This diversity of mammalian carnivores is by no means exceptional; Europe, Asia, Africa and South America either did or still do support similarly diverse carnivore guilds. In all these regions, the broad cat and dog niches are subdivided according to size, prey type and habitat, allowing many species to coexist.

Biologists have long speculated on the cause of the imbalance in the Meganesian mammal fauna. One of the most important limitations known to affect carnivores is simply the size of the landmass they inhabit. Although Australia, which comprises the bulk of Meganesia, is indeed the smallest continent, it is still about 3 million square miles in area. Yet the Meganesian carnivore assemblage is not much richer than that of the island of Madagascar, which is only one-twentieth the size of Meganesia.

Another school of thought holds that marsupials, having relatively small brains, were unable to evolve into successful predators. A quick look at the fossil record of South America, however, disproves the hypothesis that a connection exists between brain size and predation skill. Many species of dog-like marsupials, in a variety of sizes, lived in South America during the Tertiary period, about 65 to 2 million years ago. A remarkable subfamily of carnivorous marsupials evolved into cat-like animals, resembling North American sabretooths, that were capable of killing the largest of prey. The group that includes the ancestors of the American opossum also produced large flesh eaters. While all of these beasts became extinct when placental carnivores arrived in South America over the past 5 million years, they thrived for many millions of years, preying mainly upon large placental herbivores.

Since there appears to be no intrinsic bar to meat-eating marsupials, perhaps the environment holds a clue to Meganesia's paucity of large carnivorous mammals. Meat eaters sit at the apex of a broad-based food pyramid and are thus the most vulnerable of life forms to disturbances in the food chain. An area of grassland that supports billions of individual grasses, for example, may sustain only a few thousand large herbivores. These, in turn, may be able to support fewer than one hundred large carnivores. If the environment is poor, large herbivores will be rare and thinly spread, and a critical point may be reached where the density of prey is so low that a population of large meat eaters cannot be sustained. If further impoverished, such an environment can no longer support any large carnivores.

Australia is notoriously infertile. An old continent with a stable geological history, it has experienced no widespread glaciation, mountain building, or volcanic activity—the forces that create new soil—over the past 50 million years. As a result of its quiet past, Australia is a land of old, thin and leached soils. In the country's semi-arid zone, soils have about half the levels of nitrates and phosphates of equivalent soils elsewhere. The amount and quality of arable land is another good measure of productivity, and even the 10 per cent of Australia's total land that is considered arable is marginal when compared with other landmasses. Other indications of poor soil come from Australia's plants, which have developed a variety of strategies, including slow average growth rates, to cope with the lack of nutrients.

A contributing environmental factor is El Niño, or the Southern Oscillation cycle, which influences rainfall with a periodicity of roughly a decade. In some years, Australia receives high levels of rainfall, and productivity peaks, as it did in 1990. But in El Niño years, such as 1992, rainfall is reduced and prolonged droughts are likely. On no other continent does the cycle have such an extreme impact. Its effects can readily be seen in the high degree of nomadism and non-seasonal breeding in many Australian animals, particularly birds. When such variability is superimposed on a system that is already marked by low productivity, top-order carnivores are subject to exceptional stress.

These climatic factors have so shaped the biology of the region that even areas of rainforest lack big carnivores. The largest area of rainforest in Meganesia is in New Guinea, which is even more noteworthy than Australia for its lack of meat-eating mammals. Here we have no evidence of indigenous large cat-like or scavenging predators. Before human settlement, New Guinea supported some two hundred species of rather small mammalian herbivores and insectivores, but was home to just one large warm-blooded carnivore, the thylacine. Today, apart from humans, the largest predator is the bronze quoll, a one-kilogram, civet-like species.

If large meat-eating mammals are disadvantaged in such an ecosystem, might animals that require less food and energy fare better? Reptiles eat far less than mammals do, having no need to create inner body heat. They can survive long periods of food shortage and can exist at higher population densities than mammals, relative to their prey. Cold-bloodedness thus becomes a great boon to survival. I believe this is what has happened in Meganesia, home to a remarkable array of carnivorous reptiles. Before the arrival of humans, the largest carnivores in the region were *Wonambi*, a fifty kilogram python-like snake with a thirty centimetre girth; a giant land crocodile known as *Quinkana*; and a goanna—a kind of monitor lizard—called *Megalania*. Weighing as much as a tonne, and more than six metres long, *Megalania* would have dwarfed present-day reptiles. Its nearest living relative is the Komodo dragon, which survives on a few small Indonesian islands adjacent to Australia. Although it weighs only a fraction as much as *Megalania*, the Komodo dragon is capable of killing goats, calves, and even humans. *Megalania* would have been powerful enough to subdue diprotodons, the rhino-sized marsupial plant eaters that were the largest of all Australian mammals. *Wonambi*, the snake, occupied a far different ecological niche. It lived much further south than large snakes do today and its remains are often found in rocks and caves. Its head was large and its jaws were filled with hundreds of tiny teeth. It may have fed upon wombat- and wallaby-sized mammals. The least known of these reptiles is the three-metre long, 230-kilogram crocodile, *Quinkana*. It seems to have been quite independent of water, for its fossils have been found in caves that contain only remains of terrestrial species. *Quinkana* had a large, box-like snout and compressed, serrated teeth. It may have competed with young *Megalania* for the now extinct kangaroos and smaller diprotodons.

Are the climatic patterns of the Pleistocene and more recent times an aberration in the history of Meganesia? Palaeontological research suggests that during much of the 'age of mammals', and certainly since about 20 million years ago, Meganesia has been relatively resource poor and lacking mammalian carnivores. On the other end of the spectrum, leading into historic times, Meganesia has been colonised by humans and, more recently, by animals introduced by them. How have the predators among them fared? The number of humans in Meganesia since people first crossed the sea from Asia some 40,000 years ago remained small prior to European settlement.

Adaptable and omnivorous, humans also became the top-order predators; their hunting prowess probably led to the extinction of all terrestrial vertebrate species that exceeded them in size, including all land carnivores larger than the thylacine. The dog known as the dingo, introduced some 3500 years ago, apparently drove both the thylacine and Tasmanian devil to extinction on the mainland. The success of other smaller, introduced predators such as the fox has been detrimental to native predators such as quolls.

Humans, dingoes and foxes have not caused a net increase in the number of mammalian carnivores in Meganesia; they have simply replaced the few existing warm-blooded carnivore species. But today, Australia, Tasmania and New Guinea can still boast a rich supply of reptiles—ten species of goannas and a further ten species of pythons that weigh at least 4.5 kilograms. This remains a record number of sizable cold-blooded carnivores.

The case of the Meganesian meat eaters opens up new areas for exploration while reinforcing the view that because of its unusual climatic conditions and long isolation, Meganesia is truly a separate experiment in evolution.

A Telefol bow hunter emerging from the mist of Miptigin Ridge, located above Telefomin, Sandaun Province.

Irian Jaya's New Tree Kangaroo: Just the Tip of the Ertzberg?

Nature Australia, WINTER 1995

In the early 1900s, the great British explorer Alfred Wollaston led a team into the heart of Dutch New Guinea. In the preface to his 1912 account of the expedition, it was noted: 'There can be no doubt that when the higher ranges between 5000 and 10,000 feet [about 1500 to 3000 metres] are explored, many other novelties will be discovered.'

But until very recently, much of the higher regions of Irian Jaya's Carstensz Mountains, which Wollaston knew to be so potentially fruitful, remained biologically unexplored. Time did not pass the area by, however, for in 1936 a Dutch geologist discovered the Ertzberg—a literal mountain of copper—just below the Meren Glacier. Mining commenced in the 1960s, and the modern mining town of Tembagapura, equipped with all conveniences, is now situated on the southern slopes of the Carstensz Mountains.

In May 1994 a joint Australian–Indonesian expedition set out to document the fauna of part of this vast and poorly known region. Our survey was to be the first ever to explore the mammals of the high forests of the Carstensz Range.

We hoped—somewhat vaguely, since we had so little to go on—to find some trace of an intriguing, possibly new species of marsupial we had provisionally dubbed the pied tree kangaroo.

In 1990 the South African photographer Gerald Cubitt sent me a series of colour photographs he had taken in Irian Jaya of a Dani man holding an odd-looking mammal. In his accompanying letter, Cubitt asked if I wouldn't mind identifying the animal for him. My reply was that I wouldn't mind in the least, except that I couldn't. I could see that it was a juvenile tree kangaroo, entirely black but for a white chest flash, and with a short tail. It resembled none of the described species, although the possibility always existed that it was simply an unusually coloured individual of a previously known kind.

Cubitt's photographs did, however, make some sense to me. The previous year I had collected an artefact among the Dani people of the West Baliem River, some 150 kilometres to the east of where Cubitt took his photo. A hat worn by a senior Dani hunter incorporated the fur of an animal that was clearly a tree kangaroo, but its colour pattern—black with a vestige of pure white—was different from that of all known species. This hat and Cubitt's photographs were the only evidence known to Western science that tree kangaroos existed over the entire 400-kilometre-long Irian Jayan section of the Central Cordillera. I suspected that the young animal in Cubitt's photograph and the fur of the adult animal in the hat were one and the same species.

Following up such tenuous leads is no simple task. One can speculate upon such things at great length from museum collection rooms, but getting to the place and physically looking for the animal is another matter altogether. Who, for example, would offer the necessary funding for an expedition based solely on a few snapshots and a disreputable-looking scrap of fur? Not surprisingly, the idea wasn't overwhelmed by takers. The fur and the photos went into a drawer.

A solution came four years later, from an altogether different quarter. I received another letter with photographs, this time from Irian Jaya itself. An executive working for the mining company P. T. Freeport Indonesia in Tembagapura discovered, after reading my book *Mammals of New Guinea*, that an animal given to him as a pet appeared to be the rare great-tailed triok (*Dactylopsila megalura*). Would I mind, he asked, coming over and having a proper look?

Within a few months we had organised an Australian Museum–Zoology Museum Bogor team of three to conduct a preliminary faunal survey of the southern slopes of the Carstensz Range. It was the region that had beckoned so enticingly to Wollaston all those years ago, but which, for him, had remained so frustratingly out of reach.

For those who enjoy a good bedtime story along natural history lines, Wollaston's account of his expedition is compulsive reading. It is elegantly written, brimming with acute observations and sprinkled with a peculiarly gentle but effective humour that frequently leaves one weak with mirth. There is pathos, too, related in close-lipped stoical lines, clearly written from the midst of the most appalling circumstances. His trip began in disaster when the esteemed collector Wilfred Stalker was drowned the day they arrived at their base camp at Wakatimi. Subsequently, they lost to disease many of their 260 Malay carriers and Gurkhas (Nepalese soldiers); they had their campsites and equipment carried away by flood at least twice; and Wollaston wrote more than once of standing all night in a campsite flooded up to his chest. Compounding these disasters was the frequently dismal state of the expedition members' health and the difficulty of traversing the almost impossible terrain. Despite all this, Wollaston's expedition struggled on for fifteen months. They never managed to ascend higher than about 1400 metres, even though the snow-capped peaks were sometimes in view.

Many times during our survey I had cause to feel guilty at the ease with which we reached our destination. A quick two-hour jet flight from Cairns took us to Timika in southern Irian Jaya and from there, following formalities, it was only thirty minutes by helicopter to the famed Meren Glacier itself.

Our search for the tree kangaroo, however, was not destined to go as smoothly as our arrival. The first task was to contact local hunters who possess extensive knowledge of the large marsupials of their homelands. We soon learned that there were two kinds of tree kangaroo in the area. One, known to the Damal people as *Naki*, was golden-brown in colour. The other, *Nemenaki*, was reputed to be black and white. Accounts of it tied in well with Cubitt's photographs and our piece of skin.

The identity of *Naki* was soon resolved, for it is a common species that occurs in less rugged country. It proved to be a subspecies of Doria's tree kangaroo (*Dendrolagus dorianus*) that occurs as far east as the Star Mountains of western Papua New Guinea. Indeed, in 1990 Lester Seri (from Papua New Guinea's Department of Environment) and I had named the subspecies *stellarum*, meaning 'of the stars', in reference to its initial discovery in the Star Mountains.

The identity of *Nemenaki* proved more difficult. Very few Damal hunters professed to have real personal acquaintance with it. Our first week of searching was lost as we were working with a group of young, relatively inexperienced hunters who were concentrating at what would turn out to be too low an elevation. We had combed the relatively high beech forest that grows at 2300 to 2700 metres elevation to the south of Tembagapura. Despite a vast effort, and encounters with several *Naki*, our work yielded no results.

It was only when we met accidentally with Jonas Tinal, a young but experienced Dani hunter, that our luck changed. We were searching for frogs and other small game at nearly 3000 metres elevation in mossy forest below the vast Grasberg Mine. I was absorbed in the hunt at this lonely place when I noticed shadows moving in the mist. They turned out to be Jonas, his two wives and a scrawny beast that Jonas referred to as his 'four million rupiah dog'—so called because its value as a securer of game was enormous: literally a million rupiahs (about US$600) per canine tooth! The party had walked up to this remote spot to hunt, and we arranged to meet several days later to examine what they had caught.

Imagine our dismay when we met up with them and they were carrying not a complete animal, but the damaged partial skins of two *Nemenaki* specimens. Being hungry, they had eaten their catch and so the chance to undertake valuable biological research had been lost. Still, the scraps of skin and bones provided data from which to evaluate just what kind of creature *Nemenaki* was. We also learned that *Nemenaki* occurs very high in the mountains. Indeed, it is most abundant at 3200 to 4300 metres elevation—within view of the glacial ice itself.

A few days after Jonas returned to his village, a fresh bunch of Dani hunters we had employed located an animal. They had been working with their dogs (one of which was called Photocopy, as its appearance was deemed by its owners to be a poor copy of the real thing) high up on Gunung Ki, in an extremely difficult and rocky area. Photocopy and his companions had got away from their owners when the distinctive call of New Guinean hunting dogs was heard. When the hunters finally caught up with the dogs, they found that they had located and badly bitten a female *Nemenaki*. By the time we had caught up with the hunters, the animal was dead.

Despite our disappointment, I was fascinated to see *Nemenaki* at last. My first impression, when I saw it being carried out of the ever-present mist on the shoulders of a hunter, was that it was not a kangaroo at all. It was about 8.5 to 9 kilograms in weight, that of a medium-sized dog, and was boldly patterned in black and white. No other kangaroo is similarly coloured. Just as striking as its colour was its relatively short tail, a bold white stripe that runs around the base of the muzzle, and a white star on the forehead. These features give it more the appearance of a small bear or panda than a kangaroo.

As the weeks wore on we learned more of *Nemenaki*. The Dani, who avidly hunt it, know it as *Wanun*. Experienced hunters described how it rarely climbs trees and, unlike Doria's tree kangaroo, it never jumps from the canopy but always descends backwards, like a person. All agreed that it was ridiculously tame. One hunter described how he caught them by slipping a noose over their necks and then led them away. Another tempted the creature within his reach simply by offering it a bunch of choice leaves. The Dani also described how, when first encountered, *Wanun* would raise its arms above its head and emit a clear whistle. This distinctive behavioural response to a threat makes the individual clearly visible and may have the advantage of warning others of danger.

Towards the end of our expedition we decided to visit Pogapa, a settlement of the Moni people who live to the west of the Dani.

A missionary who, fortunately for them, had grown up in Irian Jaya and was extremely sympathetic with their traditions and way of life had Christianised the Moni. Traditional beliefs are still strong among them, and the black-and-white tree kangaroo, known to Moni as *Dingiso*, lies at the very heart of their culture. It is thus afforded strict protection by many and, because it is common, its habits are well known.

Moni hunters confirmed the fact that when *Dingiso* is alarmed it whistles and raises its arms, revealing its white belly in the process. Other tree kangaroos are silent or produce a low grunt, though other species have a similar arm-raising display. Furthermore, Moni hunters were unanimous in indicating that it was largely terrestrial (another feature unique among tree kangaroos). Later examination of its skeleton showed that in certain ways it is more similar to terrestrial kangaroos than other tree kangaroos and that it is incapable of leaping out of the canopy as other tree kangaroos do, for the bones are too fragile.

Initially, these terrestrial adaptations had made us think that it may have been a very primitive kind of tree kangaroo. But further analysis has revealed that it is probably a highly specialised kind of tree kangaroo that has reverted to life on the ground. This is an extraordinary evolutionary reversion, given that kangaroos as a whole are derived from tree-dwelling, possum-like ancestors, and that the first tree kangaroos evolved from terrestrial ancestors.

The discovery of the black-and-white tree kangaroo was doubtless the highlight of our expedition. But much more resulted from our six-week survey of Irian's high forest. Of the forty-two mammal species found by us, over 25 per cent were entirely new records for Irian Jaya. Three animals—the black-and-white tree kangaroo, an alpine rat found just below the Meren Glacier, and a bat mist-netted in dense mossy forest nearby—were discoveries entirely new to science. Many mammal species were photographed for the first time, while for many more the expedition resulted in the first insights into their obscure lives. Clearly, the great mountain range that once cradled the Ertzberg will continue to produce extraordinary discoveries for many years to come.

Dingiso, *1995. This young* dingiso *was captured when it wandered into a machinery shed at the Freeport Mine in Irian Jaya. It was half-grown, and was completely tame.*

Men of the Forest

FROM *Tree Kangaroos: A Curious Natural History*, 1996

The worlds of tree kangaroos and men are largely separate. The lives of men centre upon villages, gardens and rivers, and upon the gentler and more easily hunted closer slopes of the mountain ranges. The world of tree kangaroos is often perched high above. It is one of precipices and swirling mists—a cold, dank and dangerous world. The infrequent flashing moments when tree kangaroos and men meet, however, are full of meaning and excitement. Their importance is out of all proportion to their brief duration, for they shape the lives of both the hunter and the hunted long after they have passed.

In New Guinea, the man who has successfully hunted a tree kangaroo has greatness bestowed upon him. He has conquered the largest, most prestigious and human-like marsupial known to his people. In sharing its meat he wins brides and cements alliances. In wearing its skin, in warfare or on grand occasions, he reminds all present of his prestige. Thus the successful hunter of tree kangaroos has status, and often many children. People listen to him: the knowledge a hunter gains during those precious few moments when he sees a tree kangaroo face to face are recounted over and over to an eager audience. And in the mind of the hunter they are added to the retold experiences of father, uncles and grandfathers.

The knowledge of many coalesces to form a detailed understanding of the lives of these most obscure animals.

For tree kangaroos, too, the moment of encounter with a hunter is a crucial one. Those that tarry too long, not realising the danger they are in, meet a swift death. Likewise, those whose belly is a little too pale and easily seen in the canopy from below, or those that are careless in choosing their daytime roost, will pass on no more genes. This has happened over 20,000 tree kangaroo generations, as human hunters have pursued their prey. Throughout this time tree kangaroos have also stored up knowledge, not in memory but in genes. Those with the right behaviours and colours have survived to pass on their traits. A tree kangaroo's behaviour, and even its appearance, if read properly, presents a catalogue of its predator's behaviour as detailed as the predator's is of the tree kangaroo as prey.

I have hunted tree kangaroos in two ways: by accompanying New Guineans who have searched for tree kangaroos using traditional methods, and by tracking tree kangaroos with radio-tracking devices. Even so, my first-hand experience of wild tree kangaroos is limited, and much of what I know has been learned from consummate hunters whose knowledge encapsulates the experience of many lifetimes.

HUNTING WITH SKILL AND MAGIC

In February 1984 I was lying sick in a rough hunting shelter high in the Victor Emmanuel Range of far western Papua New Guinea. I had just spent four weeks in the lowlands near the Irian Jaya border hoping to learn something of tree kangaroos. I found to my chagrin that I was at too low an elevation, and rather than return home empty-handed, I decided to devote my last two weeks to working with Telefol hunters high in the Victor Emmanuel Range.

At Telefomin I met Dan Jorgenson, an anthropologist who had spent many months among the Telefol. He directed me to two experienced older hunters, Tinamnok and Amunsep. Tinamnok was in his forties and a superb hunter. Even he, however, professed no skill in hunting *D'bol*, as the Telefol know Seri's tree kangaroo (*Dendrolagus dorianus stellarum*). To do that I would need to consult Amunsep, and he was up-country. Dismayed, I decided to accompany Tinamnok into the high country on the Sol River, a day's walk away.

Almost as soon as I arrived at the little lean-to Tinamnok used as a shelter when he was hunting, I fell ill. At Yapsiei I had contracted what I now know was giardia and had been laid low for days. Its return on the Sol River left me helpless. Tinamnok would go out hunting for two or three days at a time, sleeping in hollow trees or napping on a sunny riverbank by day, finally to return with his booty. It took all my strength just to weigh, measure and skin the specimens he brought to me.

One night, after about a week's work, a dog walked casually into camp. Presently, another, then another followed it. Some minutes later a man arrived. Amunsep was in his fifties. He had a broad face with a typically large Melanesian nose and frizzy hair which was greying at the temples. Over one eye was a boil the size of a hen's egg. He wore ex-army shorts and a beret, but had doubtless spent his early years dressed in *kamen* and *autil*, the traditional Telefol penis gourd and cane waistband. Over his shoulder he wore an exquisite string bag or *billum*, made with care and an eye to utility that only Telefol women possess. It was decorated like no other, for the tail tips of at least twenty *D'bol* adorned its outer surface. Around Amunsep's neck hung a miniature *billum* even more beautiful than the first. This looked impossibly small to be of any practical use.

Doubtless Amunsep was surprised to find someone at the camp. Perhaps he thought me too lazy or incompetent to follow Tinamnok. Whatever the case, I found it difficult to disabuse him of his opinions, for Amunsep was a traditional man who spoke neither English nor Pidgin.

It took time for him to respond to me, but one evening, nearly a week after first meeting, I greeted him with the customary phrase *'Ngum saro'*, which he returned before sitting by the fire. After an awkward silence I fished out of the ashes a cooked sweet potato (our principal food) and passed it to him. Then, as he ate, I began to read aloud the list of Telefol animal names given to me by Tinamnok.

With each name correctly pronounced, Amunsep would mime the animal's behaviour, give its call and indicate, by pointing, its habitat. There was *Bogol*, as the Telefol know the New Guinea harpy eagle (*Harpyopsis novaeguineae*). So powerful is this bird that it is reputed to carry off young *D'bol,* and even human infants neglected momentarily by their mothers. Its call, like the release of a tense bowstring, is followed by the low clucking call of its mate. Amunsep imitated it perfectly. The mimed terror of its descending talons and the fierceness of its eye had my heart in my throat.

Finally, I came to *D'bol*. Instantly, Amunsep made the animal come to life for me. Its immensely powerful forearms, its fearfully sharp claws, its imperious stare as it looks down at its assailants from high in the canopy—all were conjured up. The snuffling sounds and grinding of teeth signifying annoyance were there, as was its peculiar posture and hop. It was nearly 2 am when the performance finished. I looked up at the starry night, which promised good hunting on the morrow.

I was woken, not by the first grey strands of dawn, but by acrid smoke. Amunsep was already up, kindling the fire for warmth. As I watched from my wet sleeping bag, feeling sicker than ever, Amunsep took the tiny *billum* from around his neck. From it he extracted what appeared to be some native tobacco. He rolled it into a tiny cigar, lit it and inhaled deeply. Grabbing the nearest dog by the foreleg, he roused it from slumber by blowing smoke into its nose. The whimpering animal was released and the process repeated on the others. Next, Amunsep took the pale, scented bark of a plant known to Telefol as *tabap kal*. This he chewed until it was pulp. Again he took up the dogs and blew the white fragments into each one's face. Finally, he took from the *billum* a pebble of beautiful deep-red agate, rolled smooth and pellet-like by a stream. This stone, called *nuk terap*, he rubbed gently on each dog's forehead, all the while chanting under his breath. Then Amunsep was gone and I was left alone in the forest for another two days.

On the third afternoon Amunsep and Tinamnok returned to camp. They had the usual kinds of cuscus, but *D'bol* had eluded them. At last I felt well enough to walk, and together we descended from the world of *D'bol* into the world of men.

It was to be another two years before I would meet *D'bol* face to face. Amunsep suffered a serious knee injury soon after our work on the Sol River and was never to hunt the rugged country again. And so I tried hunting with several other men.

One group of young men had a dog by the name of Rocket. Rocket was reputed to be a paragon among the canines. According to his owner, Rocket was such a diligent hunter that he was wont to go out by himself at night, secure a cuscus and carry it back to camp, placing it under his master's head to act as a pillow, thus augmenting both slumber and breakfast. But while I was with him, Rocket proved to be a fizzer, for he did not aid in the capture of a single game animal. Instead, I suspected him of stealing rats from my traps.

Quite by surprise, one afternoon in April 1986 a group of young men came into my camp on the Sol River carrying a young male *D'bol*. It had probably been caught while travelling out of its natal area in a search for territory not already guarded by an adult male. Perhaps it had chosen some less rugged slope for its new home and had been spotted there by the hunters.

That evening the camp was alive with activity. I was busy measuring, taking samples and skinning. In the evening, our largest pot was filled with the meat of *D'bol* along with various greens picked from the surrounding vegetation. Late that night, the cooking finished, I was handed some meat. It was delicious, not as gamey as kangaroo, and as tender as could be wished. In my enjoyment of the meal I failed to notice that no one else was partaking. Early that morning the still-full pot was carried down into the village.

I later learned that the meat of *D'bol* was considered such powerful food that only the most senior Telefol men could eat it. It seemed that no one in my camp was eminent enough to partake, but as an honoured guest and a *Tablasep* (white man), I was exempted.

RADIO-TRACKING

In 1985 I was conducting a faunal survey near Wigotei Village in the Torricelli Mountains of western Papua New Guinea when I fell sick with scrub typhus. This misfortune terminated my survey, but not before I had obtained the claw of a tree kangaroo.

The claw was the solitary neck ornament of one of my stretcher-bearers, a local village man who helped carry me to a mission station to receive medical treatment. Travelling through the bush in an uncharacteristically horizontal manner, my eyes (when I could force them open) would light upon many strange things, some real, others undoubtedly imagined. But my gaze kept returning to the object gently swaying from a string around the neck of the man beside me. At the end of our peculiar journey, I summoned the presence of mind to purchase it from him. When I returned to the Australian Museum in Sydney some weeks later, I examined the claw and found that it was unlike that of any known species.

It was to be three years before I could return to the Torricelli Mountains, but when I did in May 1988 I obtained a juvenile specimen of a black tree kangaroo. The Olo people called this animal *Tenkile*, meaning 'I stand' in their language. To a biologist, it was clearly a species new to science, one that had a very limited distribution. I obtained grant funds to return to the area to undertake research and a conservation program.

Conditions in the Torricellis are among the most difficult I have ever experienced for long-term field work. Before leaving Australia I had visited Roger Martin, a biologist undertaking a detailed study of Bennett's tree kangaroo near Cooktown. Roger had lived for months in a waterless camp, which was little more than a tarpaulin stretched over some sticks. He had endured insects and abject, interminable isolation—with the exception of wandering cattle—before being able to place a radio collar on a tree kangaroo. Roger is clearly a tough bushman, yet when he visited the Torricellis, he found it almost unbearable.

I had engaged Viare Kula, of the Papua New Guinea Department of Conservation and Environment, to undertake most

Roger Martin, Viare Kula and me, tracking the Tenkile *in the Mount Somoro area, 1988.*

of the radio-tracking work. Each day during the month or so I spent with Viare, we struggled up and down a succession of near-vertical slopes some 500 metres high. The rain was incessant, the food repetitive and limited. We were never dry. And we saw one of our radio-collared animals only the once. Over the hour I observed it, the *Tenkile* sat impassively, only occasionally twitching an ear. This highlight could hardly sustain us for the months necessary for the study.

The broken topography and wet conditions made it close to impossible to source radio signals, even if one spent all day chasing them. Sometimes we would hear a distant thump as the animal being tracked detected us and jumped from its tree into a steep gully. When we found two of the tracked animals dead, we decided to terminate the program. Dogs had probably bitten the two when they were first captured and after some months they had succumbed to chronic infection, despite being given antibiotics as a precaution against this upon initial capture. The despair that comes with killing rare animals that one has worked so hard to preserve defies adequate description. It makes the continuous, chill drizzle of *Tenkile's* habitat more biting.

HUNTING WITH DOGS

Rocket isn't the only four-legged tree-kangaroo hunter I have worked with. Others include Photocopy, Dingo and, the finest hunter of them all, Sime of Wilbetei. Photocopy, well named, looked like a good hunting dog, though he did not act like one. His companion Dingo, however, was an outstanding hunter and therefore especially valuable. Both dogs were owned by Jonas Tidal, an Ilaga Dani man living at Tembagapura. Jonas had named Dingo in honour of an Australian friend. This dog caught the first

Dingiso (*Dendrolagus mbaiso*, a new species of black-and-white tree kangaroo) I ever saw, but like many thoroughbreds he was temperamental.

Wishing to help Jonas and his wives, who had spent several days living in the bush, I offered them a ride in a vehicle back to their village. Hunters, wives and dogs duly entered the cabin—all, that is, except Dingo. He ran off and hid in a drain instead. For days rumours flew about that he had been caught by Bugis miners from Sulawesi and that they had turned him into curry. Others had seen his poor mangled body on the road, smitten by a vast mining truck. All hope appeared lost until one day, nearly two weeks later, Dingo appeared back at the village, fat and sleek. He had merely been hunting for himself for a change.

Sime was the best four-legged hunter I have ever met. He was already old when I knew him in 1989. A distinct greying on the face betrayed his age, but he still had a sleek and muscular physique. Despite having been deprived of his masculinity, Sime walked with a confident swagger possessed by few dogs in New Guinea. He never ran in fear, as other dogs did when someone scowled or shouted, and he was aloof with strangers. Although we spent months in camp together, Sime never allowed me to touch him.

Sime's canines were worn almost to stumps. He doubtless relied on the younger dogs (his acolytes) to make the kill, but it was his wealth of experience and keenness of attention that brought success in the hunt, for without him, hunting was a highly uncertain affair. Whenever we hunted with Sime in the Torricelli Mountains we met with success. One time he bagged four Finsch's tree kangaroos (*Dendrolagus inustus finschi*). On the triumphant walk back to the village, Sime wore a wreath of victory, made with leaves from the forest.

Sime, the best hunting dog in the Mount Somoro area of Sandaun Province, 1992. He's returned from the hunt wearing a victor's wreath.

The lives of most dogs, even good hunting dogs, are often difficult in New Guinea. Sometimes the best hunting dogs are, by virtue of their predatory temperament, a danger to village chickens and piglets. Among the Goilala, such dogs are progressively whittled away from behind for their crimes. A first offence results in the loss of half a tail, while a second (if male) means the testicles go. The third results in a finely cropped wagger. Any further breaches and the offender is usually dispatched to the stew pot.

One of the finest tree kangaroo hunters of all time was a dingo named Balnglan. The explorer Carl Lumholtz travelled high into the mountains near Cairns in 1888 to meet the animal, having heard much of his expertise. Balnglan was in a class of his own as far as tree kangaroo hunting went. Lumholtz's triumph in obtaining a *boongary* (later to be named the Lumholtz tree kangaroo), and Balnglan's part in it, is best told in the explorer's own words:

> I had just eaten my dinner, and was enjoying the shade in my hut, while my men were about smoking their pipes, when there was suddenly heard a shout from the camp of the natives. My companions rose, turned their faces toward the mountain, and shouted 'Boongary, boongary!' A few black men were seen coming out of the woods and down the green slope as fast as their legs could carry them. One of them had a large dark animal on his back.
>
> Was it truly a 'boongary'? I soon caught sight of the dog 'Balnglan' running in advance and followed by Nilgora, a tall powerful man.
>
> The dark animal was thrown on the ground at my feet, but none of the blacks spoke a word.

Lumholtz's joy, however, was short-lived. After skinning the tree kangaroo and lacing the skin with arsenic, he made the fatal mistake of leaving the skin in the roof of his hut. The number of specimens I have lost to pole-climbing, lid-lifting or similarly acrobatic dogs that could reach specimens stored in seemingly impossible places is horribly high. Imagine Lumholtz's dismay to find, upon his return, that his unique specimen had disappeared!

> I was perfectly shocked. Who could have taken the skin? I at once called the blacks, among whom the news spread like wild-fire, and after looking for a short time, one of them came running with a torn skin, which he had found outside the camp. The whole head, a part of the tail, and the legs were eaten. It was my poor boongary skin that one of the dingoes had stolen and abused in this manner.
>
> Everyone tried to convince me that it was not *his* dog that was the culprit. All the dogs were produced, and each owner kept striking his dog's belly to prove its innocence. Finally, a half-grown cur was produced. The owner laid it on its back, seized it by the belly once or twice, and exclaimed '*Ammery, ammery!*'—that is, 'hungry, hungry!' But his abuse of the dog soon acted as an emetic, and presently a mass of skin-rags was strewed on the ground in front of it.

The biologist's preference for arsenic as a preservative was to lead to the tragic death of Balnglan. Lumholtz had rubbed arsenic on a ringtail possum and left it as bait to catch a large carnivorous marsupial known to the Aborigines as *Yarri*. Balnglan found the bait.

In 1889 Messrs Cairn and Grant were dispatched from the Australian Museum to the forests of north-east Queensland to obtain tree kangaroos. They soon realised that they could not do this without help from the local Aborigines and were apparently delighted to find that 'natives had been brought in by the police at Atherton ten miles from [their] camp'.

The collectors employed some of the Aborigines to obtain mammals for them. These hunters knew Lumholtz's tree kangaroo as *Mappi*, and they used an interesting method to catch it:

> On finding one in a tree, [they] build a sort of brush-yard round it a few feet from the roots; one of the natives then climbs up until he is above the animal, which he compels by pelting it with sticks to descend to the ground, where being unable to jump any height it is easily killed with waddies.

Hunters in the Torricelli Mountains of Papua New Guinea have described a variant of this method to me, whereby a fence is built much further out from the base of the tree. The hunter then climbs the tree and either attempts to get the tree kangaroo to leap to the ground, or throws it down by grasping its tail. Hunters and dogs waiting below then dispatch it. Hunters always claim that tree kangaroos always try to flee downslope when hunted in this manner. Sometimes, if there are plenty of people, the fence is done away with and a ring of people and dogs is used instead. In her behavioural study of Lumholtz's tree kangaroo, Elizabeth Proctor-Gray placed a fence made of fishing net in a six-metre radius around the tree and shook the tree kangaroo out.

Tree kangaroos are powerful animals, which, if handled carelessly, are capable of inflicting considerable damage. The

Aboriginal hunters who obtained Lumholtz's tree kangaroo for the Australian Museum in the nineteenth century made a fence around the tree in which a tree kangaroo was found. They would not enter the fence, and instead grasped its tail from outside, for fear of its powerful claws. Males of Bennett's tree kangaroo, which are much larger animals than Lumholtz's tree kangaroo, have a reputation for pugnacious behaviour. Early explorers in the region found that many Aborigines were fearful of approaching them. Residents living in the area today tell of male tree kangaroos climbing out of trees to fight with dogs that are baying at them from the ground below. If the fight were one-on-one, I am uncertain which would come off the better.

Mr Bob Whiston, an Irish durian-grower who lives on the Bloomfield River near Cooktown, recorded a three-way tussle between a male Bennett's tree kangaroo, a dog and a human. In a letter to me dated 28 July 1995, he related the following:

> My notes from 28-9-74 as follows: Adult male, [one] mile [east] of Hook's Crossing on Gap Creek. Heard grunting and sounds of a scuffle, thought pig caught by dingo but large male climber [a tree kangaroo] baled up by dog.
>
> Climber held both hands in air, palm outwards. Chased dog, grabbed tail of climber and said to Ruth, 'I think it's surrendered', but [it] brought both arms down with stunning speed and slashed my wrist cleanly and deeply (about three stitches' worth). First time we've seen the obviously effective defence. Bad cataracts but in good nick generally.
>
> The little female would sometimes accompany the 'I surrender' gesture with a little hop forward, but always

silently and with the face as devoid of expression (no teeth bared, etc.) as only tree kangaroos and the English are capable.

Golila hunters in Papua New Guinea told met that Doria's tree kangaroo (*Dendrolagus dorianus dorianus*) is a powerful adversary and will kill hunting dogs either by crushing the dog's snout with a paw or by ripping open the abdominal cavity. A rather lightly built Mianmin hunter I met in 1984 recounted that he had wrestled with a *Timboyok* (*Dendrolagus goodfellowi buergersi*) and was forced to beat a retreat. The story occasioned much mirth among his fellow hunters.

Mianmin have also told me how, when a hunter wounds a *Timboyok* with an arrow, the animal will pluck the arrow from its flesh and fling it back at its assailant, sometimes even hitting its mark. This behaviour seems unlikely but is widely believed among Mianmin and other New Guinean people.

Roger Schifferle, who lived for some time in a village near Lake Murray, Western Province, found lowland tree kangaroos (*Dendrolagus spadix*) living in uninhabited swamp forest to the south-east of Lake Murray. He pursued them on several occasions with local hunters, who were quite wary of them—adult males were particularly feared. The locals told him how lowland tree kangaroos band together to hunt wild pigs, just as people do. Indeed, these people recounted that much of the country east of Lake Murray remained uninhabited through fear of these creatures, which had driven out the original human inhabitants! While this story may seem ridiculous to biologists, it indicates how hunters relate to this large, and in some ways anthropomorphic, marsupial. It also neatly illustrates that where there are people, there are no lowland tree kangaroos, and vice versa.

The Western Dani, Amungme and Moni people of Irian Jaya have an intriguing way of cooking tree kangaroos. Evidence of such feasts is readily recognisable, for the stone ovens created for the occasion are large, consisting of a fireplace made of stones with a stone-lined oven pit alongside. The first stage in the process is to light a large fire and to singe the fur off the animal. The carcass is then butchered, the extremities (hands, feet and part of the tail) often being tossed into the fire. The tail tip and some claws are often retrieved for ornaments. Next, the various portions are wrapped in leaf packages.

While the butchering is going on, men are busy collecting large river stones to be placed on the fire. A cooking pit is dug near the fire, and the stones are wrapped in strong leaves and used to line the pit. They are then handled with wooden 'tongs'. From the forest, women bring fern fronds and edible green plants, which only they know how to find. These, along with the wrapped meat, are placed on top of the stones in the pit. More hot stones are placed on top of the food, and then everything is covered with large fern fronds. The meat and vegetables are thus slowly steamed and ready for eating within an hour.

Frenchmen Dreaming

Sunday Times, 1997

Just a short drive north of the Western Australian town of Busselton is the Vasse River. It is an unpretentious waterway that winds through salt flats before debouching languidly into Geographe Bay. It's a forgotten place, for there is not even the customary name sign on the South Western Highway where the bridge crosses the waterway. You would never know that the fate of empires was decided here. Yet, had things been just a little different 196 years ago, Australia's southern coast—from Busselton to Bass Strait—might now rejoice in the name *Terre Napoleon*. It's also just possible that its inhabitants would be speaking French.

In 1801 two French corvettes, the *Astrolabe* and *Geographe*, made their first Australian landfall off the river mouth. The ships were crammed with scientists in what was arguably the grandest and most ambitious exploring expedition ever sent to the great south land. They had left France eight months earlier, dispatched by Napoleon himself—a patron of exploration with a personal interest in Australia. Their discoveries, he hoped, would immortalise an empire, and in time its emperor. Tragically, the revolutionary foment of the times limited the fame of the expedition, even in France itself.

François Péron, a scientist on the expedition, left a vivid account of the expedition's landfall at the Vasse River. He enjoyed what he called 'the sport of waves' as the longboat toiled through the surf and came to a grinding halt against the sand. The strand was then, as today, strewn with seashells, cuttlefish bones and driftwood. But then all was new. No European eye had ever beheld the shells and plants. Here was a whole new world to explore, and the French set about cataloguing, collecting and studying.

Péron, however, had other things on his mind, for he was the first person ever to glory in the title 'field anthropologist'. He followed the river, hoping to find signs of human habitation. What he discovered was a structure he dubbed 'a garden-temple':

> Twelve large trees formed a semicircle, the two extremities of which terminated on the bank of the river. Within the area of the semicircle formed by these trees were three other semicircles each ending similarly with their extremities outwards towards the river. The outer semicircle was two feet in width, and consisted of a lawn of fine grass, raised six to eight inches above the ground. This elevated lawn was scalloped on the side which faced the river [forming] 27 'seats'. The next semicircle was a bank of turf two and a half feet wide and covered with black sand then a semicircle of rushes in a regular line and cut to the height of six inches. The third and last semicircle was covered by fine white sand…a vast number of rushes had been planted to form figures. Lastly, on the very edge of the river was a single large tree. The grand patriarch of the bower.

The trees were evidently great paperbarks, which had been stripped of their outer bark to give their trunks a smooth, silvery sheen.

This curious structure was my first clue that the Aborigines of the south-west of Western Australia were somewhat different from those of the rest of the continent. George Grey, who explored in Western Australia between 1837 and 1839 and was later Governor of South Australia, described them as a relatively settled and numerous people. As a region, the south-west has some of the most infertile soils in Australia, yet there are a few small areas where soils are reasonably fertile. Here, the Aborigines seem to have practised a sort of prototypical root-crop agriculture. The south-west is an exception to the rule that Australia is an El Niño dominated land of drought and flooding rain, for it experiences reliable winter rainfall. Could this account for the unusual Aboriginal cultures encountered by Grey?

The peculiar ecology of the south-west may have had other effects on these rather different Aborigines, for like New Guineans, they lived by the law of 'payback'. Here is what George Grey had to say of this aspect of their culture:

> The natives do not allow that there is such a thing as a death from natural causes [and] the first great principle with regard to punishment is, that all the relatives of a culprit, in the event of his not being found, are implicated in his guilt.

As I read Grey's account I began to wonder whether it was just coincidence that 'payback' was such a prominent feature of the culture of the south-western Aborigines, or whether it was related to other aspects of their lifestyle that are echoed in New Guinea.

I also began to wonder whether the 'bower' seen by Péron was further evidence that the Aborigines of the south-west were somewhat different—a more settled and numerous people than most. Curiosity as to whether anything remained of it led me to the mouth of the Vasse River almost 196 years to the day after Péron stepped ashore.

The Vasse River I encountered was not the place of my imaginings. The second I stepped from the car I found myself facing down a ferocious nor'-wester. The open bay, whipped into a fury, offers no protection from this direction. Sand and grit filled my scalp as I bent forward, searching for shells like those the French had seen. The water of the bay was stirred to a grim-looking chocolate by the madness of the breakers that drowned out all sound. The grey horizon beyond was empty, except for scudding clouds and angry sea.

And so it was for François Péron 196 years ago. The scientists had not noticed the wind shift, but Captain Baudin had. Fearing being caught on a lee shore, he had the vessels stand off. The wind continued overnight and into the next day, wrecking the shore party's boat. Baudin cursed the naivety of the scientists, with their penchant for collecting seashells. Yet something had to be done to rescue them.

Finally, with no respite in sight, Baudin ordered the cream of French seamanship into the *Geographe*'s longboat to pick up the scientists. The 'sport of waves' had turned into a nightmare, but through a miracle the shore party was picked up without incident. Then, when the rescue seemed all but complete, disaster struck.

Seaman Vasse, who had heroically manned the longboat's tiller throughout, was still at this duty as well as lending a hand to the scientists as they boarded the *Geographe*. As the last scientists clambered to safety, a huge wave hit the longboat, swamping it, and the brave French seaman was ejected into the briny.

Vasse struggled against the waves, time and again, to reach the ship, only to be defeated. Eventually he disappeared from view. The sailors and their captain were incensed. The life of their most heroic companion had been sacrificed by rescuing shell-collecting scientists who had failed to keep an eye on the weather. Already riven by internal dissent, from this moment on resentment between sailors and scientists exploded. Before long, the discord would all but tear the expedition apart.

The stormy weather and fast approaching winter added to the expedition's woes. Their orders were to chart *Terre Napoleon*, the great unknown southern coast of the continent, yet after the storm in Geographe Bay, Baudin turned north to Timor to await the summer. Consequently, Matthew Flinders beat the French to their long-desired south coast survey.

Despite their misfortunes, remnants of the French expedition persist in names such as Geographe Bay and Vasse River. More recent connections are found in the burgeoning vineyards of the south-west. Like the Aborigines of the area, the lives of the region's grape growers are shaped by the region's unusually reliable winter rainfall. Rain is liquid money and, when delivered on time and in just the right quantities, it makes growing grapes of the highest quality that much easier. When I asked one vintner about the effect of droughts on local production, he scratched his head for a moment and replied, 'Droughts? Oh yes, I've heard they get those east of Albany.'

Following my pilgrimage to the Vasse River, I stopped off at Killerby, a tiny family-owned vineyard located at the very bottom of Geographe Bay. Tuart forest grew on the site until it was cleared for pasture. Today, a few hectares of vines nestle in a small swale, at the bottom of which soil has accumulated, and this is just a little richer than the sterile sands of the surrounding dunes. The vines struggle in the sandy soil, and as a result produce grapes of unusual intensity of flavour.

As I entered the cellar, I noticed that the barrels of French oak were labelled *Tronçais*. The village of Cérilly, nestled deep in the Fôret du Tronçais, was the birthplace of François Péron. Peron retired there following the great expedition, broken by tuberculosis. In a vain attempt to restore his health, he resorted to a local folk remedy and took up living in a cow shed. There, in the winter of 1810, he died. All that remains today to remind one of Cérilly's greatest son is a monument in the village square, decorated with images of Australian flora and fauna. The villagers themselves have long forgotten its significance.

The fine barrels of Tronçais oak that fill the Killerby cellar would have been a familiar sight to Péron, but he could never have imagined them being exported to Geographe Bay to mature wine, which would rival France's finest. Nor could he have imagined paying $1400 for each barrel, as winemakers do today.

As befits an agricultural enterprise in fragile Australia, everything at Killerby's is done with an eye toward sustainability. Lucerne is planted between the vines to supply nitrogen naturally to the soil. Sunflowers are planted when the grapes are ripening to distract the birds. And the barrels of Tronçais oak are recycled when their usefulness to the winemaker has ended. They are then turned into elegant furniture that is impregnated with the scent of the best Western Australian wine.

On a sunny day, the mouth of the Vasse River is still beautiful—but only just. A quaint colonial farmhouse nestles behind the dunes in a bend in the river near, perhaps, where Peron's Aboriginal 'temple' once stood. It would look just as attractive and at home in rural France.

No sign of the bower remains, nor even the stately paperbarks that surrounded it. Unfortunately, the local Aboriginal culture was altered so rapidly following European settlement that it is not possible to say how different it was from that of the rest of the continent, nor what the bower's precise significance was. Yet all is not lost, for Aboriginal culture is undergoing a revival in the south-west. While in Busselton I heard a rumour that somewhere to the south of the Vasse, local Aborigines had recently made a replica of the structure sketched by Péron, using his published drawing as a blueprint. Péron would, I'm sure, have been as surprised as he would be delighted at this use of his work.

A hundred metres south of the Vasse River mouth a very different construction project is taking shape. A hideous canal development scars the landscape. Great bulldozers have gouged the salt marshes—once home to scores of waterbirds and irreplaceable biological values—into uniform, concrete-sided canals. Mansion-like brick houses are sprouting up on the windswept piles of saline mud heaped between them. These temples of the white Australians are dedicated to a lesser, more pecuniary god than the structure that graced the site 200 years earlier.

Ironically, the only tribute I could find to the French in the whole region was in an advertisement above the canal estate's sales office. It features a caricature of a rueful Napoleon. 'Sacré bleu,' the emperor laments, 'how did we let this Port Geographe slip through our hands? The land is selling so fast.'

As for the Aborigines, it is as if their 40,000 years habitation in the area had never existed. This environmental and heritage catastrophe unfolding at the mouth of the Vasse River will scar Australia irreparably, for the place is one of enormous cultural significance for both Aborigines and Europeans. Instead we are treating it like a sewer.

Western Australia, like much of the rest of the nation, seems to be going through a period of deep schism in its attitude to the environment. On one side are enterprises like Killerby's, who are clearly there for the long haul, and who are pioneering new ways of living sustainably in this demanding land. On the other are the slash-and-burn developers, who will walk away from the mess and the environmental debt they have created just as soon as the last block is sold. Unfortunately, government policy often seems to encourage the latter.

Years after the return of the Baudin expedition, the French newspaper *Le Moniteur* published a story that somehow seaman Vasse had survived and had made it ashore, there to live happily ever after amongst the Aborigines. Searches were made, but no evidence was ever found of this Vasse Felix.

I have since wondered whether things would have turned out better had Baudin turned south instead of north, and France had successfully colonised Australia's west. I doubt that they would have treated their 'story places' as neglectfully as us, but if their environmental record in the Pacific were any guide, they probably would have destroyed nature at least as thoroughly. Perhaps it is in the synergy of the French oak barrels, an Australian love of good wine, and a respect for the land as deep as that of the Aborigines that we will find our way forward.

Sydney Gone Wrong? It's Werrong

Sydney Morning Herald, July 1996

The city of Sydney has taken root in a very special place, for it is situated in the centre of one of the planet's greatest concentrations of biodiversity. There are more eucalypt species of different types growing within a 200-kilometre radius of Sydney than anywhere else on Earth. For this alone, I have heard botanists talk of nominating the region as a World Heritage area.

Add to this waratahs, gymea lilies and thousands of other unique species of plants, reptiles and insects as well as our marine ecosystems, and one begins to appreciate just how extraordinary the immediate Sydney environment is.

And yet, for all this, we continue to treat Sydney as another European city. London plane trees line our streets. They support nothing. I have never seen so much as a leaf chewed by an insect on any of them. Eucalypts, in contrast have between 6 to 40 per cent of their leaves damaged by insects. This very high percentage is testimony to the riot of life each eucalypt shelters. Thousands of insects are dependent upon them, which in turn support countless birds and mammals.

I have seen a visiting Hungarian entomologist moved to tears at the beauty of the beetles he found in a native tree growing in

Hyde Park. Yet we who live here seem to be blind to that beauty. Every year sees more backyards and open spaces subdivided, more trees destroyed.

I am sick at heart when I see that our best response is to plant more English plane trees or other exotics in the few remaining places suitable for trees in our streets. We have 25,000 native species from which to choose. Must we continue to choose our street trees from the 6000 or so species to be found in Europe?

Our urban parks have also been tragically neglected. The last place on mainland Australia where one could see eastern quolls was Nielsen Park, near the very centre of the city. They were allowed to become extinct in the early 1970s. No attempt to save the priceless colony was made. Our parks have lost countless hundreds of such species. Many species, from quolls to waratahs, could be successfully reintroduced to bring some semblance of the region's original biodiversity back. With judicious management, these introductions would thrive.

Our marine environment is likewise impoverished. Cape Town has a highly visible colony of sea lions living right in the city's polluted inner harbour. They are fed fish in lean times. Why could not Sydney have managed a return of seals to our harbour?

The reason lies, I think, in our fundamentally European cultural orientation. Even though we call ourselves Australian and are privileged to inhabit one of the world's most wondrous environments, we still expect our parks to have lawns, deciduous trees and introduced pigeons.

Worse, our inappropriate cultural baggage allows us to destroy our inherited natural beauty with impunity. English law, derived from its class-dominated, hierarchical society, has always permitted the landed gentry to do pretty much as they will with their property.

Here in Australia, with our unique, fragile and highly interconnected ecology, this brings disaster. It is also fundamentally at odds with our Australian sense of social obligation and 'a fair go'.

Recently, I lost something very dear to me in an outright theft. A hotel built a large extension, snatching from me my view of Sydney Harbour. The developer then sold my view to someone else. It was a theft as brazen and hurtful as any break and enter, except that every day I must look at the thief. Nearby are other developments under construction sporting billboards, which state 'own the view everyone comes to see'. Our laws, derived as they are from another ecology, another social system, condone such thefts, and yet prosecute vigorously far more trivial offences.

Even our language may need to change to accommodate our new environment. Is not 'land development' in this context more appropriately referred to as land exploitation? Were we to view it this way, we might set up a register of sites that could be exploited, rather than a register of those that cannot. Whatever the case, we should demand that the exploiters at least leave the site more biodiverse, with greater bulk of native biomass, than when they found it.

If we wish to retain the beauty and biodiversity of this extraordinary city, we need to adapt quickly to life in Australia. It is for this reason that, in my internal dialogue, I can no longer call this city Sydney. It is Werrong.

Werrong is a city of hybrid origin. Grafted from British stock, it will, I hope, adapt to the abrupt cliffs and poor soils of the land on which it is built. Its inhabitants will, perhaps, one day feel genuinely at home with its ecology, and yearn no more for another ecology, another continent.

What Is Love?

Sydney Morning Herald, JANUARY 1997

The biology of love makes depressing reading. This is because our genes are designed to make us do things that make us miserable. Still, it's best to know the game plan of the enemy, for without that you have very little chance of defeating him. So steel yourself for a briefing.

Genes are the job sheet by which we are made, and as far as they are concerned we have but one purpose—to ensure their immortality. Given this, it is not surprising that our genes take a special interest in our love life. Although we are largely unaware of it, they try to dictate, in the most imposing manner, with whom we shall fall in love, when we will fall in love and even when we shall fall out of it.

If you remain sceptical of this, consider the issues of with whom you fall in love. Because of the genetic defects associated with inbreeding, it is best for our genes if we do not fall in love with our siblings, and they have gone to elaborate lengths to make us avoid this. An extraordinary study of 2769 marriages among the children of kibbutzim (who, although unrelated, live together from birth to adulthood), revealed that only thirteen marriages were contracted between children from the same kibbutz.

But even these thirteen were the exception which proved the rule, for they all involved children who had arrived at the kibbutz after age six. Even more amazing, there was not a single instance of heterosexual activity between same-kibbutz kids. This shows astonishing restraint on the part of nearly 6000 hormone-loaded boys and girls! Only an in-built incest taboo devised by our genes could achieve such a thing.

It is also good for our genes if we don't fall in love with someone or—something—too different: a chimpanzee, for instance. Those thirteen couples that married after meeting at age six or later open the way for an understanding of how our devious genes achieve this. Age six, it turns out, is the critical time for imprinting our future mate. In short, your partner is likely to resemble the kids you played with at that age. Our genes have chosen this age because our six-year-old playmates are likely to be similar to, but not closely related to us. This maximises genetic fitness.

The impact of this 'age six sex imprinting' is particularly evident among people who spent this part of their childhood in a foreign culture. A woman I know spent this critical period in Fiji. She has fallen for dark-skinned men ever since. Once again the exception proves the rule.

Having got us in the right general ballpark as far as a mate is concerned, our genes then ensure that we choose (or try to choose) the partner who suits them perfectly. For male and female genes, the attributes of the perfect partner are very different.

For male genes, the perfect mate is youthful and beautiful. The obsession with youth is straightforward. Our genes would prefer us to mate with a young woman because she has more reproductive years for them to exploit. Beauty, however, reveals a more devious side of genes.

What is beauty? It is simply the average. An ingenious researcher discovered this when he developed a computer program which 'averaged' the features of a human face. It superimposed one randomly picked face upon another, then melded the two images. He produced a series of images resulting from the averaging of between two and nine faces. When he asked his subjects to choose the most beautiful face, without exception they considered the face with the most superimpositions as the most beautiful.

But why should genes prefer the average? Because the average 'evens out' asymmetries and odd features. Body asymmetries are a good clue to the presence of genetic abnormalities. Our genes don't want us mating with someone who is carrying those defects.

That beauty is 'average' is commonsense, really. If beauty consisted of anything other than an appreciation of the average, natural selection over a million years would have resulted in human faces as bizarre as the plumage of the birds of paradise.

The fact that heterosexual men generally find large breasts and broad hips attractive is also plainly due to the male genes' desire for reproductive success. Large breasts promise an ample milk supply, while broad hips promise an easy birth. Male genes stand to be tricked on this count, however, for large breasts and buttocks could result from obesity and not reproductive fitness. It is possible that male genes then began to select for females with a narrow waist as a sort of 'certificate of guarantee' that breasts and buttocks were not the result of obesity. Thus the hourglass figure.

This 'guarantee', though, is yet another dupe. The breadth of female hips does not correlate with ease of birth; the underlying bony female pelvic structure does. Broad hips are the result of fat deposits. They are false advertising. Male genes, it seems, are not yet smart enough to have discovered this.

And what do female genes desire in a man? Generally, they are not so choosy about looks or age; but height, status and wealth are all highly attractive to them. So, curiously, are honesty, kindness and generosity. The benefits of height, status and wealth are obvious, but what of the rest? For a woman's genes to optimise their chance at immortality, they need to attract a mate who will continue to contribute to her children throughout life. Perhaps honesty, kindness and generosity are some guide to a man's propensity to do this.

But why does love exist at all? Do chimpanzees love? I think not, or at least not as we love. This is because humans are the only higher apes which form a pair bond. We do this because the division of labour between male and female results in a benefit greater than either could achieve alone. Men bring home the wild boar, while women hunt by hand and gather the greens. Love ensures that we continue to benefit from this co-operation.

And yet the genes do not want a perfectly harmonious system. The genes of men may be better served by him leaving his partner when the children are old enough to survive without his input, then starting another family with a new, younger partner. This genetic treadmill sees octogenarian millionaires marrying ever-younger women. A woman's genes, likewise, may not be best served by fidelity. She may find the security she needs in one partner, but the recipe for success in another. Her genes can have the best of both worlds if she indulges in a moment of infidelity. Little wonder that around 10 per cent of children in Western societies are estimated not to be the children of their putative father. Such is the genetic treadmill made for us. How can we get off it?

Fortunately, genes don't have it all their own way. They made a terrible mistake when they invented the human brain. Suddenly the creature they created to launch them into eternity could think for itself. It had its own feelings, needs and desires. It might decide, for instance, that it just does not like the richest, tallest, most successful man in town, or that it is happy with life-long monogamy. It might decide that it would be happiest without reproducing at all.

Worse, from the genes' point of view, we have discovered how we are made, and have developed powerful technologies. We might even decide that we dislike a particular gene, and snip it out with gene shears.

So if you are at a party chatting to an average-looking person, and that person says something that goes straight to your heart, and you feel that he or she might be the one for you, tell your genes to go to hell.

Australia: Overpopulated or Last Frontier?

Politics and the Life Sciences, SEPTEMBER 1997

The spectre of a declining population causes alarm amongst economists, demographers and politicians. To many biologists, however, it is a natural process that is probably inevitable, on the global scale, in the coming centuries.

Kenneth Smail has given this important issue the coverage it deserves in his article 'Beyond Population Stabilisation'. A key aspect of his case is that there are few if any 'frontiers' to be exploited by a growing population. The only realistic option is, therefore, to reduce population. My work on population-related issues has been undertaken largely in what is considered to be an underpopulated land—Australia.

Australia is a continent of 7.6 million square kilometres— about the size of the contiguous forty-eight states of the United States of America. Australia controls an exclusive fishing zone of over 10 million square kilometres. Its population is currently about 18 million.* By contrast to the United States, it appears to be underpopulated. For over fifty years the Australian government has been acting to increase population. But what is the reality?

---

* Today this is about 21 million.

The Minister for Immigration recently announced that Australia's population will reach 23 million by 2025, if immigration policy and fertility projections remain unchanged. This represents about a 25 per cent increase in just over a generation. Immigrants will comprise about half this number and their children a smaller, additional percentage.

This increase follows a period of extraordinary population growth in Australia's postwar history. Between 1986 and 1996, the Australian rate of population increase exceeded that of China, Canada and the United States. It continues to approach or even exceed that of many developing countries. This rapid growth is occurring in the absence of a national population policy.

In my book *The Future Eaters*, I suggested that Australia was already overpopulated, and that given current technology and affluence, its optimum population probably lies somewhere between 6 and 12 million. This finding was initially met with disbelief and derision. It is now, however, not so outlandish as it formerly appeared.

In December 1996, the Australian federal government published its first comprehensive 'State of the Environment' report. For the first time, Australians had an accurate, up-to-date account of the health of the environment, much of which was presented in real dollar terms. The results were shocking.

Australians have long believed that exploitation of their marine resources could be extended significantly. The continent has one of the largest exclusive fishing zones on the planet, yet its fisheries rank only fifty-third in size. The bad news is that even this modest achievement has come at the cost of gross overexploitation of the nation's fish stocks. The report found that virtually no Australian fishery was being conducted sustainably. Many of the most important were already in collapse (and a number that have collapsed over the past fifty years are not showing significant signs of recovery).

The situation on land is just as dire. Forest resources are becoming depleted, with access to the last remnants being savagely disputed between industry and conservationists. Supplies of timber products seem to be insufficient to satisfy demand over the coming decades.

Just 3 per cent of Australia's surface area is suitable for growing crops. Even here, the soils are characteristically poor and fragile. Much is already stricken by significant soil degradation. Until the 1970s, Australia exported about $20 million worth of wheat per annum. In the 1990s it managed to export as much as $60 million worth for some years, but only half that for the one that followed. It is becoming clear that farmers are planting wheat in ever more marginal areas, and that inter-annual variability in crop yield is increasing as a result. The damage done to fragile, marginal lands by this practice is enormous.

Rainfall is more variable in the eastern two-thirds of Australia than almost anywhere else on the planet. This means that rangelands are easily overgrazed, water catchments and reservoirs must be enormous to cope with droughts, and water quality can decline precipitously following drought or flood. Sydney must have the capacity to store three Olympic-sized swimming pools of water per head of population as a result—a far greater volume than that of other Western capitals. The closer catchments are now used to capacity, and even distant ones such as the Darling are utilised.

Despite the enormity of the water problem, the authors of the government's reports did not see it as being the most serious concern. That, they agreed, was the loss of biodiversity. Many of Australia's ecosystems are in collapse, and species loss is the result.

Many Australians hope that increasingly sophisticated technology will remedy these difficulties, but there are few signs that this will happen. Indeed, earlier attempts at 'improving' things, such as damming rivers and fertilising soils, have themselves added to the problems. The few success stories so far have involved enterprises which work with the environment rather than against it, and have placed less demand upon resources.

Successive droughts, floods and persistent economic problems have pushed people from the rural areas into the cities. As a result, Australian society is one of the most urbanised on the planet. Many of Australia's cities are now so large that they face daunting problems. On some days each year air pollution in Sydney and Melbourne already approaches the levels of that in New York and Tokyo, and both cities will spend billions in the future to ameliorate air and water pollution. Perth and Adelaide will suffer severe water shortages in the future, while transport and other infrastructure in many cities is straining under rapidly increasing demand.

Sydney, in particular, is finding its infrastructure and amenities strained under the burden of 4 million inhabitants. Its own river system, the Hawkesbury, is severely degraded and can no longer cope with the demand placed upon it as both a drain and a water source. The city's wildlife is being elbowed out by increasing development. The harbour catchment's last bandicoot colony is currently under threat from a housing development, while concrete is replacing greenery at many locations around the foreshore.

Australia's immigration policy grew out of postwar xenophobia and a desire for national greatness. It was originally designed to deliver a 2 per cent population growth rate per year. So ingrained were beliefs concerning its benefits that until recently there was almost no rigorous analysis of the program.

Doubts concerning the value of large-scale immigration are now widespread. Because immigration intakes are not justified within the context of a population policy, they cannot be defended as being demonstrably in the national interest. This situation has provided fertile grounds for racists. Those opposed to all immigration, especially that from Asia have flourished, causing enormous societal strain and personal hardship.

For all these reasons, there is an urgent need for Australia's immigration policy to be determined in the context of a national population policy. This policy should be based upon an estimate of the optimum population size for the continent. This approach would result in an intellectually defensible immigration intake, which could be shown to be in the national interest.

Should that population policy indicate the need for a population decline, Australia should be ready to countenance it.

A Hostile Land

New Scientist, JANUARY 1998

Politics and science are sometimes too comfortable as bedfellows. When the British Empire was at its height, it was widely assumed that the native races in colonies such as Australia would, as if by a law of nature, give way to the inherently superior British colonists. In the same way, Australia's marsupials—primitive pouch-bearing species such as kangaroos and koalas—were expected to vanish before the advance of colonising fox, sheep and rabbit.

The recent turmoil over land rights in Australia clearly illustrates that colonial views about the inevitable demise of Australia's Aborigines were mistaken. Now, the discovery of a tiny fossil jaw in southern Victoria has shaken the long-accepted view that placental mammals (which feed their young through a placenta—such as cows, dogs and whales) are superior to and tend to replace marsupials when the two groups compete. The finders of the jaw have named it *Ausktribosphenos nyktos*.

The importance of the fossil is that it apparently belonged to a placental mammal that lived in southern Australia 120 million years ago. This makes it the oldest, well-dated placental on the planet, opening up the possibility that our distant placental relatives first evolved on the southern continents. As if that weren't heretical enough—placentals were thought to have evolved in the northern hemisphere, where they dominate today—the find also implies that placental mammals became extinct in Australia while the supposedly primitive marsupials, and even more superannuated egg-laying mammals like the platypus, survived.

This week [late November 1997], publication of the find has provoked intense controversy. Some scientists have suggested that it is a strange monotreme, but the supporting evidence is almost non-existent. Others have suggested that while the jaw looks like that of a placental, it must have belonged to its own, hitherto unknown group of mammals, which closely resembled placentals. I suspect that if the find had been made outside Australia, neither of these possibilities would have been raised.

I am reasonably satisfied that the jaw did indeed belong to a placental, but a placental that was living in the wrong place and time to conform with current dogma. And I do not find it so surprising that placentals should have failed in the race for survival in Australia.

Australia is very different from the other continents. Its infertile soils and extremely variable climate make it a hostile place for any species requiring a high input of energy from its food. As a result, cold-blooded creatures such as reptiles have done particularly well there. Placental mammals have greater energy requirements than similar marsupials. They also have larger brains, which is a good thing if you can afford it. The trouble is that the brain is the greediest of all organs in the body. In humans, it weighs a mere 2 per cent of the body mass, yet requires 18 per cent of our energy input to maintain it. In places where food is hard to find—which includes much of Australia—such an organ can become a fatal burden.

The placental mammal jaw may well be telling us that the current distribution of mammals is the result of differential extinction rather than dispersal. It appears possible that both marsupials and placentals were widely distributed on all continents towards the end of the age of dinosaurs. In the rich northern continents, the placentals could out-compete the marsupials, because resources were sufficient to support their extravagant needs. Conditions were poorer in South America, and marsupials there became predators while the placentals became herbivores. I believe this occurred because less energy reaches the top of the food pyramid, so the miserly marsupials could survive in that ecological niche. Australia, however, was so nutrient-poor that the low food requirements of the marsupials and monotremes gave them such a great advantage that they could utterly out-compete the placentals—that is, until invading placentals met a naive marsupial fauna in the nineteenth century...

Well, that's the new view from the antipodes. But the find has given human Australians more to ponder than mere evolution. For it suggests that our distant placental ancestor failed to survive on this strange continent. Amazingly, each Australian currently uses as much energy as five sperm whales. Our catastrophic environmental record reflects this. Perhaps it is time that the Australian government reconsidered its stance on greenhouse gas emissions and looked at new, energy-efficient ways of surviving on what is clearly a challenging continent.

The Day, the Land, the People

AUSTRALIA DAY ADDRESS, JANUARY 2002

Two hundred and fourteen years and one day ago, a rowboat tentatively made its way through the entrance of the harbour that lies outside these doors. It was the first European vessel ever to glide upon Cadi, as Sydney Harbour was then called, and it carried Governor Phillip, who was seeking a place to settle the 1000–odd people of Australia's First Fleet.

This is the 214th anniversary of the day Phillip discovered the pretty cove called Werrong with its run of good, clean water. He must have been delighted by the smooth-trunked angophoras that seemed to spring straight from the sandstone around it, their limbs turning bright salmon pink as they shed the last of the old year's bark. And the water was full of bream. One of Phillip's rowers, an American named Jacob Nagle, hooked a beauty while the governor was ashore examining the cove he would rename Sydney for a dithering and now-forgotten Home Secretary.

Phillip's party left the following morning, and for one last time—just a few days—the Cadigaleans had Cadi all to themselves. As they woke next morning to warm themselves by the fire, they faced, as always, the incomparable harbour that gave them their life and their name; and watched its ruffled waters, musing, perhaps, that the rowboat's visit had been a bad dream.

Doubtless they enjoyed those last few lazy summer days travelling to their favourite spots to fish. The women would take to their canoes with fishing line in hand, a fire smouldering amidships and perhaps a baby on their shoulders; while the men strolled to a sheltered cove, its surface like a mirror. There they would chew mussels, spitting into the water and spearing the fish that came to the burley. Or maybe they'd just pluck a feed of oysters from the rocks, or gather great handfuls of flowers to make a sweet drink from the nectar.

Some Cadigaleans were lucky enough to have their own private island in the harbour. These had been handed down from parent to child since time immemorial. Perhaps they'd invite friends over to enjoy a meal at this special spot; then the sounds of the corroboree would carry through the balmy night air. If conditions were right, the young men would travel to the beaches near the Heads to ride their short bark canoes through the waves, managing them with small hand paddles in feats of amazing sporting prowess.

The anniversary we're celebrating today marks the day that ruined the neighbourhood for the Cadigaleans. Within eighteen months of Phillip's return, half of them were dead from smallpox. Within a century their 10,000 years of freehold around the harbour would be denied, then forgotten. Only the bream remembered. Those crafty fish make no distinction between black and white, but treat all of us two-legged landgoers with the same suspicion.

Perhaps because we all sense in our hearts the tragedy of this, our national day carries shadows that neither ebb nor lighten with the years. We can't celebrate Australia Day unreservedly, nor can we expect Aboriginal people to celebrate it, unless we somehow come to terms with that terrible history. For a long time we denied it; until that furious outbreak recently when we screamed at each other that the black armband view, or the white blindfold one, was the more correct version of our past. Then, just over a year ago, 100,000 Australians took to the Harbour Bridge and strode across the waters of Cadi, the sky above emblazoned with a heartfelt 'sorry' to the Cadigals and other indigenous peoples of this land.

It marked, perhaps, a new beginning—one that I'd like, if I can, to carry forward today.

Australia Day is also a day for relaxing and celebrating the good life—a great Aussie holiday—and a time also to think about our origins; what it means to be Australian, and where our nation is going. Perhaps it's an Australian characteristic that until now we've been long on the leisure and short on the thinking, which is unfortunate, because it has left us with shallow roots in this continent. Our history and our ecology reveal just how superficial those roots are, for they show that most of us still live as people from somewhere else, who just happen to inhabit—sometimes unsustainably, ignorantly and destructively—this marvellous continent.

Let's look at history first. Growing up with Irish ancestry in Victoria, I've always had a soft spot for Ned Kelly, with his intolerance of injustice and independent spirit. But the more I think about him, the less I see him as distinctively 'Australian'. At heart he was an Irishman struggling with his Old World oppressors in a drama transplanted to the Antipodes, the khaki backdrop of the Australian bush making little difference. The Man from Snowy River can hardly be regarded as uniquely Australian either. Seated astride American megafauna (a horse) that had been introduced to the continent just a century before, chasing other introduced megafauna, he is a figure of a much larger history—the global cattle frontier. Exchange his Akubra for a ten-gallon hat and he becomes a cowboy. Give him chaps and maté and he is transformed into an Argentinian *vaquero*. Even most written histories of the Australian nation read like the story of a European people who just happen—almost incidentally—to stride an Australian stage. And perhaps that is, until now, precisely what we have been.

I don't mean to suggest that the European aspects of our history are irrelevant or should be disposed of—only that they reflect us as a people who have not yet developed deep, sustaining roots in the land. Yet Australia—the land, its climate and creatures and plants—is the only thing that we all share in common. It is at once our inheritance, our sustenance, and the only force ubiquitous and powerful enough to craft a truly Australian people. It ought to define us as a people like no other.

And our land is so very different from any other. The Europeans who migrated to North America found a land not so very different from the one they had left behind, but those who came to Australia sometimes felt that they had arrived on another planet. The environmental forces that have, over the millennia, shaped that very distinctive Australia—from kangaroos to gum trees and Aboriginal cultures—are currently working on us, shaping our culture. So it is worthwhile knowing a little about the forces that make Australia so different.

For 45 million years Australia has wandered in isolation across the Southern Ocean, carrying with it an ark full of ancient life forms. Over this immense period the other continents have experienced violent change—profound swings of climate that saw them transformed from tropical paradises into bare rock sheathed in miles of ice. Their nature has been irrevocably altered by multiple invasions of plants and animals, their ecological stability denied. Australia, however, has remained almost unique in its stability. Its biodiversity increased in relative peace and isolation over the eons, until today we rank eighth on the planet in the richness of our natural wonders. And because of that stability many species became very specialised, confined perhaps to just a few square kilometres, making them vulnerable to future changes.

It also seems that the evolution of life here was driven partly by a different imperative—towards co-operation for survival rather than competition. Many Australian birds, from kookaburras to blue wrens, breed co-operatively, and many species exist in symbiosis with others. This trend towards co-operation is also evident in the country's human cultures (a theme to which I will return). As a result of these trends, Australian life forms have become woven into a web of interdependence, which means that a small disturbance in one part has repercussions for the whole.

Despite its relative stability, this ancient Australia was no paradise. Its soils were by far the poorest and most fragile of any continent, its rainfall the most variable, and its rivers the most ephemeral. It was a harsh land for any creature that demanded much from it, and as a result energy efficiency is the hallmark of Australia's plants, animals and human cultures.

Our European heritage left us appallingly equipped to survive long-term in this country. It left many colonial Australians unable to see the subtle beauty and biological richness of the land, and what they could not understand they strove to destroy as alien and useless. For most of the last two centuries we have believed that we could remake the continent in the image of Europe—turn the rivers inland and force the truculent soils to yield. We knowingly introduced pests—from starlings to foxes and rabbits—

in our efforts to transform this vast Austral realm into a second England. Much of this terrible history reads as a rush towards 'development', which was then, and often still is, just a soft word for the destruction of Australia's resource base.

That arrogant colonial vision left a fearful legacy, for it actually made people feel virtuous while they dealt the land the most terrible blows. Already one of every ten of Australia's unique mammals is extinct, and almost everywhere—even in our national parks—biodiversity is declining. Australia's soils are still being mined—salination will destroy the majority of Western Australia's wheat belt in our lifetime if nothing is done—while our rivers are in great peril and sustainable fisheries everywhere have collapsed. We are reaping the bitter harvest of all of this today. The last fifty years have been marked by a return of Australians to the cities, partly because the resource base they relied on had been destroyed by earlier generations.

Yet despite all this, there are signs that things are changing for the better. Today, as the Australian environment subtly teaches those who listen to it, Australians are undergoing a radical reassessment of their relationship with the land, particularly when it comes to the basics like food, water and fire. After 200 years of destruction, revolutionary changes are taking place in the countryside as farmers and graziers strive to make primary production sustainable in Australia's unique conditions. Leading the way are people like the Bell family, who run cattle sustainably in the ultra-dry Lake Eyre Basin, or the many involved in the development of sustainable aquaculture. These people are *my* national heroes. Unlike Ned Kelly or the Man from Snowy River they're not acting out European dramas on an Australian stage but are instead throwing out old, inappropriate European-based practices and inventing distinctively Australian futures to create sustainability in this land.

I have no doubt that today many farmers are very far ahead of the majority of Australians in most aspects of environmental thinking. What's needed now is a shift in consumption patterns by city-dwellers to provide a market for sustainably produced products. As the 'buy Australian' campaigns and the advertising of many products as 'environmentally friendly' shows, there is a great desire among Australians to preserve their environment. Yet damage still continues, in part because urban-dwellers need to become better informed about what sustainability really means, and how they need to change their patterns of consumption to achieve it.

The way we use water is also slowly changing in response to Australia's unique environment. Because of our continent's great rainfall variability, Sydneysiders need eight to ten times the water storage of the inhabitants of New York or London. The economic and environmental costs of this are stupendous, and they are forcing us into new ways of thinking about water as plans for more dams are shelved and water is re-priced. This shift has the power to alter our urban landscapes—for the beloved Europe-green lawn, English rose and London plane tree are all thirsty drinkers.

Nothing seems to rouse the ire of some Australians so much as disparaging roses, lawns, plane trees and the like. Yet I really do think that they are a blot on the landscape. I used to joke that I'd shout beer all round at my local pub the day someone brought me a plane tree leaf that an insect had actually taken a bite out of. As far as Australian wildlife goes, plane trees are so useless that they might as well be made of concrete. Australia is home to 25,000 species of plants, as opposed to Europe's 6000 or 7000. Surely amongst that lot we can find suitable species that will provide shade, and food for butterflies and native birds as well? And there is another reason I dislike many introduced plants. If gardens are a type of window on the mind, in our public spaces I see a passion for the European environment that indicates that we are still, at heart, uncomfortable in our own land. If we can see no beauty in Australian natives, but instead need to be cosseted in pockets of European greenery, can we really count ourselves as having a truly sustainable future adapted to Australian conditions?

Fire is the issue of the moment. Who could imagine, having seen the heartrending destruction in Canberra over the last few weeks, that we are even beginning to understand how to manage fire in Australia? The losses in biodiversity and human infrastructure we suffered are part of a repeated pattern that shouts to us that our fire prevention practices are inappropriate.

It's worth recalling the searing summer of 1789, when Sydney was just a year old. Then the wind blew so hot from the north-west that birds and flying foxes dropped, dying, from the sky. Watkin Tench wrote that standing among the rough tents of Sydney was like being at the mouth of an oven—yet the journals of the First Fleeters mention no fire. When it came to fire management, the Aboriginal people of the Sydney region had things right, for they maintained biodiversity while reducing the risk of wildfire. While we do not know in detail how they managed things, we can surmise that they managed the land with an eye to fire all year round—not just in crises.

Three human lifetimes—about 214 years—is simply not long enough for a people to become truly adapted to Australia's unique conditions, for the process of learning, of co-evolving with the land, is slow and uncertain. Yet it has begun, and the transformation must be completed, for if we continue to live as strangers in this land—failing to understand it or live by its ecological dictums—we will forfeit our long-term future here by destroying the ability of Australia to support us.

An environmental view of culture is not what most people think of when defining themselves as Australian. Instead, things like meat pies, Holdens and Aussie Rules (or League) loom large. Holding such things dear makes some people feel more Australian than others—the citizen eating a souvlaki, or wearing a turban, or following the soccer, for instance. Yet such definitions tend to divide Australians from one another rather than unite us. I like my meat pie as much as anyone, though it's silly to define your identity around it. I look forward to the day when we forget about whether it's a pie or a souvlaki that's being eaten, and ask instead what the meat is—whether it's sustainably harvested kangaroo, or beef from a polluting feed-lot.

For those weaned on the notion of multiculturalism the concept of an environmentally based Australian identity may seem alien. Why not let a plethora of cultures from all corners of the globe exist side by side in this expansive land? And isn't the alternative simply assimilation into the great Anglo majority? While I celebrate Australia's diverse cultural mix, I don't think that multiculturalism is the future for Australia, simply because no culture can exist unmodified in a new environment. Old practices die away and new ones, those that help people adapt to their new home, spring up. At the most fundamental level that is what cultures *do*—they help us to survive in our particular circumstances. As a result, after 214 years of exposure to Australian conditions, the supposedly dominant Anglo culture is no longer truly 'Anglo'. Instead it has been steeped in the dye of Australia and it is beginning to transform into something else. The same is true for every other cultural group that has entered this continent—even the Aborigines were once newly arrived people from Asia. Whether we like it or not, all of us are in the process of a slow convergence on a yet-to-be-formed Australian culture that is suited to Australia's conditions.

The single most important change needed for our country is for all Australians to achieve true environmental sustainability. A tremendous start has already been made in the area of primary production, but much more remains to be done. The development of a population policy is central to this process and would, I believe, result in better environmental and humanitarian outcomes.

Australia's population policy should be based on recognition of the environmental constraints of our land, our economic needs, and the social desires of its people. The only way that such a policy can be achieved is for the nation to engage in a broad, vigorous and truthful debate, accompanied by a government inquiry that is charged with setting an optimum population target. Once the target has been decided we should redesign our immigration program in light of it, with an eye to more flexibility and greater fairness. Before the inquiry has done its work it is not possible to say how large the immigration intake could be, but almost any imaginable scenario would allow for a reasonable level of immigration.

The development of such a policy would remove much of the hysteria and negativity from the immigration debate, for an immigration program firmly embedded in a population policy would transparently serve the national interest, and thus have the support of most people. It would also result in a better humanitarian outcome, because the intake could be framed over a longer period than the current annual intake, allowing us to accommodate those caught up in international emergencies.

Another advantage of such a policy is that by examining environmental impacts to set the population target, we would highlight our most unsustainable environmental practices. These could then be targeted for remediation so that our overall environmental impact would be reduced (allowing for a larger population, if that is what we wish). It would be important for the population target to be reviewed every five years to help track change. Then if environmental conditions improve, we can, if we wish, increase immigration. Ideally this important national process would come under the purview of a Minister for Population rather than a Minister for Immigration. Their responsibility should encompass all things pertaining to population change, including issues such as maternity and paternity leave.

Some people have extremely negative feelings about population policies. It's important to remember, however, that our schemes of social support for parents and children, and our immigration program, add up to a de facto population policy—one that has not been carefully thought through as a whole. No one has oversight of it, it is not clearly demonstrated to be in the national interest and there is little acceptance of elements of it in the community. Others argue against a population policy on the basis that it would be preferable to reduce consumption rather than concentrate on numbers. While focusing on patterns of consumption is important, it is vital to realise that population is the great multiplier of environmental impact, and that sustainability cannot be addressed without considering it.

Just as important as making environmental sustainability a priority for our nation is recognising the role that Aboriginal people played in shaping this land. Only by doing so will we be able to address critical aspects of our troubled past.

When James Cook sailed up the east coast of Australia in 1770, he remarked that the land looked like a gentleman's park. And indeed it was, for those eucalypt groves set in grassy plains were the result of 45,000 years of careful management by Aboriginal people. They, just like the Europeans, irrevocably changed the land when they first arrived—but thereafter they crafted it with fire and hunting, creating something new. It was that 'something new' that we now recognise as the distinctive Australian landscape. Thus, in a very real sense, this land is human-made—a handicraft of the Aboriginal people.

This concept has profound implications. It means that there is no Australian wilderness and no national park that can exist in its pre-1788 form without the ongoing input of people. All of the continent must be managed. This is one reason why the depopulation of the outback is so distressing—without people, vast areas of the continent will go unmanaged. If we accept this view, it implies that there is an important management role for Aboriginal and non-Aboriginal people in all reserved lands.

We are indebted to Aboriginal people for our land in many ways, and their skills and knowledge are vital to the continuance of the Australia we know and love. Having said this, romanticising Aboriginal cultures is not helpful. Reconciliation must be undertaken on Aboriginal terms—not with some fictional or idealised people or nation, but with Aboriginal communities in their full diversity throughout this land. We need to listen carefully to what they have to say, and assist them in achieving their desires.

We also need to do something symbolic and permanent to mark our change of heart. I suggest we go back to where it all began—Werrong, on the fine harbour of Cadi. Phillip's act of sycophancy in renaming the pretty cove for Lord Sydney did its job long ago. And even back then those rebellious Irish convicts would have little to do with such toadying. They ignored Phillip's Rose Hill, instead using its Cadigal name of Parramatta. So it would be in the best tradition of Ned Kelly to return to the name honoured by 10,000 years of use on the lips of its original inhabitants and re-christen Sydney Cove as Werrong, and Sydney Harbour as Cadi.

Men and Women of Cadi! To my ear it has a fine ring to it.

Other important changes that will lead to a sustainable future involve our relations with other nations. Australia will always be thinly populated and a minor influence in a world of far larger, more powerful—as well as many far poorer—countries. And yet foreign policy is critically important to us—for it must act as our national insurance policy. This view, I think, necessitates a fundamental restructure of the way we deal with others.

Our guiding light in this matter will always be self-interest, but it must be enlightened self-interest; that is, a self-interest congruent with that of our neighbours. Corrupt and dictatorial governments will rise and fall in the nations around us, but the people will always be there and it is our good reputation with *them* that will be our greatest assurance of an untroubled future. Only one platform can deliver that: an enduring commitment to the recognition of human rights worldwide. That should be the yardstick against which we measure all of our dealings with non-Australians. The development of such a 'national insurance policy' might proceed best if we had a Minister for Non-Australians, a sort of ombudsman whose responsibility would be to ensure that the non-Australian people whom we affect—from refugees to recipients of Australian aid—are well-served and fairly treated in our dealings with them.

Several global environmental issues threaten Australia, not the least of which is a runaway greenhouse effect. Scientists studying global climate change inform us that if global temperatures rise by around 6° Celsius over the next century, it will pose the greatest threat that our species has ever faced during its half-million years of existence. This is because it will create far hotter conditions than humans have ever experienced. What this astounding rise in temperature means for Australians, or indeed anyone, is not yet clear, but the warning signs are ominous indeed. Australia needs to take a global lead in terms of its renewable technologies and the brokering of international treaties such as the Kyoto Protocol.

Education will play a vital role in the creation of a truly Australian nation, for it's the tool we use to shape our minds to give us the best chance of success in life. A commitment to education that imbues people with a real sense of place is a great national imperative. Yet in this we seem to have lost our way, and are squandering our intellectual resources as profligately as previous generations squandered the soil. Students increasingly seek degrees that will turn them into cogs in the economic machine; and universities are in crisis, with the academic expertise vital to negotiate our way forward in ever-shorter supply. Our nation needs a federally endorsed vision of what it requires of its education system, particularly with regard to higher education. That vision should then be taken up by universities and academics to help shape it, subscribe to it and make it a reality.

Finally, there is one last matter—that of our responsibility to each other. I believe that co-operation, sometimes glossed as that peculiarly Australian phenomenon of 'mateship', represents the first significant social response of the Europeans to their new land. By this I mean not just mateship as a masculine blokey thing, but something much deeper—a kind of interdependence fostered by adversity. It came about because the Europeans soon learned, as the birds and Aboriginal people had long known, that one could survive in such a difficult land only if you have helpers and friends.

In the very first Australia Day address, Thomas Keneally discussed how central the concept of a 'fair go' is to Australians, and how precious our accepting, relatively equal society is. We are fortunate that our experience in this land has encouraged the development of such a society. Yet now globalisation has brought other social models, developed in other, more competitive places, and these are beginning to influence us.

How can we engage with the world and keep our society equitable, generous and cohesive? Each of us can think of some things that will help, but all signs indicate that we are losing this vital battle to preserve the defining values of Australian society. Perhaps if we all gave some thought to the issue each Australia Day we would stand a better chance.

The darkest horror lurking in the imaginings of nineteenth-century Australians was that this wild continent might somehow claim them, or their children, to itself. As the currency lads and lasses grew up—tall, barefooted and at ease in the bush—those dark fears increased for their parents, who saw degeneration in every deviation from standard European cultural practice. The continent, they feared, somehow forced all of its inhabitants—from its seemingly half-formed marsupials and egg-laying platypus to its naked, black savages—into a base and primitive form. Right up to the time of Sir Robert Menzies and beyond, their worst fear was to return 'home' only to find that they had become uncivilised 'colonials'.

Today that same dark, lurking fear—that this wide brown land might claim us as its own—is, I suspect, our best hope for a sustainable, long-term future. We have realised that we have no other home but this one, and that we cannot remake it to suit ourselves. Instead we must somehow accept this land's conditions, surrender our 'otherness' and in so doing find our distinctive Australian way in a very different world.

After the Future: Australia's New Extinction Crisis

The arrival of the First Fleet in 1788 initiated a period of rapid change for Australia's environments. Brown rats (*Rattus norvegicus*) probably disembarked at Port Jackson along with the first convicts, and cattle had escaped into the bush by 1789. These first feral species spread quickly, and within a century they'd been joined by goats, foxes, pigs, cats, black rats, rabbits, hares, horses, several species of deer and a dozen or so bird species. Today the tide of introduced species continues to swell, making Australia home to a vast array of ferals—from starfish to carp and camels to cane toads—and each is having its own particular impact.

Paradoxically, some biologists argue that Australia's environmental problems are so bad that they can only be solved by introducing yet more exotics. One of the most controversial of such calls was made by Professor David Bowman from the University of Tasmania, who in February 2012 published an article in *Nature* (the world's leading science journal) suggesting that if Australia's ecosystems are to be returned to health, then elephants should be introduced to the outback.

His argument was that elephants would eat enough vegetation to suppress the vast wildfires that currently inflict so much damage on Australia's inland ecosystems. The discussion that followed included many acerbic objections, one coming from an African wildlife expert who pointed out that elephants are difficult to manage. Whether Australian cow-cockies would be up to the task was, to his mind, questionable. But the most fundamental objection concerned the mismatch between elephants (and indeed any introduced species) and the Australian environment.

Australia's megafauna co-evolved with the continent's vegetation for millions of years. The strange "horned" wallaby from the Nullarbor demonstrates that some plants defended themselves from being eaten by megafauna with thorns or a thicket of hard twigs, and some marsupials had adaptations that allowed them partially to circumvent these defences. Other plants doubtless used chemical defences to repel herbivores, and over the ages a balance was struck. One of the great problems with introduced herbivores is that they may not be deterred by such defences, and so can chew through Australia's vegetation as if it were a bowl of salad. Moreover, in Australia such herbivores lack predators, which means they can proliferate to the point where they degrade the ecosystem that feeds them.

I am not saying that some carefully controlled introduced herbivores may not benefit Australia's inland ecosystems by going some way to restoring the "dollar spent a day, with a ten-cent bonus" type of ecosystem that existed here in times past. It's just that we're a long way from understanding what species they might be, and how they might be managed to achieve the desired outcome. Moreover, it's self-evident that ill-conceived and poorly monitored programs, such as the proposed trials of cattle grazing in the Alpine National Park, are no substitute for such studies.

There are a few species of megafauna which, while extinct in Australia, have survived elsewhere. The Komodo dragon exists today only on the island of Flores and nearby smaller islands, yet fossils show that it was once widespread in Australia. Why did it survive on Flores? For around a million years the island was home to a pygmy human-like creature known now as the Hobbit (*Homo floresiensis*). Perhaps hunting by these metre-tall creatures (about the height of a three-year-old human) relieved the Komodo dragons of some of their naivety regarding two-legged human-like predators, and so they were wary enough to survive when the first humans arrived around 12,000 years ago.

A second such species is the long-beaked echidna of New Guinea. Fossils of similar creatures have been found throughout Australia in deposits 45,000 years or more old. The New Guinean long-beaks are gigantic (up to a metre long) relatives of Australia's common echidna, but eat worms and possibly beetle larvae rather than termites. Presumably they survived in New Guinea because the dense forest and difficult terrain made them more difficult to hunt there. The western long-beaked echidna (*Zaglossus bruijni*) inhabits the New Guinean lowlands, and may be able to survive in seasonally dry environments. It is severely endangered by human hunting in New Guinea, but might thrive if introduced into northern Australia.

Because both the Komodo dragon and something like the long-beaked echidna were part of Australia's environment for millions of years, we can be more confident that their reintroduction would not disrupt ecosystems, and would indeed fill a vacant niche. The same is true for the Tasmanian devil, which only vanished from the mainland of Australia around 3000 years ago.

We now need to turn to a discussion of direct human impacts on the environment. Since the first days of settlement Europeans have been active, felling forests, planting crops, hunting and altering watercourses. And doubtless these activities have had a great impact on Australia's ecosystems. Australians often imagine that these are the most important changes that have occurred to the environment, and that they alone are responsible for the extinction of native species. But in fact what the Aboriginal people were prevented from doing by the Europeans was equally important.

Forty thousand years is a very long time. Longer than humans have been present in western Europe; three times longer than the entire human history of the Americas. Long enough, indeed, for a human culture to become the keystone in the environment of a continent. The Aborigines acted as a keystone in Australia by carefully burning the vegetation that was once eaten by the megafauna, and by regulating the abundance of the remaining species through hunting. Take a keystone out of an arch, and the structure collapses. And so, when the European settlers began to disrupt Aboriginal land management, they removed the human keystone that lay at the heart of Australia's ecosystems. Environmental collapses can occur on the timescale of decades or centuries, and the consequences of this particular keystone removal are still being played out today.

A breakthrough in our understanding of the importance of Aboriginal land management to the survival of many Australian species was made when researchers examined what has happened in the Great Sandy Desert over the past half-century. This vast region was home to the Pintupi people, and it has a unique history that makes it a particularly valuable natural laboratory. Not only was it the last place in Australia where Aboriginal people pursued traditional lifestyles unaffected by Europeans, but it was photographed from the air in great detail as early as 1953.

The aerial photographs were taken by the military because the British and Australian governments wanted to use the region for testing rockets in a program known as the Blue Streak rocket project. They reveal a landscape patterned into a fine mosaic of vegetation, in various stages of recovery from fire. This had resulted from the burning of small patches—most only a few hectares in extent—by the Pintupi. In the 1980s, some of the people who had done the burning were interviewed by scientists who wanted to know how they burnt, and why. The Pintupi said that they burnt every day, and that while fire served a variety of purposes, hunting was the main one.

The last of the Pintupi to follow their traditional lifestyle walked out of the Great Sandy Desert in 1985, so ending 40,000 years of indigenous fire management. But the system had begun to break down earlier than that. Aerial photographs taken in 1973 reveal that there were then too few people to maintain the tight mosaic of small burns, so larger fires were beginning to break out. By 1981, large, hot fires had gained such a hold on the landscape that four huge ones burnt 90 per cent of the study area. What had happened? As the Pintupi left the desert, the vegetation built up until large fires became inevitable. For the mammals and many other desert creatures, the results were catastrophic.

To understand how catastrophic, imagine being a creature the size of a bandicoot or a small wallaby in a harsh desert environment. Each day you must find shelter from the climate and predators, and each night enough food to survive. Where fires are small, you can easily move from an unburnt patch that provides shelter to a freshly burnt one that provides new green shoots. But if a great, hot fire burns through your habitat, even if you survive the flames by sheltering in a burrow, you're likely to emerge to a devastated field of ashes that stretches to the horizon all around. You'll either be picked off by a predator or starve. Some of the wildfires that erupted in central Australia following the end of Aboriginal fire management were large enough to burn through three Australian states, and to be seen from space. And with them went the fertility of the soil, the variety of vegetation so many creatures needed to survive, and the tight mosaic of old and newly burnt vegetation that provided food and shelter. Now the fires have become so large and hot that even some of the fire-sensitive desert vegetation, like mulgas and some desert eucalypts, are endangered by them.

For a while there was hope that some of the mammals of the Pintupi homeland could be saved. Andrew Burbidge is a mammalogist who told me that when he met some Pintupi people who had recently come in from the desert, he was astonished to learn that they had regularly hunted and eaten a number of mammal species that scientists assumed were long extinct. Andrew excitedly arranged an expedition to take the people back to their tribal homelands, hopefully to find some of the long-lost mammals. The Aborigines, too, were excited at the prospect of returning home, as they had not seen their country for a decade or more. But almost immediately upon arriving, they became dismayed. "All gone," they said. There were no tracks of any of the creatures in the sand, and the vast field of uniformly aged vegetation that had developed disgusted them. It needed to be "tidied up," they said. As soon as they got out of the vehicle, they began lighting fires.

As I explained in *The Future Eaters*, I think that there is a direct link between the extinction of Australia's megafauna and the historic extinctions of creatures like the bandicoots and wallabies that recently vanished from the Pintupi country. After the great herbivores vanished, wildfire should have led to the extinction of the smaller mammals. It was only Aboriginal fire management which prevented that. The management was an act of environmental stewardship that involved the lifetime efforts of countless millions of long-forgotten Australians, who passed down, in an unbroken string of learning and action, daily practices that became the keystone in Australia's drier ecosystems. Every species given life by that stewardship should be looked upon as the most precious gift imaginable—a gift of rare beauty, diversity and ecological health bequeathed by Australia's indigenous people to those alive today.

Tragically, the kinds of extinctions seen in the Great Sandy Desert in the 1970s are now devastating vast regions of the continent, including some of Australia's most valued national parks. The situation is particularly dire in northern Australia, where, over the past decade or two, the second extinction wave is beginning to break and is sweeping away the small to medium-sized mammals as effectively as the first wave did in southern Australia a century ago.

At 19,804 square kilometres, Kakadu National Park is arguably the jewel in the crown of Australia's reserve system. World Heritage-listed, it received $18 million for operating costs in 2008–09, much of which goes to managing the influx of tourists. Yet, unless it is to become another marsupial ghost town, more needs to be spent on biodiversity protection. Between 1995 and 2008 the abundance of small mammals found in the park declined by 75 per cent, and a third of the species that were recorded there in 1995 can no longer be found, and appear to be locally extinct. One, the brush-tailed rabbit-rat (the last surviving relative of the white-footed rabbit rat of southeastern Australia), may even be extinct nationwide. As the researchers who reported these dismal findings surmised:

The current rapid decline of mammals in Kakadu National Park and northern Australia suggests that the fate of biodiversity globally might be even bleaker than evident in recent reviews, and that the establishment of conservation reserves alone is insufficient to maintain biodiversity. This latter conclusion is not new; but the results reported here further stress the need to manage reserves far more intensively, purposefully, and effectively, and to audit regularly their biodiversity conservation performance.

The ongoing extinction of northern Australia's medium-sized mammals, such as bandicoots, quolls, rabbit rats and tree-rats, while catastrophic in itself, is just one symptom of an ecosystem in extinction freefall. As the extinctions continue, vegetation communities are changing and simplifying, while populations of reptiles and birds, such as the Gouldian finch, are also being affected. These shifts are occurring on such an awesome scale and proceeding so fast that they resemble a local version of the dinosaurs' extinction. What has changed in recent decades across the north, including in Kakadu, the most highly protected region of Australia?

The main driver appears to be changes in fire regime, compounded by the presence of feral cats, and shifts in the abundance, in some habitats, of large feral herbivores such as cattle and water buffalo. The water buffalo had been introduced from Asia in the nineteenth century, and by the 1970s were wreaking havoc with aquatic ecosystems. They would crowd the billabongs in the dry season, destroying water lilies and reeds, and stirring up mud until the waterholes became mud wallows, the buffalo using them looking like so many maggots in a sore when viewed from the air.

There was thus good reason to cull the creatures, but the cull may have had unfortunate consequences. While the dynamics of the situation are still being worked out, I gained a small insight into one aspect of it in the mid-1990s. I was filming an ABC documentary when a parks ranger explained to me that a program to eliminate water buffalo from the park had changed the fire regime. Adult water buffalo each eat around twenty kilograms of dry grass per day, such that prior to the cull they removed much flammable material from the Kakadu floodplain. With the buffalo gone, hot fires began to consume the uncropped grass. Fuelled from the floodplain, extremely hot and large fires then began to sweep deep into the surrounding escarpment country.

I recall standing beside one victim of the flames, a gigantic *Allosyncarpia* tree, its eighty-centimetre-thick trunk still smouldering, its once dense canopy a mess of browned leaves and ashes. This giant must have been hundreds of years old, and had been growing in a moist fold in the sandstone escarpment, where it had been safe from fire all its life—until, in the absence of both grazing by water buffalo and Aboriginal fire management, its trunk was burnt through and it collapsed. Tragically, it was not alone. The whole area was being transformed by the enormous, extremely hot fires.

If we are to fully understand what's happening to Australia's biodiversity, we must also consider the assault of cane toads, feral cats, pigs, cattle, horses, donkeys, noxious weeds, and in southern Australia foxes, cats, rabbits, camels, deer and goats. In all, seventy-two vertebrate species have established feral populations in Australia, and when combined with the fires, their varied impacts are making our national parks unsafe for native species continent-wide. Those living close to the land have long understood this, as was recently highlighted in Adelaide at a public meeting convened by Bob Debus to discuss the federal government's billion-dollar biodiversity fund. Debus had been talking about the need to connect up national parks by creating corridors which would allow species to migrate as Australia's climate changed. An Aboriginal elder from Cape York responded that it sounded like a great idea—in theory. But the fact was that many of the national parks in his region were infested with feral pigs, which would use any corridors that were created to spread and thereby inflict even more damage on the environment.

Medium-sized native mammals are critically important to Australian environments. They include the largest burrowers in many habitats, and their burrows provide refuge for many other species. Moreover, the spoil heaps created by digging bring fresh nutrients to the surface, providing important habitat for many ecologically important plants. Rabbits burrow, too, but they also destroy the plants. Moreover, some marsupials are fungus-eaters, and they spread fungal spores that are important to forest health. Others disperse seeds, eat insects that can kill trees if their numbers build up, and distribute nutrients such as phosphorus across the countryside. Take out these vital functions and you end up with sick ecosystems.

What is to be done? At the highest level, it's clear that Australians today must take up the role, forged over 40,000 years, of acting as a keystone species in Australia's varied environments by managing fire, regulating the numbers of feral animals and eliminating weeds. If this is not done, then northern Australia will lose many of its important species, while in the south the last remnants of the medium-sized mammal fauna will be lost. Just where this would lead over time is unclear, but both ecosystem stability and productivity are likely to be affected.

With Australia having over 22 million people in a continent of nearly 8 million square kilometres, it is fair to ask if these things can be achieved within an affordable budget. A partial answer to this question comes from a recent assessment of endangered species in the Kimberley region. A study of 637 vertebrate species showed that 45 mammals, birds and reptiles were likely to become extinct in the next twenty years without action being taken to manage fire, feral animals and weeds, and grazing. Yet the cost of all actions to avoid the extinctions was just $40 million a year—a startlingly small sum given the many benefits that flow from fire management and control of pests in one of Australia's most valuable tourist regions.

We need not rely on theoretical studies alone as a guide to the cost-effectiveness of protecting endangered species in the Kimberley. The Australian Wildlife Conservancy (AWC) is a not-for-profit organisation funded principally through donations from the public. It was established by Martin Copley, whose vision to protect Australia's endangered species has had an enormous impact. (Here I must declare a personal interest: I've been involved with the AWC since its inception, and now serve on its board of directors.)

In little over a decade the AWC has grown to the point where it manages over 3 million hectares. Its reserves are scattered throughout the nation, with particularly significant holdings in the tropical north and centre. On this land, the organisation conserves around two-thirds of Australia's threatened mammal species, and 70 per cent of its threatened mainland bird species. And it manages to do this on an annual budget of around $12 million— just two-thirds the budget of Kakadu, which occupies an area half the size of the AWC's holdings.

The operations of the AWC vary in accordance with the needs of the region, but the challenges it faces are particularly diverse and urgent in northern Australia. Mornington Sanctuary in the central Kimberley is the headquarters of the organisation's research program, and the place in northern Australia where it has been operating longest. When the AWC commenced scientific management of the property in 2004, the wildlife responded almost immediately. In fact, the abundance of native mammals more than doubled in the plots sampled between 2004 and 2007.

In the early days at Mornington the most immediate task was reducing the impact of cattle and horses by removing them from vulnerable habitats. But it was clear that a fire strategy was also urgently required. So, in 2007, the EcoFire project was initiated. It's already clear that the EcoFire program is essential to the continued survival of small mammals, as well as several bird species, in part because it has resulted in a significant increase in the extent of old-growth vegetation (defined as vegetation which has grown for more than three years since the last controlled burn). Moreover, this old vegetation is scattered in a fine-grained pattern across the region.

Partnerships with indigenous people play a vital role in the EcoFire project, as well as in other AWC initiatives.

In southern Australia, the challenge of environmental conservation is significantly different, and requires other measures. Many of the medium-sized mammals, such as woylies and rabbit rats, that once abounded in the south are now extinct or survive only as remnant populations on islands, where they have lost all wariness of mammalian predators. In these circumstances feral-proof enclosures offer the best method of conservation. This involves fencing areas, eliminating cats, foxes, rabbits and other ferals, and reintroducing the endangered species. These fenced areas effectively act as arks, keeping the survivors safe from extinction and genetically diverse until better options are developed.

To maintain viable populations of some species, truly enormous feral-proof areas need to be created. At Scotia Sanctuary in western New South Wales the AWC has created an 8000-hectare fenced area—the largest in the country, and vital to species such as the numbat and bridled nailtail wallaby. Fencing involves a significant up-front investment, but over the long term costs compare favourably with alternatives such as ongoing baiting for cats and foxes.

Why has the AWC been so successful at conserving biodiversity? Clarity of vision is important. The organisation's sole objective is the protection of Australia's biodiversity. Moreover, it is committed to creating and maintaining a strong scientific base, which means that it can establish appropriate goals, monitor progress and report accurately to stakeholders. This gives the AWC a very different internal structure from its peers. For example, the AWC devotes around 84 per cent of its total budget to field-based staff and operations, including its science programs. Among other not-for-profit organisations in the environmental sphere, and indeed in comparable government agencies such as parks services, 40 per cent or less of total funding is typically spent on field-based staff and programs, and very little on science. The focus on science is also reflected in staff expertise: the AWC employs twenty-five ecologists (a dozen of these with PhDs) and has about fifteen students, from doctoral to honours level, at work at any time, as well as running a very popular internship program for recently graduated ecologists who are seeking field experience.

A good example of how science guides the AWC is its approach to protecting one of Australia's most spectacular birds, the Gouldian finch. At the time the AWC's Gouldian finch program was instigated, there were thought to be fewer than

2500 adults in the wild, and the species was declining towards extinction. Research showed that this was due largely to changed fire patterns, which had altered the availability of the grass seeds upon which the species feeds, which also meant that during the breeding season birds were becoming stressed by the great distances they had to travel between their nesting hollows and the nearest seeding grasses.

This may sound like a simple finding, but establishing the facts and eliminating other possibilities required a sophisticated program of scientific research that took several years to complete. With research completed, AWC staff started to burn parts of their properties in ways that encouraged the seeding of grasses near nesting hollows of the finches. Today, as a result of the program, Gouldian finches are thriving on Mornington, and blood analysis shows that nesting females are far less stressed than in years past and therefore more likely to survive into a second breeding year. The program also benefits other species that share the finches' habitat, and indeed is emblematic of how protecting a species can lead to healthier ecosystems.

A strong scientific basis means that the AWC can account for its successes and failures. It also means that it is today the only conservation organisation in Australia able to provide reliable estimates of the population sizes of each endangered species in its care. The ability to demonstrate the success of its operations is also a great magnet for staff: talented young people are keen to work for such a body because they can be sure that their work is effective.

The AWC is not the only organisation succeeding in protecting threatened species. In Western Australia, Wildlife Research and Management has had success in protecting the burrowing bettong at Heirisson Prong on Shark Bay, demonstrating that community-based initiatives with some government funding can be effective. Nonetheless, the sheer scale of the AWC programs, and their high rate of success, is impressive.

It is reasonable to ask if not-for-profit organisations can be charged with protecting Australia's biodiversity in the long term. After all, being dependent on donations, they may be thought to have a tenuous existence. But overseas some not-for-profit organisations have been operating successfully for a century or more. Such organisations suffer ups and downs as the economy expands and contracts, but so too do government departments. Indeed, one AWC staffer recently told me that employees there feel far more secure in their jobs than do their government-employed peers.

It may also be argued that the AWC has a particular vulnerability in that much of the land it manages consists of pastoral leases, and so it does not enjoy the legislative protection of national parks and nature reserves. Yet, as we have seen, even lands protected under legislation are not exempt from being resumed for development. And the AWC is increasingly managing land on behalf of others, making it less vulnerable to changes in tenure, and ever more capable of using its expertise to preserve biodiversity in a wide variety of circumstances.

With biodiversity in Australia's national parks in decline, there's a crying need for state governments to reach out to organisations like the AWC for help in managing the problems that they can no longer adequately address acting alone. Were an organisation like the AWC to be given a role in managing feral animals, weeds and biodiversity in national parks, the state could hold it responsible for achieving a clear set of mutually agreed goals. If they were not met, the state could sack the organisation and employ another to do the job.

Some may object that letting private enterprise into the state-owned realm will only lead to a further hollowing out of government expertise. But public–private partnerships are hardly new, and they've proved useful where governments alone lack the means of achieving results. Moreover, the risk to the environment of this initiative failing could be minimised if it were trialled first in national parks or nature reserves where biodiversity values are already low. The truth is that things are now so dire that we cannot afford to persist with business as usual: a change of direction is essential if we're to head off the great impending wave of extinctions. Australia needs several organisations like the AWC, which would compete for funding and the privilege of conserving our endangered fauna and flora.

PART TWO

On Other People's Words
1999–2012

Wonders of a Lost World

New York Review of Books, DECEMBER 1999

The Ambonese Curiosity Cabinet, Georgius Everhardus Rumphius, translated, edited, annotated, and with an introduction by E. M. Beekman, Yale University Press, Hartford, 1999.

In the year 1698 a blind German merchant sat in a whitewashed cottage on a tropical island in the southern sea, dictating intricate descriptions of crabs, sea-snails, 'metals, stones and other rare things' to an amanuensis. Four years later, as its author lay dying alone on his tropic isle, the manuscript was journeying towards publication in the bustling city of Amsterdam. A further three years later, in 1705, *The Ambonese Curiosity Cabinet* was finally published. Although reprinted twice early in the eighteenth century it has been unavailable ever since. Now, after an interval of more than 250 years, Yale University Press has seen fit to reprint the work. Why should anyone bother reading, let alone reprinting or purchasing such a book? Because it is glorious, just glorious!

Georg Rumphius lived most of his adult life on the spice island of Amboina (now Ambon) in the Indonesian archipelago.

It's a place where one naturally turns to the sea, for its waters are startlingly blue, all encompassing, and full of extraordinary life. The wonderful detail and deep insights contained in Rumphius's descriptions of sea creatures should not surprise us, for other naturalists have also been inspired by Ambon.

The co-founder of the theory of evolution, Alfred Russel Wallace, visited the place in 1857 and described its harbour as:

> One of the most astonishing and beautiful sights I have ever beheld. The bottom was absolutely hidden by a continuous series of corals, sponges, actiniae, and other marine productions, of magnificent dimensions, varied forms, and brilliant colours. The depth varied from about twenty to fifty feet, and the bottom was very uneven, rocks and chasms, and little hills and valleys, offering a variety of stations for the growth of these animal forests. In and out among them moved numbers of blue and red and yellow fishes, spotted and banded and striped in the most striking manner, while great orange or rosy transparent medusae floated along near the surface. It was a sight to gaze at for hours, and no description can do justice to its surpassing beauty and interest. For once, the reality exceeded the most glowing accounts I had ever read of the wonders of a coral sea. There is perhaps no spot in the world richer in marine productions, corals, shells and fishes, than the harbour of Amboyna.

For thirteen years Rumphius lived on the beautiful Hitu coast of this enchanted isle, at its westernmost point, surrounded by the natural world. There he lived, as one visitor observed, 'like a Prince, and with greater repose than many a King', following his profession as a merchant and his passion as a student of nature. Then, in

April 1670, a terrible catastrophe struck. At the age of forty-two, and over a period of a few weeks, the great man was blinded by cataracts. It was, in his own words, a 'terrible misfortune [that] suddenly took away from me the entire world and all its creatures'. Just four years later a second, even greater catastrophe was to befall him, when an earthquake in the town of Ambon (where he then lived) killed his wife and youngest daughter.

From that time on, Rumphius had only his work, but his pursuit of it was to be dogged with misfortune. Before his blindness Rumphius had begun composing his best known book, the great *Herbal*, in Latin, a language he spoke fluently. At 1661 folio pages and with 695 plates, this was a masterwork. Yet following his blindness, he had to throw away what he had done and begin again—this time in Dutch—for there was no one on the island to whom he could dictate Latin, and no one who could read what he had already written.

Further misfortunes followed. In 1687, Rumphius's original drawings for the *Herbal* were consumed by fire. By 1690 the first six books had been rewritten and were sent off to Amsterdam, but they never made it, for the ship carrying them was attacked and sunk by the French fleet. A complete copy of the work finally made its way halfway round the world to Amsterdam, but it was ignored for years. It was not until 1750, after being laboriously translated into Latin to make it acceptable to the scholars of the day, that it was first published in full.

Rumphius's dotage was spent, as far as we can tell, worrying about whether either of his voluminous works would ever be published—such were the vexations of the seventeenth-century natural history writer. He shared his cottage in Ambon town with a small Bengali slave named Cour, and a Javanese mongoose that could 'stand up, walk, and sit on his two hind legs, like a monkey, and if he has nothing to do, he puts [his paws] on his chest, like a poor sinner.' Rumphius died on 15 June 1702, without holding either of his books in print.

Rumphius's island of Ambon lies in a unique zoogeographic realm known as Maluku. It is a land between the great zoogeographic provinces of Asia and Australia, and in honour of Wallace's work it is often referred to as Wallacea. Because of its location, the people of Wallacea have long found benefit in trading the treasures of the East in the markets of the West. Among the most valued of all the products at their disposal were nutmeg, cloves, the oil of the *kulit lawang* and *kayu putih* trees, and plumes from birds of paradise. All of these items are harvested from plants and animals with venerable Australian/Gondwanan pedigrees, some from as far away as the mountains of New Guinea, then to be sold in the markets of the Spice Islands. This trade had occurred for millennia, for cloves were known in Europe by Roman times, despite the fact that they grow on only a few islands in Maluku.

The reasons that the Australia–New Guinea islands are so rich in such tradeable goods are curious. The birds of paradise, for example, can thrive in all their diversity and cumbersome plumage because the region lacks carnivores, such as cats and ferrets, which dominate the other zoogeographic realms of the planet. Instead, these islands are the home of marsupials such as possums and kangaroos. Its plants—including the clove and nutmeg—are encouraged by the region's poor soils to develop chemical defences against insects, and it is these chemicals that put the spices in our lives.

What the Australia–New Guinea region lacked, however, were manufactured goods; and feathers and spices were traded for metal and porcelains, which abounded in Asia. It was cloves and nutmeg that brought the Dutch East India Company to Ambon, and it was this company that employed Rumphius, initially as a soldier then later as a construction engineer and merchant.

Rumphius wrote *The Ambonese Curiosity Cabinet* before the world had ever heard of that great methodiser of nature, Linnaeus, and a full century and a half before the word 'evolution' fell from Darwin's or Wallace's lips. As such it is an anomaly in the modern world, where science and natural history are virtually synonymous. Thus if you wish to learn about the taxonomic relationships of molluscs or crabs, *The Ambonese Curiosity Cabinet* is not for you, for it confounds the living and non-living worlds, and lumps together such unrelated species as squid and violet-snails, sea cucumbers and anemones. If, however, you revel in the struggle of humanity to come to terms with the vastness and beauty of nature, and if you can see the world, even briefly, through another's eyes, then this book will repay you a thousand-fold.

The translator of this edition, E. M. Beekman, quotes the Earl of Roscommon in the opening pages, revealing the sentiments that guided him in what is clearly a labour of love:

> Examine how your *Humour* is inclin'd
> And which the *Ruling Passion* of your Mind;
> Then, seek a *Poet* who *your* way do's bend,
> And chuse an *Author* as you chuse a friend.
> United by this *Sympathetick Bond,*
> You grow *Familiar, Intimate* and *Fond;*
> Your *Thoughts,* your *Words,* your *Stiles,* your *Souls* agree,
> No longer his *Interpreter,* but *He.*

Just as significantly it reveals that Beekman regards Rumphius not just as a natural historian, but as a poet as well. It's a quality the two clearly share, for Beekman's translation retains all the freshness, curiosity and vividness of the original. If you have never seen the *Nautilus tenuis* or ruma gorita, here is part of Rumphius's description of it:

> The fish that lives there [in the shell] is notably similar to a *polypus* or Many-Feet. Its flesh is entirely soft, supplied with eight beards, of which the six front ones are short, white and covered with warts like all seacats, and which it spreads out like a rose when swimming. The two back ones are the same length, which it stretches forth along the curl of the back, lets them hang down in the water and steers its little boat therewith; for they are round and smooth, but at the end as wide as the blade of an oar, the colour of silver. One will find that when this fish goes sailing it stows most of its body towards the rear, keeping only the two aforementioned rudders on the outside for steering; but when there is no wind, it will bring all its beards out, lowers the prow again, and rows. When it notices any kind of danger or ambush, it will pull all its flesh on board, turn the stern up, so that the little boat will take on water, and in this manner it goes to ground. If one wants the shell complete with fish, one has to approach it very quietly in the wind and skillfully scoop it up; but this happens so rarely, that fishermen consider it a great boon if they catch one, which is only likely to happen when there is a great stillness after a thunderstorm.

And so is the paper nautilus, known to most of us solely as an empty shell sitting on a mantelpiece, rendered a living thing.

Rumphius conjures it to us, rowing across its slick tropical sea in the silent stillness that is only felt after the fury of a tropical storm has passed.

Rumphius's account of his 'Sea-Gellies' Boats' is, if anything, an even more remarkable poetic tribute to nature, for it reveals a more familiar creature—the purple sailor shell—in what is, quite literally, a new light.

> The animal that lives in there [the shell]…is like a kind of Sea Gelly that stands up straight like the joint of a finger, when it drifts out on the open sea; this little Sea Gelly is perfectly clear, like a little crystal, with a blue sheen, and it consists of nothing but slime, that is surrounded by a little skin, and if one keeps it but for a single day, it will surely pass away. These little boats are seldom seen, at least at Amboina we had them for the first time in August and September, anno 1682, at the end of the Harvest, when they came drifting up in large schools from the East, on the open sea. The little boat laid there with the opening up, and the Sea Gelly stood upright like a small pillar, appearing to sail with a feint breeze, wondrous to see that such a fleet of easily a thousand little ships, could sail so agreeably together. When one took them from the sea and put them in a dish of water, the little Sea Gellies did manage to stand upright for a day, emitting a wondrously beautiful repercussion of light, as if the dish were filled with precious stones.

Sceptical, perhaps, at such fantastic description, Rumphius's printer added in 1704: 'What are the Sea Gellies and Sealungs, and what is their origin, since we are not certain at all?' The difficulty the European mind had in accepting the astonishing beauty and diversity of tropical life was to remain an obstacle for Rumphius and other natural history writers for decades. Indeed, when Louis Renard published his *Poissons Ecrivisses et Crabes . . . que l'on trouve autour des Isles Molucques* in 1754, so sceptical was the audience that he was forced to include a letter from a highly respected Reverend who had resided in the Moluccas, stating that the fish he painted actually existed!

Rumphius's naive wonder at many of the more obscure creatures of the sea is delightful. Among the most troublesome to classify were the phallus marinus and its lowlier kin. He notes that they belong to a class of organisms that 'come very close to plants and stones, and hardly show anything that looks alive, but nature is so confounded by the Element of water, that one finds things in it, which can hardly be assigned . . . as if they were remnants of the original chaos'.

The phallus marinus, Rumphius ominously warned, is 'very like the male member, 6 or 7 fingers long, more than an inch thick . . . pointed in front though tapering roundly, where they pull a round little head in and out, from which they squirt a water that looks like whey'. The Dutch, he notes, call them *Kaffir Pricks*; the Malays, *Buto Kling* (which translates as Indian's Pricks). These strange creatures share a page with the equally odd Tethyis, described as:

> The colour of flesh, like nipples or finger. If one grabs hold of them too hard, they will provoke a burning or itching in one's hand. Inside, one will see nothing more than pipes that look like veins, and which are filled with water, which one can press out of them, as with nipples.

Here, I think, we see Rumphius floundering. What God, he might have asked himself, would have filled Ambon's seas with such blatantly sexual 'remnants of the original chaos'? It's as if the creator had been overly fond of genitals, and fashioning too many, had tossed the excess into the briny, where they took on independent life. It is somewhat disappointing to realise that marine biologists have solved the mystery for us, for these apparently cast-off body parts are nothing but sea cucumbers (relatives of starfish) and sea anemones respectively.

If sea cucumbers confused the blind seer of Ambon, then the medusas struck fear into his heart. Rumphius described the Bulu Aijam (meaning 'chicken feathers' in Malay), as a 'monstrous sea animal, dreadful to behold, and not easily touched by those who have never seen one'. It has, he says, the head of a spider to which are joined five pairs of limbs. These limbs divide and subdivide, until hundreds if not thousands of tiny tentacles are produced. When the beast moves, Rumphius declares, it 'is of such a ghastly appearance, that one would hold it to be a clump of millipedes or tiny little snakes'. If one tries to grasp it, he added, its arms curl upwards and grasp the offending hand. How sensibilities have changed, for today the beautiful gorgonians (a type of crinoid) are a staple in undersea natural history films, and are more often likened to flowers than snakes.

The clams also disturbed him, though perhaps for different reasons. The smaller clams of the seashore he described as 'dreadful to behold, because if one looks upon one that is gaping, one sees nothing but a taut skin, full of black, white, yellow and lead-colored veins; painted like a snake's skin'. The giant clam is, he tells us:

3 to 4 and 5 feet long. They gape almost always when on the ground, especially in order to catch the little fishes that come in multitudes to swim and play therein, until all of

them together are suddenly locked in there, and come to serve as the beast's food: This lumpish beast always has a little comrade with it, which is its guard, being a kind of little shrimp . . . which pinches its flesh when it sees that there is a great deal of prey in its house, whereupon the shell snaps shut, and one believes that the beast cannot live, if that little pinna guard happens to be away from it, because the Beast cannot see, and cannot be on guard for robbers.

This wonderfully acute observation—even if combined with erroneous deduction—reveals perhaps the personal feelings of the great man. Who was the blind Rumphius's pinna guard, one wonders? Perhaps the wife killed in the earthquake? Certainly it is such tiny details of biology, read by Rumphius in terms of loyalty, protection and friendship that lend his work some of its greatness.

The Ambonese Curiosity Cabinet is divided into three parts. The first concerns the 'soft shellfish' such as the crabs, lobsters, starfish and worms. The second deals with the molluscs, while the third part is dedicated to stones and metals. A curious combination finds its way into these latter pages, from gold to fruit pips, fossils and ambergris. This final section, more than the others, reveals the seventeenth-century experiential mind at work. It opens with a merchant's preoccupation of assaying precious metals, and of weights and measures suitable for them. We learn how gold is 'falsified', and how clever the Moluccans are at this practice. We are then made privy to a series of tests that Rumphius has developed for detecting various frauds. It's quite a shift from the style of the earlier parts.

The strange metals and alloys of the East are discussed, and our seer must admit defeat in his attempts to create the *Tambagga*

Suassa of the Malays. We then come to the thunder stones. These, Rumphius declares, all come from the sky during thunderstorms. Some of the objects illustrated are clearly meteorites, but others are neolithic stone axes and adzes, and yet others metal instruments from Asian cultures. At the same time that Rumphius dismisses as superstition the Malay belief that such stones are the teeth of the thunder giant, he informs us:

> that all of mankind's arts and sciences, and the tools that go with them, and which serve man in this temporal life, were originally an astral influence ... wherefrom one may conclude, that the astral smith who informed mankind how to make hammers, chisels and other tools for the smithy, could also make such tools in the thunder fire that he commands.

The author is a little closer to the mark in his discussion of fossils, for he recognises them as the remains of shells and fish that have been petrified, but then goes sadly astray in his discussion of dishes that can detect poison in food and other such mysteries. And what are we to make of his inclusion of 'white water' in this section? 'Twice a year,' he says, 'the sea around the Banda Islands turns white and shines brightly.' Again we see the animate and inanimate co-mingled. Further on, we read of 'stone files, stone bullets and stone fingers.' Clearly the geological sciences were sadly behind the life sciences in the eighteenth century.

The book closes with a discussion of the various kinds of ambergris, bezoars, pigs' balls, stones found in certain fruits, and 'stones which happen to have an unusual shape'. There are stones where 'people go in secret in order to transact that cursed thing called *Batappa* [possibly mortification of the body], when they request something from the *Djing* or devil, such as luck in war, good fortune in gaining riches, whoring and other such things.' As for the stones of various fruits, the bezoars and their supposed properties, and the pigs' balls, I'll leave the joy of discovering their nature to the reader.

The Ambonese Curiosity Cabinet represents a European, or perhaps hybrid European–Malayan folk taxonomy of sea creatures and stones of the Ambon region and is full of what was then useful knowledge. We discover what every kind of crustacean looks like in its cooked and uncooked state, which ones are believed to be poisonous, and how to prepare the flesh of everything from a sea-lung to a giant clam for dinner. Detailed notes are also given on the preparation of shells for the curiosity cabinet, and how much to pay for various objects. The roles of shells, food and stones in Malay ritual are all documented, with Rumphius often uncritically passing on tips about the supposed medicinal qualities of the various denizens of the deep.

All of this is accompanied by a series of black-and-white plates that are useful for helping one determine exactly what creature is being discussed. The copious notes are also highly useful in this regard, as is the introduction, setting out what is known of Rumphius's life and works. So thorough and well researched is Beekman's work that it appears to be both the labour and the passion of a lifetime. Yale University Press is to be congratulated on the handsome production—well bound and presented.

As I read this wondrous work I became saddened by our modern world. I have often sailed down Ambon Harbour, yet I have seen no coral gardens, no medusae, no fishes. Today the water stinks and is thick with effluent and garbage, and as one enters the town one is greeted by rafts of faeces, plastic bags, and the intestines of butchered goats. The town itself has grown prodigiously. It is now a sprawling and grubby city, no longer the village of Rumphius's day. It is also a troubled city. As this review goes to press the people of Ambon—Christian and Muslim—are killing each other, while a corrupt and vicious military holds these remote islands in the thrall of a Javanese empire.

I have been a practising biologist all of my life. As a student I've sat in lectures as the wonders of the sea were explained to me, only to come out with a head brimful of facts and names, and a sense of curiosity and wonder utterly stifled. To my shame I must admit that I've taught students the same way, dissecting, ever dissecting nature, until tiny pieces of knowledge are passed on in what becomes an arcane ritual. Despite its egregious errors, were I to teach again, I think that I would do so with *The Ambonese Curiosity Cabinet* by my side, for enthusiasm and a sense of wonder are worth more to a biologist than a decade of learned 'facts'.

Glow in the Dark

New York Review of Books, July 2001

The 13th Element: The Sordid Tale of Murder, Fire, and Phosphorus, John Emsley, John Wiley, New York, 2000.

Histories of seemingly obscure things—from longitude to cod—have recently become extremely popular. But until last year, when John Emsley wrote his history of phosphorus, no chemical element had been so dignified.

What makes the best of such histories fascinating is their potential to allow us to see the world anew, reflected in the light of their humble subject. Emsley could not have done better in choosing phosphorus, for, as he says, this thirteenth discovered element is at once the source of one of the most terrifying means of mass destruction ever devised and one of the most useful aids to humanity ever discovered. It is, according to Emsley, 'the supreme ruler' of life on earth.

A secretive alchemist, the self-styled Herr Doktor Brandt, made the initial discovery of phosphorus in Hamburg around 1669.

One imagines that Brandt envisioned a golden future as he toiled over his vats of urine, following the 'golden stream' in pursuit of the philosopher's stone. What he discovered instead must have shocked him deeply. As he heated the residue in his retort, glowing fumes filled the vessel. Then a shining drop appeared at its end, which immediately burst into flames, filling the room with a pungent, garlic-like smell. When he caught and stoppered a drop in a glass vessel, he found that it solidified. Hours later it was still glowing with an eerie, pale-green light, waves of flame seeming to lick its surface. Brandt never published an account of his discovery, and most of what we know of him comes from letters written by his wife. He did, however, sell samples of his newly discovered element, and even passed on something of the method of its making to various German alchemists.

By 1677 news of the marvellous discovery had crossed the Channel and come to the attention of the Honourable Robert Boyle, co-founder of the Royal Society and of the discipline of modern chemistry. A confirmed bachelor, Boyle lived with his sister, Lady Ranelagh, at her home in Pall Mall. 'He is charitable to ingeniose men that are in want,' wrote his contemporary John Aubrey, 'and foreigne Chymists have had large proofe of his bountie, for he will not spare for cost to gett any rare Secret.' Nothing, it seems, fascinated him as much as things that glowed, glimmered or shone.

Boyle's researches into luminosity had begun by 1663, the year he reported on a 'carbuncle'—a diamond that glowed when heated. The strangest of such carbuncles were the 'virgins'—those that glowed only on the first heating and never thereafter. When Boyle finally obtained a specimen from diamond dealers in Amsterdam, he withdrew with the prize to his four-poster bed, where he 'brought it to some kind of glimmering light' by 'holding it a good while on a warm part of my naked body'. This excitation of the carbuncle delighted Boyle, who was six feet tall, temperate and frugal, and well aware that his constitution 'was not of the hottest'.

For all of its quirkiness the experiment was significant, and in 1948 the observation was put to use when scientists realised that the carbuncle's glow came from electrons trapped in the flawed diamond's crystal lattice. By counting the number of trapped electrons they could estimate the length of time the stone had been buried. This knowledge laid the basis for the dating method called thermoluminescence, now one of the more advanced tools for research in prehistory.

Not all of Boyle's researches into things that glowed were as inoffensive as his escapades with the carbuncle, and on occasion were doubtless trying for Lady Ranelagh. He made earnest efforts to obtain living specimens of 'the shining Flees, called Cucuyes' that pestered the settlers of Virginia, but since these proved impossible to obtain he resorted to studies of rotting fish, which also glowed in the dark.

His greatest breakthrough occurred one Saturday evening in September 1677, when the German alchemist Daniel Kraft arrived at Ranelagh House and introduced Boyle to phosphorus. To demonstrate the strange new material to the assembled fellows of the Royal Society, Kraft took a piece that glowed with a 'mixture of strangeness, beauty and frightfulness', which he broke into fragments and scattered onto Lady Ranelagh's fine Turkish carpet. Boyle, perhaps recalling other incidents in which the 'fellows' had disturbed domestic harmony, called for a candle to examine the condition of the precious possession that, fortunately, was unharmed.

Lady Ranelagh may well have forgiven the strange odour resembling sulphur and onions that pervaded the house following Kraft's demonstration, but her patience was limited, and she soon banished brother Robert's experiments to a shed she had built in the backyard. Her timing was impeccable, for Boyle became obsessed with phosphorus and was determined to make some. He offered a handsome sum to Kraft for the recipe, but the German remained tight-lipped, only letting slip that it was 'somewhat that belonged to the body of man'. This led Boyle to suspect that the source may lie in the 'golden stream'.

At this time a curiously named Mr Bilger manned Boyle's backyard laboratory. He was given the task of collecting the chamber pots of the neighbourhood and boiling up the contents. The hours spent by Bilger toiling over vats of steaming urine were unfortunately wasted, for he succeeded in creating only an unsavoury black lump. Boyle, suspecting they were on the wrong track, decided that the back door might prove more fruitful than the golden stream, and the unfortunate Bilger was sent out again, this time in pursuit of vast quantities of faeces. These were boiled, baked and burned—but again with no result.

While the olfactory challenge of life in Restoration England was doubtless greater than today, one can hardly imagine that the efforts of Bilger and Boyle went unnoticed by the residents of Pall Mall. In any case the whole thing appears to have been too much for Bilger, and soon there was another assistant, one Godfrey Hanckewitz. Boyle returned to the golden stream and, by heating urine residues until they were red-hot, was soon successful.

Boyle's formula for making phosphorus was finally published posthumously in the journal of his beloved Royal Society in 1680. While it is not as eccentric as some other formulas (which direct the manufacturer to 'let the urine lie steeping, until it putrify and breed worms') it does specify the use of 'Man's urine'. Ironically, urine is a relatively poor source of phosphorus, containing just 1.4 grams per litre, as opposed to bone with 11 grams per kilogram. Until this fact was recognised in the 1750s, phosphorus was rare and expensive, which was just as well since its main use was then medicinal, and phosphorus is highly toxic and useless as a medicine.

The nineteenth century saw a great increase in the manufacture of phosphorus, which, until a mineral source was discovered in the 1860s, was derived from bones. Most was used in the production of matches. Emsley takes us on a ramble through the history of these everyday objects, from the awful fate of the nineteen-year-old Archduchess Matilda, who burned to death after stepping on a lucifer (as pre-safety matches were called), to the development of safety matches and the ravages of phossy jaw. This disease, thankfully no longer with us, was chronic among matchmakers. It attacked the jaws, literally eating them away and exposing the bone through foul-smelling ulcers. Its cause is still not entirely understood, but it is clear that exposure to phosphorus was the key risk factor. Phosphorus poisoning occasionally occurred in stranger circumstances, such as the case, reported in 1890, of a young girl who succumbed after a fake medium smeared her with a phosphorus-based rat poison so that she would glow in the dark at a séance.

Despite such unfortunate incidents, it was in the twentieth century that the true potential of phosphorus as a killer was realised. One of its earliest large-scale uses was in the manufacture of phosphorus bombs. Emsley provides a rare firsthand description of what it is like to be assailed by them in an account by a young German woman who took refuge in a public toilet during the

Allied bombing of Hamburg. A bomb burst at the door, splashing phosphorus over the people packed inside. The burning fragments could not be put out with water and ate into the flesh of three wounded soldiers, who resorted to suicide rather than face a more agonising death.

As horrendous as the phosphorus bomb is, even more sinister uses were soon found for the versatile element. As the Russian army advanced into Germany in 1945 it encountered a heavily defended chemical plant in Prussian Silesia that had been producing a strange new chemical at the rate of one thousand tons per month. Upon analysis it was found to be a cyanide–phosphorus compound known as tabun, one of the most toxic gases ever produced. By the end of the war, enough tabun had been manufactured to kill every person on earth. The only reason it was not used was that the Nazis feared (wrongly as it turned out) that the Allies had similar plants and that the retaliation would be catastrophic.

Research on phosphorus-based toxic gases (commonly known as nerve gas because they attack the central nervous system) gained pace after the war, sometimes through truly heroic experimentation. Emsley tells us of Dr Bernard Saunders, who tested the effect of diisopropyl phosphorofluoridate on himself. He sat:

> in a sealed room, put a drop of the vapor on a glass dish and then simply waited. After an hour, during which nothing appeared to have happened, an assistant went into the room to ask Saunders how he was feeling; Saunders replied that he felt very strange and was wondering why the room had gone dark.

Just 0.36 parts per million of this compound was found to be deadly to rats if breathed for ten minutes.

Emsley is a chemist by profession and co-author of the definitive textbook *The Chemistry of Phosphorus*. While his prose can be rather pedestrian, he lends an easy, explanatory style to *The 13th Element* that allows even the chemically naive to understand how nerve gases work, how phosphorus compounds are structured, and how phosphorus is used in living bodies. Much of this more technical material is included in break-out boxes.

The link between nerve gases and insecticides is closer than many might think. The phosphorus-based nerve gas called sarin was once tested on the plant louse phylloxera, while other members of the organophosphate group are currently the world's leading herbicides and insecticides. The use of these chemicals, therefore, is not without risk.

Some veterans of the war in the Persian Gulf claim to suffer from Gulf War syndrome brought on by exposure to insecticides, while farmers are also occasionally affected. One of the most famous sufferers is the Countess of Mar, who was accidentally poisoned by organophosphates in sheep dip in the summer of 1989. A member of the House of Lords, she is now a strident campaigner against the chemicals. Emsley's book, incidentally, documents strange cases of antipathy between female European nobility and phosphorus, of which the Countess of Mar's poisoning is one of the less hair-raising examples.

Inevitably, perhaps, phosphates have been used in murders as well as war. Emsley gives us an account of some of the most famous ones, including the celebrated case of Dr Bowers of Baltimore, who was accused of murdering three wives between 1865 and 1885. His perfidy is matched by that of Mrs Mary Wilson, who did away with two husbands, and possibly a third, by skilful administration of beetle killer mixed with Worcestershire sauce. She was tried at Leeds Winter Assizes in 1958 and sentenced to death.

Despite its efficacy in killing, phosphorus was hardly the ideal medium for a would-be murderer. Often the poisoner was given away by the corpse (or on occasion by its internal organs), which would emit an unearthly glow. Phosphorus can also persist for long periods, and coroners' inquests would sometimes find traces up to a year after interment. Things could also go wrong at earlier stages, such as in the case of the German housewife who tried to murder her husband by lacing his food with phosphorus rat poison. The plan was foiled when the husband noticed that his soup glowed in the dark.

Phosphorus is such a protean substance, and its influences on humanity so varied, that Emsley must be congratulated on producing such an inclusive work. The discussion of one major question, however, leaves the biologist in me unsatisfied. Chapter twelve, The Supreme Ruler, deals with phosphorus's significance to ecosystems. It begins with a quote from one of Isaac Asimov's works of non-fiction: 'Life can multiply until all of the phosphorus has gone and then there is a inexorable halt which nothing can prevent.'

Asimov is pointing to the fundamental limit that the availability of phosphorus places on life, and nowhere is that limit more perilously approached than in Australia.

Australian landscapes are so ancient that the zone of deeply weathered rock (the regolith) in many places is over one hundred metres deep. This zone has lost most of its nutrients, and is virtually phosphorus-free. It is now clear that the rise to prominence of Australia's distinctive eucalypt forests, along with that of the rest of its hard-leaved vegetation, has come about as a result of a lack of phosphorus. Most species have developed highly specialised methods for capturing what little phosphorus there is. Some Australian gums extend their roots right through the regolith; not solely in search of water, but also of fresh rock that might contain phosphorus. This continent is also world headquarters for many carnivorous plants, because insects are the easiest source of phosphorus available to them.

It is perhaps unfair to expect a chemist to cover such topics. Emsley does, however, give us a splendid account of the limiting character of phosphorus in English agriculture. Crop records extending back to the Middle Ages have been kept for fields in the Oxford region. They reveal that crop yields were in decline because phosphorus was being 'mined' from the soil. The vital role of phosphorus is also revealed by the longest-running agricultural experiment in the world—at Rothamstead, fifty kilometres outside London—where crops have been grown on the same soil, with precisely measured fertiliser, for 150 years. There is even a plot of land where no fertiliser is used, and it annually produces around a tonne of wheat per hectare, about the medieval yield. The phosphorus comes from two sources—the breakdown of rock to create new soil, and car exhaust, whose phosphorus is dissolved in rainwater.

Emsley's last chapter is a surprise, for it deals with a topic more usually associated with the paranormal: spontaneous human combustion. After giving some gruesome examples of bodies thought to have spontaneously combusted (including that of the Countess Cornelia Baudi of Cesena, who went up in flames in 1731), Emsley gets on the chemical trail. He argues that the key to the phenomenon may be a little-known derivative of phosphorus called diphosphane gas, which will burst into flame upon contact with air. The making of diphosphane gas is tricky and energy-intensive, and until recently it was believed that it did not occur in nature. But in 1993, Dr Günter Gassmann of Hamburg (the very town where phosphorus was discovered, and the first to be destroyed by phosphorus bombs) found that it could be synthesised by certain as yet unidentified microbes. The appositely named doctor, who published his work in the leading chemistry journal *Angewandte Chemie, International Edition in English*, pursued a strangely familiar yet antiquated research technique. Diligently scraping the nappies of eight-month-old infants, and procuring adult faeces as well, Gassmann was able to show that a kilogram of infantile excreta contained 160 nanograms of diphosphane, while in adults a disappointing 80 nanograms only was present.

Emsley posits that diphosphane gas might be produced in considerable quantities, particularly among the costive and overweight, and that this may be the source of the mysterious ignitions that initiate spontaneous combustion. To bolster his case he marshals testimony from a number of witnesses, each of whom observed a mysterious flame erupting from near the nether regions of victims as they caught alight. Disappointingly for Emsley, one suspects, none of the surviving victims confessed either to severe flatulence or constipation in the lead-up to the frightening episode. His diphosphane theory remains in the air.

Emsley writes that early chemists such as Boyle were fascinated with phosphorus because 'it proved that beneath the surface of things there was indeed another world'. It's a fascination that almost every child of my generation experienced when given a toy chemistry set. Things that went *bang* or gave off foul odours were particularly prized by my fellow experimenters, which is probably why chemistry sets were restricted before falling out of favour with a more safety-conscious generation. With *The 13th Element*, Emsley restores the wonder of chemistry, and for that he deserves a wide readership.

The Mneme-ing of Life

The Times Literary Supplement, OCTOBER 2001

In *The Selfish Gene,* biologist Richard Dawkins coins the term 'meme', which he defines as being the cultural equivalent of a gene. The concept provides a new way of examining how ideas behave in human societies, but like many innovative and challenging hypotheses its central tenet—that memes are cultural analogues of genes—is fiercely debated. Are some memes, for example, 'selfish', maximising their spread to the detriment of their human bearers? Even more intriguing is Dawkins's idea that memes have a physical reality. Do ideas leave some actual 'impression' on the brain that receives them? Despite the currency of Dawkins's meme hypothesis and the modernity of our appreciation of how genes work, such ideas and questions are not new. Indeed the concept that ideas resemble physically inherited traits (expressions of genes) in such ways is at least a century old.

One early and brilliant pioneer in the field was German biologist Richard Semon. His two books on the subject, *Die Mneme* (1904, in English as *The Mneme* in 1921) and *Die Mnemischen Empfindungen* (1909), contain fundamental insights into the issues raised by Dawkins. In *The Mneme*, Semon investigates how cultural transmission of experience operates. In some ways his findings are closely parallel to those of Dawkins. Yet Semon's mnemes were doomed to early extinction in the fields of human memory, while Dawkins's memes thrive. The reason for this seems not so much to do with the ideas themselves as with the social milieu into which they were born.

Semon was fated to publish his most significant advances in the decade prior to the outbreak of the Great War, and he died shortly after it finished, in Munich in 1919, aged sixty-one. Anti-German sentiment delayed publication of the English edition of *The Mneme* for seven years and probably poisoned the fertile mental furrows in which it may otherwise have taken root. Worse, the principal experiments on which Semon drew became the focus of a furious battle between neo-Darwinians and neo-Lamarckians. Slurs and accusations of fraud muddied the scientific waters, ending in the humiliation and suicide of one of Semon's most esteemed colleagues and the unfair discrediting of a body of work central to Semon's thesis. Only in Australia is Semon widely remembered, and there solely for his book *In the Australian Bush and on the Coast of the Coral Sea*, which is a popular account of his experiences as a young biologist in Queensland during an expedition in the late nineteenth century.

Researcher John Laurent has questioned the independence of Dawkins's memes and Semon's mnemes. He debates the etymological origin of Dawkins's term, which is given as the Greek *mimeisthai*, to imitate. Laurent identifies a more straightforward source—mneme—referring to a unit of memory and 'taken from the Greek *mimneskesthai*, to remember (and ultimately from Mnemosyne, the Greek goddess of memory)'.

Laurent cites a curious early use of the term mneme: Maurice Maeterlinck's 1927 book, *The Soul of the White Ant*. Maeterlinck was a Belgian dramatist, essayist and amateur entomologist who studied termites. His book was tremendously popular and was reprinted thirty-four times to 1948. Laurent writes:

> Nowhere does Dawkins refer to 'mneme', but it is difficult to believe that he had not come across the term, especially since he has much about termites in both *The Selfish Gene* and *The Blind Watchmaker* and cites a number of works about these creatures (though not Maeterlinck's) in both books.

Laurent notes that Maeterlinck cites Semon as his authority for the term, but so obscure are Semon's books on the subject that they eluded Laurent's search. In light of the growing interest in the field of memes/mnemes, Semon's contribution deserves re-examination; but both Semon and his ideas need to be seen in their historical context if they are to be properly understood.

The latter part of the nineteenth century exposed vast horizons to the inquiring naturalist. New geographic fields of exploration existed around the globe, discovery of new species of birds and mammals were mundane, and profound insights into the workings of nature seemed to be there for the taking. Spurred on by the idea that ontogeny recapitulates phylogeny, Semon travelled to Australia in the hope of discovering 'living fossils' whose development might reveal ancient evolutionary pathways.

To the European imagination Australia was a land of primitive relics, including mammals that laid eggs, pouched marsupials and archaic invertebrates. Semon lived for a time with a group of Aborigines of the Burnett tribe of southern Queensland: there was Jimmy, Mackenzie, Johnny, and 'fat, lazy Old Tom' who assisted him by catching the creatures he wished to examine. His work with the egg-laying echidna was particularly arduous, for it is secretive and rather uncommon. He added materially to its rarity, locally at least, by killing more than 250, sixty of which were pregnant females vital to his studies.

No species, however, held out as much promise to Semon as the mysterious *Ceratodus* or Queensland lungfish, which had been recently discovered by Gerard Krefft, director of the Australian Museum. Krefft's discovery was made in rather unusual circumstances—on a platter at the home of a Mr Forster who, unaware of its antediluvian status, served it at supper for the doctor's culinary delectation. When news of the discovery of such a primitive creature—seemingly intermediate between fish and the tetrapods—reached Europe in 1871, it caused a scientific storm. Semon found them to be common and easily captured, and studied them extensively. Unfortunately subsequent research has shown that *Ceratodus* (or *Neoceratodus* as it is now known) is not part of the tetrapod lineage after all; but Semon's work was not entirely in vain, for his monograph on its embryological development remains definitive.

Semon's later researches resolved themselves into a quest for a grand unifying theory of 'reproduction', which included physical and mental transmissions of experience. He wrote that, 'instead of speaking of a factor of memory, a factor of habit, or a factor of heredity, I have preferred to consider these as manifestations of a common principle, which I shall call the Mnemic principle'. It was a quest that could only have been undertaken at a time when understanding of the mechanism of inheritance was opaque, and when there was still room in the most respectable scientific circles for non-Darwinian explanations of evolution.

Semon's all-encompassing theory possessed what is, from a contemporary perspective, a fatal flaw, for it necessitated a Lamarckian element in evolution. Semon viewed this as complementary with, rather than opposed to, Darwinian principles. He devoted a whole chapter of *The Mneme* to a discussion of how physical stimuli experienced by an individual can be passed on to succeeding generations, leaning heavily upon the work of a brilliant young biologist, Paul Kammerer of Vienna. He commences with a discussion of experiments conducted on the fire newt (*Salamandra maculosa*). Pregnant females were kept from water, thereby inducing them to give birth to fewer, more advanced young. This characteristic, it was claimed, was passed on to the next generation, despite their having free access to water. Herr Kammerer also experimented on the black alpine newt (*Salamandra atra*), which normally bears just two well-developed young. By providing pregnant females with access to water he induced them to have larger broods of less-developed young, again claiming that the effect persisted into the next generation despite a reversion to drier conditions.

Other experiments were conducted too. A Miss V. Chauvin so manipulated the environment of some axolotls as to force her subjects to develop lungs rather than retain gills. Their offspring, she observed, frequently surfaced to gulp air, something normal axolotls will do 'only at an advanced age and in water deficient in air'. Semon also reported on experiments with tiger moths (*Arctia caja*) and other creatures, but the trouble with these is the possibility that some degree of genetic selection biased the results. With the tiger moth, for example, the experimenter induced melanisation by lowering the temperature during pupation. It was claimed that succeeding generations were also melanistic; but these had been bred from just the most melanistic pair of more than 150 moths.

Semon examined other sorts of genetic memory. How does a creature 'remember' how to develop, grow eyes in the right place, and to mate in the appropriate manner? Here the experiments he cites look positively bizarre by modern standards. The indefatigable Kammerer leads off again, producing great triumphs with the 'obstetric toad' (*Alytes obstetricans*). Toiling over hundreds of the warty creatures, he persuaded them to forgo their predilection for having sex on land by keeping them 'in a room at high temperature, until induced by the unaccustomed heat to cool themselves in a water trough . . . here the male and female found each other'. Once enamoured in the aqueous environment, Kammerer reported, the toads mated in the normal anuran manner rather than in the fashion usually favoured by obstetric toads (where the male helps squeeze the eggs from the female, then wraps them around his hindlimbs). This Semon interpreted as the toad 'remembering' the ancestral way of having sex (which incidentally was also claimed to persist in subsequent generations).

Even after producing such extraordinary proofs of Lamarckian evolution as this, the amphibia were allowed no rest. In another experiment Dr Speman made the '*Bombinator*' toad grow eye lenses on the back of its head—a feat remarkable in itself, but surpassed by Dr Elkman who induced green frogs (*Hyla arborea*) to grow eye lenses anywhere 'with the possible exception of the ear and nose primordia'. This, Semon argued, demonstrated that frog skin 'remembered' how to grow eyes if appropriately stimulated.

Kammerer's experiments may seem eccentric to twenty-first century eyes but the work of some of his laboratory colleagues puts them into perspective. Herr Dr Finkler, for example, devoted himself to transplanting the heads of male insects onto females. They showed signs of life for several days but, perhaps unsurprisingly, exhibited disturbed sexual behaviour. By the standards of the time Kammerer's work was painstaking and convincing, yet by the 1920s he was under severe assault. The trouble was that his findings presented a serious challenge to neo-Darwinian orthodoxy, which was then championed by William Bateson, the originator of the term genetics and thus a direct 'memic' ancestor of Richard Dawkins.

Bateson's attacks were vitriolic and obsessive, and it has been suggested that he had personal reasons for wishing to see Kammerer's work discredited. Remarkably, despite the furore, no one tried seriously to replicate Kammerer's intricate experiments, and even as late as 1971 that vital step had not been taken. In 1926 it was discovered that one of his specimens had been tampered with. This was held up as evidence that his lifetime's work was suspect. With his reputation in tatters, Kammerer shot himself.

Semon's book suffered greatly from this vicious neo-Darwinian backlash. As a result the baby was thrown out with the bath water, for Semon's deductions on the human brain, memory and the transmission of ideas is a classic case (perhaps *the* classic case) of Lamarckian evolution. Admittedly, Semon sounds idiosyncratic to twenty-first century ears, but his analysis is solid enough. He argues, for example, that stimuli are constantly bombarding us and that consequently mnemes must occur as 'highly composite exitation complexes' that may or may not function as a whole. By way of example he reminisces:

We were once standing by the Bay of Naples and saw Capri lying before us; near by an organ-grinder played on a large barrel-organ; a peculiar smell of oil reached us from a neighbouring 'trattoria'; the sun was beating pitilessly on our backs; and our boots, in which we had been tramping about for hours, pinched us. Many years after, a similar smell of oil ecphorised [brought to mind] most vividly the optic engram [memory] of Capri. The melody of the barrel-organ, the heat of the sun, the discomfort of the boots, are ecphorised neither by the smell of the oil nor by the renewed experience of Capri.

In defining the mneme, Semon states: 'This Mnemic property may be regarded from a purely physiological point of view, in as much as it is traced back to the effect of stimuli applied to the irritable organic substance.' This was true, according to Semon, whether the mneme was a memory or an inherited aspect of a body.

Dawkins says of his memes: 'If memes in brains are analogous to genes they must be self-replicating brain structures, actual patterns of neuronal wiring-up that reconstitute themselves in one brain after another,' adding that 'Memes should be regarded as living structures, not just metaphorically but technically.'

Thus both Semon and Dawkins suggest that memes/mnemes must have a physical reality. Any impression of difference is due in large part to the language of their respective times—Semon talking of 'an impression on an irritable substance', and Dawkins of 'neuronal wiring'. It is at this crucial juncture, I think, that Semon's 'mnemes' and Dawkins's memes display their closest convergence.

While some might call forth Sheldrake's theory of morphic resonance to explain such coincidences (in this Kammerer himself might have agreed, for he was also author of a book foreshadowing Sheldrake's theories), Laurent suspects borrowing—that Dawkins must have heard of Semon's mneme. I can subscribe to neither view, for it seems to me that—as both Semon and Dawkins point out—the way ideas are transmitted is still something of a mystery. All indications, however, are that Richard Semon would have been disinclined to believe that Richard Dawkins had any knowledge of *The Mneme*, for he commenced his *magnum opus* with the observation:

> The attempt to discover analogies between the various organic phenomena of reproduction is by no means new. It would be strange if philosophers and naturalists had not been struck by the similarity existing between the reproduction in offspring . . . and that other kind of reproduction we call memory.

Who Came First?

New York Review of Books, JUNE 2003

The First Americans: In Pursuit of Archaeology's Greatest Mystery, James Adovasio and Jake Page, Random House, New York, 2002.

America before the European Invasions, Alice Beck Kehoe, Longman, New York, 2002.

Before ever a word was written, at least 5000 generations of people had lived out their lives on this earth, among them extraordinary innovators and adventurers who planted the first crops and discovered and settled entire continents. Yet except in the most extraordinary circumstances, nothing but stone tools and broken bones remain to tell us of their lives and triumphs. Archaeologists delve into the earth to shed light into this void, and as you might imagine, the stories they emerge to tell are open to many interpretations. Few, however, have proven as contentious as those concerning the peopling of the Americas.

The very first human discovery of the Americas must have unleashed enormous opportunity for those tribes that crossed from Asia, for at a swoop 28 per cent of the globe's land surface, including some of its richest, most diverse and most spectacular landscapes, fell to them and their descendants. Today the details of that conquest have been obscured by the mists of time, and so scientists continue to argue the basics of whom, when, and how.

The traditional view is that people arrived in America around 13,200 years ago, via a narrow land corridor then opening up in the ice sheet that had long divided temperate North America from Asia. Recently, however, archaeologists have begun investigating the possibility that the first Americans had arrived at least 16,000 years ago, and that they skirted the ice barrier using boats. This more recent work has received a good deal of popular coverage, including a cover edition of *National Geographic*.

Over the past few decades, archaeological opinion has crystallised around two basic positions. The traditionalists argue that a pioneering human culture known as Clovis, which came into being around 13,200 years ago, constitutes the earliest human presence in America. Other researchers, however, believe that the first Americans arrived at least 16,000 years ago, and they have recently become more vocal.

While inherently interesting, the debate also has wider dimensions, for the traditionalists think that the Clovis were big-game hunters who exterminated America's megafauna (including the mammoth, mastodon and other ice age beasts) much as the buffalo hunters of the historic frontier did the buffalo. The champions of a pre-Clovis presence, on the other hand, read into bones and stones the story of a gentle people who caused no detectable environmental disturbance. Yet it is becoming clear that the debate is about even more than that, for it touches upon the very way we conduct our science.

James Adovasio is a passionate believer in a pre-Clovis human presence in America. *The First Americans*, which was written with the assistance of Jake Page, a former editor of *Natural History* magazine, presents what the authors claim to be indisputable proof that people inhabited the Americas some 16,000 years ago.

Adovasio has spent much of his professional career excavating a single site—the Meadowcroft rock shelter in south-western Pennsylvania—and this site provides the bulk of the evidence presented in his book. His team began work there in 1972, and over the past thirty years they have dug through eleven identifiable layers, recovered more than 2 million artefacts and obtained fifty-two radiocarbon dates. Consequently, Meadowcroft rock shelter is today the litmus test for a pre-Clovis human presence in North America. If it and its sister site of Monte Verde in southern Chile (excavated by Tom Dillehay of the University of Kentucky) are falsified, the core data supporting a pre-Clovis presence in the Americas would collapse.

The First Americans commences with an interesting, speculative overview about the origins of the Native Americans. The extensive mounds built in the Ohio River Valley were one of the first places to generate interest in the subject. Thomas Jefferson undertook the first scientific excavation in the history of archaeology when, in 1784, he probed one such mound—four metres high—on his property near the Rivanna River, Virginia. Other early inquirers were not so rigorous. In 1839 Cornelius Mathews penned the novel *Behemoth: A Legend of the Mound-Builders*, which posits that the civilisation responsible for the mounds was all but destroyed by a rogue and monstrous woolly mammoth. Another fanciful nineteenth-century theory was that Noah's ark came to rest on the mounds. The Mormons also posit a biblical involvement, holding that the Jews came to America around 600 BC and built great cities atop the mounds, after which one group of Israelites fell from the ways of God and became red-skinned. Adovasio writes that well into the second half of the twentieth century, Mormon missionaries were assuring Native Americans and blacks that this history was proof that their skins would whiten if they joined the church. American prehistory, it seems, has always served political ends.

American archaeology long remained an insular, unscientific field dominated by amateurs, but by the beginning of the twentieth century rigour and professionalism were beginning to make their mark. William Henry Holmes, an artist turned geologist, was employed by John Wesley Powell (who was then director of both the US Geological Survey and the Smithsonian's Bureau of Ethnology) to investigate claims of an ice-age human presence in America. Through patient research and close observation, he was able to dismiss all such claims, thus distinguishing North America from Europe, where a considerable body of evidence for an ice-age human presence had been accumulated.

By the early 1920s it was looking as if humans had entered the Americas as recently as four or five thousand years ago, but then a black cowboy made an extraordinary discovery. George McJunkin was born into slavery and when, aged fourteen, he was freed by Union forces, he had not had a single day's education. Like so many possessed of slim prospects he decided to 'go west', settling on the Crowfoot Ranch, New Mexico. Once there, he got the sons of the rancher to teach him to read, and eventually became ranch foreman, as well as a much sought after fiddler, surveyor, astronomer and instrument maker. But George's real passion lay in the study of natural history. He kept a small museum at his home that included fossil animal bones, and one day in 1908 he spotted something protruding from the side of a gully. It proved to be the bone of an enormous extinct bison, and he wrote to friends telling them of the find. He returned frequently to excavate at the place, but it was not until 1926—four years after McJunkin's death—that a team from the Colorado Museum of Natural History organised their own dig. They unearthed the near-perfect skeletons of several giant bison, and between the ribs of one lay a beautifully crafted stone spear point. This association of now vanished giant fauna with human artefacts convinced even the most sceptical that humanity had a long pedigree in America.

And the extraordinary 1933 discovery of the even earlier Clovis culture set the benchmark for the earliest human presence on the continent. Exquisite stone spearheads, some up to twenty-three centimetres long, are this culture's signature piece. They were made for just 300 years—between about 12,900 and 13,200 years ago—yet these deadly, beautiful weapons have been found across much of the lower forty-eight states and Mexico. To me they are deeply evocative of the deadly beauty of those quintessential tools of the historic frontier—the Colt pistol and Winchester rifle. Just as production of these weapons coincided with the demise of the buffalo and passenger pigeon, so does Clovis coincide with the extinction of America's megafauna—the mammoth, mastodon and other ice age giants.

Adovasio's work at Meadowcroft involved wrangling a sometimes-difficult field crew. One of his crew chiefs, he says, was 'a Hells Angel type' with 'superb technical skills', but an unfortunate predilection for alcohol, who 'once into the "loon water" was capable of a Fredric March type of face change and no end of outrageous activity'. Managing large field crews is never easy, but individuals like this can make it hell, for the work is tedious and unrelenting. 'After twelve hours of trowelling thin layers of dirt and dust, you go crazy at night,' says Adovasio. 'Running, weight-lifting, drinking, fornicating, staring off into space and babbling incoherently—you do almost anything for relief. It takes a truly bizarre person to live that way for months on end, and we had tents full of them.'

'I did not think much about my nearly fanatical drive to make Meadowcroft the best excavation ever,' Adovasio continues, 'but I realise now with utter clarity that it was me showing [doctoral supervisor] Jennings that I could be even better than he at his own game.' Jesse Jennings was, by Adovasio's own account, a brutal, callous man who crushed many of those who worked with him. Adovasio called him the 'Dark Lord', and his shadow seems to have hung over his student like the influence of an abusive father.

At the core of Adovasio's pre-Clovis claim lies the Meadowcroft radiocarbon dates, which he believes represent unassailable evidence. Yet only a half-dozen or so of the dates directly relate to human artefacts in the contentious 12,000 to 16,000 years interval, and the dating was for the most part completed before the new methods (such as sophisticated carbon extraction/isolation tools and accelerator mass spectrometry) were available. These tools are critical in dealing with sites where contamination is suspected, and there have been many suspicions of contamination at Meadowcroft.

Meadowcroft rock shelter is developed in Pennsylvanian age sandstone, which elsewhere yields the coal for which the state is famous. Some researchers have suggested that carbon from ancient coal has somehow got into the samples. But how could this have occurred? Adovasio points out a fundamental difficulty, saying that to obtain the result seen at Meadowcroft, many samples would have to be contaminated in a systematic manner. There is one possible way that this could occur naturally. If groundwater carrying humic acid rose through the site, it could have deposited a gradient of contaminant through samples that already contained coal. Yet

Adovasio strenuously denies that such groundwater ever existed at Meadowcroft, and it does seem *prima facie* unlikely.

Adovasio says of the Smithsonian-based laboratory that did the bulk of the radiocarbon dating, that it was 'utterly professional and almost always totally reliable'. But history has shown that dates produced by even the best radiocarbon laboratories are far from unassailable, for many dates processed in the 1980s and before have been re-examined using modern techniques and found to be in error. Even worse, cases of negligence and even fraud have come to light, a spectacular instance of the latter recently being published in *Science*.

Sloppy reporting may have contributed to the confusion at Meadowcroft. Dates from the lowest (pre-human occupation) levels were processed by what Adovasio refers to as 'the distinguished Oxford Radiocarbon dating facility in England' that, he reports, 'explicitly stated that no indications of contamination could be found'. Dr Richard Gillespie, the chemist responsible for preparing those samples, has confirmed this, but in a rather peculiar manner. It is his belief that the samples consisted entirely of lignite, a type of coal. Thus there was 'no contamination' because the entire sample consisted of contaminant! Despite this, the report sent to Adovasio at the time reported that the sample was charcoal. While no explanation of this discrepancy has been forthcoming, it does illustrate that even the finest laboratories can 'bugger up', which makes the reaction of Bob Stuckenrath (the now deceased radiocarbon dating expert who provided many Meadowcroft dates) to ongoing scepticism seem less than professional. In *The First Americans* Adovasio reports Stuckenrath as saying, 'If they don't believe the evidence, fuck 'em', and elsewhere he reports Stuckenrath as having said 'F... 'em if they can't read.'

It is becoming more apparent that reliance on radiocarbon dates alone (even if the most modern techniques are applied) is frequently insufficient to resolve chronologies. Thankfully, a fistful of new dating techniques has recently become available. They are already being applied in Australia and Europe, but have been slow coming to North American archaeology. Amino acid racemisation dating is one such. It is an inexpensive technique particularly suited to use on eggshells (which have been recovered at Meadowcroft). It has been used in Australia with spectacular results, for hundreds of dates can be obtained quickly and cheaply. Two AAR dates have been obtained from Meadowcroft, yet little has been made of them, and there is surely scope for more work here.

Optically stimulated luminescence dating involves the dating of sand grains. It is particularly useful in dating cave and rock-shelter sediments, and has an excellent track record in helping sort out difficult stratigraphy. Electron spin resonance dating is yet another technique that can be applied to dating ancient teeth. Increasingly, two or more of these techniques are being utilised alongside radiocarbon dating. Because they are independent, they highlight flaws and errors resulting from one or other technique due to particular circumstances such as contamination.

In the final chapters of *The First Americans,* Adovasio recounts what passed when a team of experts went to examine Tom Dillehay's supposedly pre-Clovis site at Monte Verde, Chile. The site boasts some of the most extraordinary preservation found anywhere in the world: hunks of meat, hides and even human footprints have been discovered, alongside a wealth of wooden artefacts and bones. Dillehay contends that people inhabited the site around 14,000 years ago, and even possibly 33,000 years ago, so it has generated considerable interest.

In 1989 Dr Vance Haynes of the University of Arizona at Tucson began organising for a panel of experts to visit Monte Verde and so see the evidence for themselves. It would take until 1997 for the visit to materialise, however, by which time logging roads and a meandering stream had destroyed the main site. Nevertheless the visit went reasonably well—until the archaeologists gathered one evening at a bar called '*la Caverna*' in a nearby town.

Tom Dillehay and James Adovasio were feeling badgered by the detailed examination of what remained of the site, and after the pair had 'ordered up' (or 'looned down' in Adovasio's archaeological vernacular), Tom went on the offensive. He accused Vance Haynes of knowing nothing about sites such as Monte Verde, and in response to a question from another expert retorted, 'What have you done for the past twenty years?'

Talk then turned to Meadowcroft, with Haynes remarking that if Adovasio would date just one seed or nut from the lowest levels, he might believe the alleged antiquity of the site. Haynes had an important point, for seeds and nuts cannot be contaminated by coal in the way that charcoal from an old hearth can.

Adovasio burst into derisive laughter at the suggestion before replying 'Horseshit', adding that he would never accede to any more dating requests from Haynes. He and Dillehay then stormed out of the bar.

Rarely have we been given such frank insider accounts of how debates in science are slugged out. But why in this case has the debate become so bitter? Stakes in the discovery of the first Americans are high, for researchers pin their reputations, credibility with funding partners, and even their careers on site interpretations. But this is equally true for much cutting-edge science, so it is an insufficient explanation in itself.

The First Americans is as much an autobiography as it is an account of the peopling of the Americas, and what Adovasio has to say of himself goes a long way towards explaining the tone of the debate: 'I have always pretty much responded in kind to bullies and other people who knock the work of my colleagues, teammates, and students'. He attributes his pugilistic style to growing up in Youngstown, Ohio, 'a mob town' with the highest rate of car bombing in the US where, he tells us, he associated with some pretty hard cases.

As you might imagine, Adovasio can be tough on his colleagues when they disagree with him. Stuart Fiedel published a detailed re-analysis of the Monte Verde site, which Adovasio says contains a 'thinly disguised inference that some evidence had been faked'. Adovasio characterises Fiedel as 'a man whom very few archaeologists had ever heard of…with a company that engages in what used to be called salvage archaeology, on contract with highway departments, local governments, federal agencies, and so forth'. What goes unsaid is that Fiedel is also author of the highly esteemed *Prehistory of the Americas*, published in several editions by Cambridge University Press. Adovasio also quotes from what appears to be a beautifully written manuscript by Vance Haynes describing how the Americas might have been settled. The source is given as 'Manuscript for review, on file, Mercyhurst College, 2001'.

Several things about Meadowcroft rock shelter seem anomalous. The pollen from layers supposedly dating to 16,000 years ago is characteristic of plants growing under warmer conditions than are thought to have prevailed over Pennsylvania at that time. Adovasio suggests that this is simply evidence that climatic conditions close to the ice sheet that then existed just north of the site were variable. Meadowcroft also lacks any remains of the megafauna that was so abundant in America until 13,000 years ago. This could be due to chance, or a bias by the people and animals that brought the remains into the cave. But the nature of the posited pre-Clovis people is another cause of concern. Adovasio writes, 'We do not have what archaeologists would call a pre-Clovis culture: we have a number of pre-Clovis cultures, none of which appears to be the parent technology of Clovis or even a distant relative.' Taken alongside the absence of any evidence for a human impact on the environment, this lack of connection with the confirmed cultural record rings a warning bell.

Another difficulty lies in the idea that the pre-Clovis humans entered North America at least 16,000 years ago; yet for 4000 years after, humans remained so rare that only two well-investigated sites have been discovered in all of the Americas (in southern Chile and Pennsylvania). The rareness of putative pre-Clovis sites has been attributed to the supposedly unproductive nature of North America before 13,000 years ago, and the idea that pre-Clovis cultures had a rudimentary stone tool technology that is difficult to recognise. There is a perfect test for this hypothesis—one that shows its inadequacy. Australia is a continent the size of the lower forty-eight states. Most of it is highly unproductive desert, and its indigenous peoples had a rather rudimentary stone tool technology. Yet Australia's few archaeologists (Australia has a population of just 19 million) have documented nearly 200 archaeological sites older that 13,000 years.

Clearly the most rigorous dating program afforded by modern science needs to be applied at Meadowcroft. Yet today the excavations have been closed. This seems to be because Adovasio is content that he has achieved near-total victory over his opponents.

He says that the 'handful' of remaining doubters remind him of 'a bumper sticker that had a brief run in the late seventies and the eighties which said STOP CONTINENTAL DRIFT'. Just in case the reader still hasn't got the message, Adovasio includes a cartoon of three people gathered around a gravestone inscribed with 'Clovis First 1933–1999'. Disturbingly, the book's final chapter reports on a whole raft of supposed, but as yet unconfirmed, pre-Clovis sites. It provides a pile of tantalising clues but no real data, and is about as useful in clarifying the situation as throwing a handful of clay into a glass of clean water. The entire feel of the book is one of Adovasio triumphant, a man who sees no need for further tests or dates. In other words, an end to science.

How do other prehistorians deal with Meadowcroft? Alice Beck Kehoe's *America before the European Invasions* dismisses the site in a single sentence, stating merely that samples seem to have been contaminated by ancient coal dust, though just how this occurred she does not speculate upon.

Kehoe's book does, however, give a splendid overview of the development of human cultures in North America north of Mexico. Its strength lies in the author's deep empathy with the people who lived their lives in vanished and barely imaginable civilisations, as well as with contemporary indigenous cultures. Each chapter deals with a coherent geographic region and a time period, but the bulk of the book is focused on the cultures that developed over the last 2000 years. Chapters end with 'research puzzles' pointing to the ambiguities and uncertainties of the archaeological record, while those dealing with historic cultures include accounts by Native Americans of their own origin stories and histories.

The politics of prehistory, Kehoe acknowledges, have been particularly vicious in the US. The doctrine of Manifest Destiny saw the indigenous Americans dispossessed and characterised as primitive tribes and savages. Yet as she points out, some of the political entities encountered by the early Spanish and the Virginia colonists were as large and sophisticated as the European states and principalities that the colonists had departed from.

In prehistory, of course, much larger entities existed. The mound builders of Cahokia (near modern-day St Louis) created vast edifices and clearly had far-reaching cultural influence. Kehoe likens North America after the collapse of Cahokia in the twelfth century to Europe following the collapse of Rome. By the time Columbus arrived, truly large empires existed only in Mexico.

My one regret with *America before the European Invasions* is that it does not extend its subject south of the Rio Grande. As Kehoe points out, Mexico has long been the engine of cultural change for much of North America. Crops, captive birds such as macaws, and even cultural concepts and people originating in the south long have found their way deep into the North American hinterland. Startling evidence of this influence was recovered from the only mound to be carefully excavated at Cahokia. Known as mound 72, it was a mere three metres high and fifty metres long, yet within it were buried the carefully arranged bodies of a nobleman and 260 adults, most of them young men and women. That number echoes both the number of human sacrifices made at the Feathered Serpent pyramid in Teotihuacán (a Mexican cultural centre which flourished several centuries before Cahokia), and the 260-day Mesoamerican ritual calendar.

Intriguingly, a few skeletons recovered from Cahokia possess filed front teeth. Tooth filing is unknown in the US except for those few individuals from Cahokia and a few others from the Chaco region of the American south-west, but the practice was widespread in Mexico. Kehoe posits that these individuals were visitors, perhaps traders or technicians from the south, who carried cultural innovations into the vast northern hinterland.

America before the European Invasions provides a great service to Americans. For decades the issue of race relations in the US has been focused tightly on black and white. Elsewhere in the world, including Australia, Canada, South Africa and the Middle East, people have been struggling with the legacy of colonialism and the dispossession of indigenous cultures. Given the sorry treatment of the indigenous cultures of the United States, it is time that their voice was heard a little more clearly in mainstream America.

The Lady or the Tiger?

New York Review of Books, OCTOBER 2003

Monster of God: The Man-eating Predator in the Jungles of History and the Mind, David Quammen, W. W. Norton, New York, 2003.

'There are always a few tigers roaming about Singapore,' the naturalist and evolutionary theorist Alfred Russel Wallace noted in the 1860s, 'and they kill on average a Chinaman every day.' Not too long ago only slightly less shocking statistics prevailed over much of south-east Asia, as indeed they still do in parts of India. Such figures give the impression that big predators and humans have waged an eternal, bitter struggle for survival. Yet, as David Quammen reveals in his latest book, *Monster of God*, the relationship between man-eaters and their potential prey is far more complex and interesting than that simple gloss suggests.

Anyone who has been on an African safari, or even visited a zoo, will know something of the relationship between our species and those that make us food. These animals' eyes stare with such engagement, readiness for action, and such propriety as to be almost unbearable. The stark terror evoked by those burning bright eyes has, I suspect, been seared into us over countless generations of natural selection, for our ancestors feared—or they did not survive. Here I can speak from personal experience.

In the 1980s I was a member of a committee charged with investigating the death of a zookeeper. The zoo's facilities were old, the 'carnivore house' a dark, dripping place. A narrow corridor painted with yellow lines on the floor accessed the service area. Beyond those lines, the claws of bears and big cats could drag you to mouths waiting at the iron grilles studding both walls. We were shown where the tiger had advanced on the young keeper as she photographed its cubs, all the while feeling secure in the knowledge that the mother was safely locked away. The tigress attacked from behind, its canines piercing the keeper's skull and breaking the neck, but leaving her conscious as it dragged her round the cage like a limp doll. Another keeper tried to drive off the animal with a spade, and finally succeeded, but too late.

That terrifying knowledge was fresh in my mind as I walked the corridor, tracing the maze of ropes and counterweights that controlled the opening and closing of numerous doors and grilles, trying to determine how the fatal accident had occurred. Suddenly the whole building shook and the air was filled with an indescribable sound as the iron grille before me was struck with the full force of a charging male lion.

He was stopped there, a metre from my face, roaring furiously, blasting me with his wet breath, clawing at me through the bars. Caesar hated men, a keeper explained. Over the twenty years I explored in New Guinea I'd faced death on several occasions— seated in a failing aircraft, standing at the wrong end of a Papuan arrow—but this was different. This was a terror that could not be sublimated, diverted or denied; this was a primal fear that simply takes you over.

There are relatively few creatures that can kill and eat an adult human. The tiger and lion, brown and polar bears, some sharks and crocodiles almost complete the list. Yet for much of human history, most people have coexisted with one or more potential man-eating species. Underlying that coexistence is the eternal possibility of being caught in the wrong place and time and becoming meat: a stark possibility that, David Quammen indicates, is only the beginning point in our relationship with the man-eaters.

The oldest direct evidence we have of how people feel about predators was discovered on the afternoon of 18 December 1994, when spelunkers stumbled across more than 400 paintings in a cave near Chauvet in south-eastern France. The art, which is extraordinarily realistic and dynamic, was made around 35,000 years ago and includes numerous depictions of the European lion. In the innermost grotto a pride of the great cats stare out intently from the wall, as if towards herds of bison, rhino, horse and mammoth depicted nearby. Elsewhere a pair of lions engages in sexual foreplay. These paintings, Quammen argues, are not inspired by blind terror or loathing, but rather by close observation and respect. But could people who share their environment with big predators ever feel that way about creatures that can turn them into supper? In order to answer that question in our greatly altered world, Quammen travels to remote regions where big predators and people still coexist.

It's to the last surviving lions outside Africa that Quammen turns first. Lions evolved in east Africa about 3.5 million years ago, but by around a million years ago they could be found across a great arc of the planet, from England to Siberia and on into North

America. Today they survive outside Africa in just one place—the Gir Forest on the Kathiawar Peninsula in far-western India. Their restriction is relatively recent, for as late as the nineteenth century lions still roamed across much of northern India, Iran and Iraq.

Today the Gir lions share their last home with a group of pastoralists known as Maldharis. These people follow their herds of cattle and water buffalo through lion territory armed with nothing more than a shepherd's wooden staff. The lions occasionally attack the livestock, and a Maldhari attendant will then drive off the lion with stones or his staff. Here, it seems, lions and people have devised a common understanding, allowing lions to survive and people—even young boys—to wander among the big cats, at ease and almost always unharmed.

Things are not always so rosy in the Gir forest, however, for on occasion both sides attempt to cheat on the pact. A pair of male lions (presumably brothers) has been known to attack two cows simultaneously, thereby leaving the Maldhari shepherd in a quandary. Errant lions are sometimes killed, too; yet the balance is somehow maintained. The real trouble comes when lions wander away from the forest and come into contact with people who do not know the rules. Then, people as well as livestock and dogs run an increased risk in being eaten.

The diversity of attitudes that the Maldharis hold in relation to lions is astonishing. Some individuals, even those who have been mauled by lions, bear no enmity towards them, while others would like to see them finished, and the sooner the better. This, it seems, reflects the individual's social status and economic security, as well as their generosity and self-confidence.

From India, Quammen takes us to northern Australia, where the saltwater crocodile (*Crocodylus porosus*) is the most dangerous big predator. At Crocodylus Park, a zoo and breeding facility near Darwin, he meets Dr Graham Webb, whose crooked-toothed grin bears more than a passing resemblance to that of his charges. Webb is a vocal advocate of the 'use it or lose it' school of wildlife management, arguing that people must extract some benefit from wildlife, especially creatures as unpleasant as crocodiles, or they will not tolerate them. He has devoted his career to the development of a sustainable trade in crocodile products—from crocodile-claw backscratchers to croc-burgers—and his philosophy works well in this region where Western-style enterprises have to coexist with dangerous wildlife. But when Quammen travels to Arnhem Land, the vast Aboriginal lands that cover most of the north-eastern corner of the Northern Territory, he discovers that there are other models of human–crocodile interaction.

At Maningrida, deep in Arnhem Land, he meets 'the professor', as the elfin Jackie Adjarral is known. A member of the Gurrgoni clan, Jackie reveals just a little of his culture's view of the great reptile he knows as Mururrba. Explaining that it's his clan's totem animal, he says that his deceased father's spirit might now dwell in a crocodile living nearby. 'He has never been attacked, never been bit by a crocodile,' Quammen writes. 'He won't be bit; he has protection, he says. Unless he makes "a mistake".' What sort of mistake that might be, Jackie won't say; an outsider might be tempted to interpret the 'mistake' as being in the wrong place at the wrong time. In Aboriginal eyes, however, there is only one reason why an ancestor would want to eat you: as punishment for transgressing the rules they gave you (such as having sex with a girl from the wrong moiety). In Gurrgoni experience, crocodiles only kill bad people.

To further regard the crocodile as good eating is not at all inconsistent with their beliefs, and the Gurrgoni happily hunt and kill the predators. The relationship is not one of avoidance. But neither is it the purely economic relationship advocated by Webb. Instead, it seems to be a deep-rooted symbiosis that has been forged over 47,000 years, in which the flesh and spiritual power of the crocodile sustain Aboriginal life and lore, while Aboriginal management of the land sustains the crocodile.

Before leaving Australia, Quammen meets with a fitter and turner turned taxidermist by the name of Andrew Cappo. Andrew is at the downstream end of the wildlife exploitation business, his workshop a bush compound near the forlorn outpost of Humpty Doo in Australia's Northern Territory. The lack of neighbours is probably an advantage for Andrew, as half-rotted crocodiles are likely to turn up on his doorstep any time of day or night. It takes months of hard work to turn them into the skulls, stuffed heads and full body mounts favoured by the Hells Angels who loom large among his customers. Stuffing crocodiles is a surprisingly dangerous occupation. Andrew once nicked his finger on the tooth of a dead croc and the resulting infection seemed unstoppable, turning into a creeping, pus-filled sore that engulfed the entire digit before it could be brought under control.

Quammen encounters a different aspect of Webb's 'use it or lose it' model of wildlife conservation when he visits Romania to learn about its abundant brown bear population. His entree is via the Muzeul Cinegetic al Carpatilor—the Carpathian Hunting Museum. Nicolae Ceausescu, it transpires, was an avid hunter, and the museum is filled with the remains of creatures he slaughtered. Despite the fact that he was known to shoot several dozen bears in a day, Ceausescu's passion for hunting was the salvation of the bear in Romania. In order to accommodate his hobby, a string of reserves was created with an entire bureaucratic infrastructure of

2226 game management units, whose duty it was to encourage the proliferation of bears. A regime of captive rearing of cubs and supplemental feeding of adults (under the shooting platforms used by Ceausescu) was instituted to ensure that the bears were large, abundant and available.

The Romanian brown bear was going the way of the rest of Europe's bears before the Communist Party climbed to power in 1948. Today, thanks to the bloodlust of a ruthless dictator, Romania has the healthiest brown bear population on the continent; though it's hard to avoid the fact that, as a result of their intensive management, Romania's bears are no longer entirely wild, free-living creatures. The business of bear shooting continued after Ceausescu himself was shot, for it brings greatly needed currency into the country and is one of the few sustainable enterprises for which the Romanian economy is equipped in the post-Communism era. Perhaps partly as a result, Romanians have an unusual interest in and tolerance of bears, to the point where urban-dwellers are pleased to have them forage in their rubbish skips.

Quammen's final foray takes him to the Russian far east, on the trail of the Siberian tiger. Here he uncovers yet more folk beliefs that speak of an uneasy truce between man and beast. 'If you take a tiger's prey, that tiger will surround you and will not give you any peace. A tiger will find its way to get revenge,' Su-San Tyfuivich, an elderly Udege hunter, tells us. 'Tiger is an enchanter. It will enchant you,' he adds. Perhaps because of such beliefs, Siberian tigers do not have a history of attacking people, though they often enter villages and carry off dogs. It's as if they know that if you kill a human, people 'will surround you and will not give you any peace'. Today, poachers kill twenty to thirty Siberian tigers out of a population of around 250 annually. And, after a long truce, tigers are once again killing and eating the odd human; the most recent incident occurred in 1997.

How do we summarise the relationship documented in *Monster of God*, the interaction between people and the last surviving big predators? The relationship, it seems to me, is not so different from the type we are used to in the world of politics and business. Where our competition knows us from long experience, and we know them, an easy, even fruitful relationship can develop. This is not to suggest any beneficence on the part of the players, for given the chance a political opponent or business competitor will ruthlessly pounce. It is just that such opportunities are presented rarely because we all know the game.

The problem arises when we lose contact with one another. The creaking industries of eastern Europe had been isolated for fifty years when, following *perestroika*, they abruptly came into competition with those from the West. The result was economic extinction for eastern enterprises. During a safari in Kenya, when I was permitted to walk briefly on the savannah, I got a sense of what the workers in those industries must have felt like. I stood there, a white rabbit on a plain that I knew was full of things that could kill me. Yet nearby, a Masai child armed with nothing but a flimsy stick stood serenely shepherding a herd of goats. The lions, I just knew, were looking at us differently, and all because that boy and his ancestors had never lost touch, never forgotten the rules of the game.

The shifting fortunes of big predators and their human prey over the past couple of centuries is the story of a steamrolling victory by the species carrying the gun. While Quammen does not mention Wallace's observations of Singapore, it's a prime example of the type of situation that informed imperial Western attitudes to big predators. These animals were seen as dangerous, almost satanic beings, whose presence allowed the big-game hunter to claim a kind of beneficence as he scoured the countryside in pursuit of 'man-eaters'. And yet, as we have seen, such a relationship is far from typical of the long history of coexistence between big predators and humans. The situation that existed in Singapore in the early 1860s marks the endgame in an interplay that had occurred for millennia. Human numbers were growing, and tiger prey was becoming increasingly hard to find. Reproduction for tigers was also increasingly difficult, for inexperienced youngsters would have almost no chance of surviving the numerous traps, baits and guns of humans. There was, however, a small population of adult tigers that had learned everything there was to know about humans, at least from a predator's perspective. And while they lived they supplemented their diet with forest workers, and doubtless their dogs. When they died of old age or were shot, the attacks stopped, and Singapore, the 'lion island', was left to its human multitudes. Flying into Changi Airport today it's difficult to believe that the place was, just 150 years ago, a fiercely contested battleground between people and nature.

Monster of God is an eclectic book that delves into literature and religion in its pursuit of the essence of our relationship with predators. Quammen contends that the epic poem *Beowulf* is based on a folk memory—almost a genetically based fear—of being eaten by a big carnivore. In this interpretation, Grendel (the monster whom Beowulf vanquishes) is that memory personified, much as in our own time it is embodied in the unnamed beast that starred in the film *Alien*. It's as if that primal fear remains with us long after the carnivores themselves have been banished, in a terror made worse by the lack of circumstance in which to measure it. Although written at a time when carnivores were more common, the Bible also includes similar manifestations. But here a more important point is made, for Leviathan is, to echo Quammen's title, truly a Monster of God, enforcing Divine will and reminding us of our place in the scheme of things.

In his final chapters, Quammen takes a look into the future. His view is 'a regretfully gloomy one', in which 'the last wild, viable, free-ranging populations of big flesh-eaters will disappear sometime around the middle of the next century'. It is a perspective largely informed by United Nations projections for world population published between 1998 and 2000, which indicate that the planet will have to support 9.3 billion people by 2050 (up from 6.3 billion today) and 10.8 billion by 2150. Quammen believes such a world will have little room for big, free-ranging predators.

Two important reports, however, support a less gloomy prognosis. One is the latest UN population projections, published in April 2003 (too late, presumably, for Quammen to use). They reveal a slow-down, with global figures predicted to reach 8.9 billion by 2050, a population decline due to initiatives increasing choices for women, and the ravages of AIDS. And the data provided by Quammen himself supports a less pessimistic outlook. All of the large carnivore populations he examines have fared relatively well over the past century, a period during which human population has doubled then doubled again. In 1913 no more than twenty lions survived in the Gir forest, while mid-century a similar number of Siberian tigers roamed the Soviet far east. Today, 350 lions inhabit the Gir and its surrounds, while the wild Siberian tiger population has risen to 250. Australia's saltwater crocodiles have staged an even more spectacular recovery, for after having been hunted to near extinction by the 1970s, they have now returned to near their pre-European abundance. But not all predators are thriving. The Amur leopard, for example, which shares its habitat with the Siberian tiger, is reduced to around thirty-three adults and is *still* being poached.

It is truly noteworthy, though, that so many large predators are doing well. After a long absence, jaguars are once again being seen in the US, while the wolf and bear populations of both Europe and North America are expanding after centuries of decline. It is true that most of these populations are managed and protected, but their recovery indicates that there is no direct correlation between total human numbers and the fate of the last remnant populations of large predators.

At one point, Quammen talks of the 'muskrat conundrum', by which he means the ethical dilemma we face in expecting Indian peasants to live with tigers and lions in a way that we ourselves would not tolerate. If some predator populations continue to recover, Westerners may once again find themselves facing the scintillating challenge of sharing our lives with things that eat us.

While reading *Monster of God*, I was struck by the pride and competence of those humans who do still live with the beasts. Perhaps, like a monopolistic corporation that has grown fat and lazy after triumphing over all competition, Western humanity has really lost something in our victory over the man-eaters.

Flaming Creatures

New York Review of Books, MARCH 2004

For Love of Insects, Thomas Eisner, Belknap Press, Cambridge, 2003.

One evening in 1966 near Lake Placid, Florida, one of North America's most beautiful moths flew into the web of a great orb-weaving spider. Trapped moths usually struggle to escape, but this magenta-hued beauty, its wings boldly spotted with black-in-white bullseyes, lay unperturbed as the spider crept ever nearer. When it reached the moth, instead of delivering a killing bite, the spider hesitated, and then gently cut by turn each of the silken threads holding the insect, until it fluttered free.

We might be tempted to read into this story a *Beauty and the Beast*-like allegory. And in a way it is, for the moth's beauty provides a very real deterrent to the many beasts that encounter it. Yet as Thomas Eisner, who witnessed this event, would discover, that beauty acts more by way of warning than heart-softening appeal, for it informs potential predators that beneath its skin-deep veneer flows poisonous blood.

Eisner is a professor of chemical entomology at Cornell University. One of the world's most eminent natural historians, he is an award-winning film-maker, author of numerous landmark scientific publications and a recipient of the US National Medal for Science. His latest book, *For Love of Insects*, tells the story of his research, along the way revealing how hard-won his acclaim is. His observation of the spider and the beautiful moth, for example, led to thirty years of painstaking research on the chemical defences of the ornate moth (*Utetheisa ornatrix*), revealing a life of extraordinary intricacy and complexity.

The moth's chemical protection is acquired from its sole source of food, the rattlepod bush (*Crotalaria* spp.). Plants of the rattlepod genus produce alkaloids to defend their leaves and seeds from herbivores. The toxin can kill most animals, but the larva of the ornate moth is immune—indeed it prefers to feed on the plant's most poisonous tissues, such as its seeds. The alkaloids thus acquired are stored in the insect's blood, and after the caterpillar has transformed into a glorious moth, the toxins are deployed in frothy blood that is extruded from near its wing-bases.

Understanding how the moth stores and uses its toxin for defence was only the beginning of Eisner's discoveries. Through a series of ingenious experiments that involved rearing some caterpillars on alkaloid-free food, he discovered that the toxin is essential to the moth's sex life. Males reared on a toxin-free diet seemed normal in every respect, yet they received a brusque brush-off from females whenever they attempted copulation. High-speed photography revealed that, when intent on copulation, male moths evert two large brush-like structures from their cloaca, which are used to stroke the female for a few milliseconds prior to copulation. High-resolution microscopy showed that the brushes consist of soft, hollow scales that are filled with a derivative of the alkaloid toxin. Only those males that tar their mates with a toxic brush, so to speak, get to have sex. This peculiar behaviour led Eisner and his colleagues into a detailed investigation of insect sex-life, the findings of which are, to the naive reader, often as startling and outlandish as anything invented in science fiction.

The ornate moth is, by Eisner's account, the sexual marathon champion of the insect world. Couples engage in the sexual act for up to nine hours at a time, which for a creature that survives in its adult form for only a few weeks is lengthy coitus indeed. Such extended couplings seem to be necessary so that the male can transfer his voluminous ejaculate to his mate. This comprises an astonishing 10 per cent of his total body weight. (Should humans be given to producing an equivalent volume, sex would be a messy business indeed, for around eight litres of fluid would be involved!) Sperm forms only a small fraction of this fluid, the greatest part by far consisting of the toxin that is so avidly consumed by the caterpillar. Within minutes of receiving the alkaloid contained in the seminal fluid, the females have transferred it into their blood, rendering themselves immune to most attacks. Then, when the time comes to lay eggs, the female withdraws some of the stored toxin and secretes it within the eggshells, thus defending her offspring from attack as well.

With sex offering such immense benefits, female ornate moths have healthy libidos. They will mate with as many chemically defended males as possible—twenty-three is the record so far. Yet no matter how many sexual partners she has, all of a female's eggs are fertilised by a single male. He is not the first one she mates with, nor the last, but the largest. Just how the female selects his sperm remains a mystery, but Eisner has demonstrated that the mechanism may be under conscious, probably muscular control. He discovered this by anaesthetising female moths after copulation, a procedure that rendered them unable to discriminate between the sperm of various males, and ensuring that their eggs had many fathers.

Insect lives are all about the basics—food, sex and death—yet the ways they have evolved to cope with life's challenges are often so ingenious and intricate that our own lives can look uncomplicated in comparison. Because chemistry plays such a large role in insects' existence, much of that complexity is invisible, and it only becomes evident to us through detailed and intricate experimentation.

Gifts of love such as the ornate moth's seminal toxin are not uncommon in the insect world. A more widespread and obvious strategy for acquiring toxins, however, involves predators that derive it from their prey, and that strategy sometimes entangles humans in the weird world of insect chemistry.

An astonishing case came to light in 1893, when a certain Dr Meynier, then attached to a French military force serving in northern Algeria, found his *chasseurs d'Afrique* suffering from an embarrassing complaint. The men were doubled up with stomach pains, thirst and painful urination, but their most surprising discomfort was '*érections douloureuses et prolongées*'. Given this last symptom the afflicted soldiers were perhaps somewhat impatient and perplexed when Dr Meynier asked them what they had been eating. Their answer, however, gave the doctor the clue he needed, for the men had been at the local river catching frogs to make that Gallic delight *cuisses de grenouille* [frogs' thighs]. Close examination of the frogs' stomachs revealed that they had been eating blister beetles (family Meloidae)—the source of the famed aphrodisiac Spanish fly. Rather disappointingly, and despite the *érections prolongées* suffered by the soldiers, Eisner informs us that the aphrodisiac qualities of cantharidin (the principal ingredient of Spanish fly) are, in the case of humans at least, greatly exaggerated.

There are, however, insects known as cantharidiphiles that, although they cannot synthesise cantharidin, find it to be a true aphrodisiac. These creatures are irresistibly attracted to the chemical, and will travel vast distances for a few grains. Some must kill to obtain it, while others lick the corpses of blister beetles (a source of the chemical) to satiate their craving. A few even sell their bodies on the insect sex market for it. One of the larger cantharidiphiles to be found in the US is a handsome red-and-black creature known as the fire-coloured beetle (*Neopyochroa flabellata*). Eisner characterises the species as 'utterly shameless and [they] usually "go at it" the moment a pair is introduced into a petri dish'. On closer scrutiny, however, he discovered that their mating is not quite so straightforward.

When male and female meet, the first thing the female does is to grasp her partner's head and insert her mandibles into a cleft which runs across his forehead. The cleft looks as if it might have been wrought by a blow from a miniature axe, and deep within it a glistening fluid can be seen. This substance contains cantharidin, and if the female is not satisfied after imbibing at the groove, mating will not take place. The amount of cantharidin she obtains this way is minute—just 1.5 per cent of the male's store, and Eisner's team was at first uncertain why a female would sell sex for such a paltry return. The cantharidin in the groove, they learned, was just a foretaste of what was to follow, for if there is cantharidin in his groove, a male will deliver a goodly dose in his ejaculate. In effect, the 'taste' of the aphrodisiac in the groove acts as the male's *bona fides*. Obtaining a store of cantharidin is crucial to the virgin female fire-coloured beetle, for she possesses none herself, yet she must have it to protect her eggs from predators.

Much of Eisner's field work has taken place at the 600-hectare Archbold Biological Station near Lake Placid, Florida. This wonderland of biodiversity is a gift to biologists from one of America's great explorers and philanthropists. Richard Archbold sponsored and participated in a series of expeditions to New Guinea during the 1930s, which were conducted under the auspices of the American Museum of Natural History. They include some of the most extended and significant biological expeditions of the twentieth century, and the results of the expedition continue to be published. Archbold acted as pilot, flying his frail aircraft into true *terra incognita*. In 1938 he took his twin-engined 'flying boat' *Guba* over the Baliem Valley in West New Guinea (now part of Indonesia). He later trekked into the region, becoming the first outsider to encounter the vibrant Dani people and their 'Shangri La' valley. Never again would such a large population be brought into contact with the outside world. So I was intrigued to read of the wonderful work Archbold supported at Lake Placid, and of his foresight in acquiring such a large swathe of a biologically valuable and threatened region.

Eisner's work has also taken him to the deserts of Arizona, to Australia, and to bogs and woodlands near his home in Ithaca, New York. Wherever he travels he seems to be on the lookout for a clue that will lead him to another chemical discovery. Complex investigations into the life histories of creatures which most of us would unthinkingly crush underfoot have been a lifelong obsession for this man.

Thomas Eisner was born into a German-Jewish family in 1929. His family was forced to flee Nazism, initially to other European destinations and then, as the threat grew, to Uruguay. *For Love of Insects* is partly autobiographical, offering intriguing insights into the kind of person who would devote his life to such work. In explaining his own enthusiasm for insects, Eisner reveals himself to be a devotee of colleague Edward O. Wilson's 'biophilia hypothesis', which is that humans are naturally drawn to living things and are born with an inherent love of them. What is needed to 'trigger' the biophilic response, Eisner speculates, is the opportunity to interact with nature during childhood. He suggests that this factor explains why there are relatively few Jewish biologists, for the ghettoes of Europe and great cities like New York offer little opportunity for children to explore natural ecosystems. In Eisner's case it was Uruguay, where he lived between the ages of eight and eighteen, that provided him with the chance to observe nature first-hand. Indeed it provided a sort of natural bonanza, for the country is exceptionally rich in biodiversity.

I am not entirely convinced by Eisner's reasoning in this regard, for even as a very young child he was clearly fascinated by wildlife. He vividly recalls seeing, at age seven, a butterfly collection kept by a Dutch uncle. Indeed so focused was he on insects that despite what was clearly a stressful early childhood, his account of his family's forced travels reads as little more than a series of opportunities to collect and observe invertebrates. This suggests that Eisner's interest in insects was largely inherent, and thankfully complemented by a highly original and ingenious mind in which deductive reasoning, patience, and a love of gadgetry have combined to allow him to undertake complex investigations. He also has a remarkable sensory capacity: he has been, as he puts it, 'nasal' from the start:

My parents recalled that when I was little I could tell from the scent that lingered in the coat closet in the morning that my grandmother had visited the night before. But now, as a teenager, I was coming to realize that I could really learn things from my nose. I learned to sniff insects carefully.

Thomas Eisner's father Hans also enjoyed exquisitely sensitive nostrils, which he employed in his leisure moments by creating perfumes, skin lotions and colognes for family and friends. In 1958 Hans retired to Ithaca where he joined his son's lab and employed his chemical talents on insect experimentation. In fact, the wide variety of Thomas Eisner's collaborators—from photographers to biochemists and family—is truly astonishing.

Eisner's first experiments in chemical entomology were undertaken at a very tender age in Uruguay. They concerned the *bicho peludo*, or hairy beast, a caterpillar that is covered in hairy spines that can inflict instantaneous pain and severe systemic reactions. Eisner recalls:

I used to raise *bicho peludos* and noticed that they lacked spines on the belly surface, so I concluded that I risked nothing if I could somehow get them to crawl onto my hand without touching the spines. I mastered the technique and would often induce panic among my buddies by approaching them menacingly with arms raised and a *bicho peludo* on each hand. I managed to scare even the neighborhood bully in this fashion. Evidently, if I made myself obnoxious enough, I too could emit warnings that were heeded by others. I remember experimenting with the spines. I cut them with scissors and noted that they were hollow and filled with fluid. I placed droplets of the liquid on my skin and quite foolishly also on my tongue, only to find to my surprise that this caused no pain. Needless to say, I conducted these experiments in utter secrecy.

After being rejected from a series of colleges (including his own Cornell—he keeps the rejection slip proudly framed on his office wall) Eisner entered Harvard University. There, he met Edward O. Wilson in 1951, whose 'ascendancy into the ranks of the truly great in science was then already forseeable'. In 1952 the pair drove 12,000 miles across the US in a 'geriatric Chevrolet', studying insects and cementing a relationship that has endured to this day. In a handsome foreword to the book Wilson hails his colleague as 'the modern Fabre', after France's pioneer observer of insect life, which is high praise indeed in entomological circles.

Despite its enjoyable reminiscences, *For Love of Insects* is first and foremost a scientific work. It is filled with schematic illustrations of chemical compounds and technical drawings that act as vital visual aids in understanding the phenomena under discussion. But it also includes glorious close-up photographs of insects. It is also packed with strange-but-true facts, some of which are perhaps too indelicate for conversation while dining. Readers may be both surprised and discomfited to learn that ant-lions (which build their pit-traps under eaves and in other dry places) have no anus and so cannot defecate until they transform into beautiful lacewings. And who would have guessed that the bombardier beetle expels its chemical defences while boiling hot, in pulsed spurts at the rate of 500 to 1000 per second? The caterpillar of the spicebush swallowtail butterfly provides further cause for astonishment. It possesses the most life-like false 'eyes' on its neck, which seem to follow the observer wherever they go. The teardrop-shaped 'pupils' of the false eyes achieve this effect, a discovery that, as René Auberjonois's *The Italian Lady* illustrates, was made by artists long before scientists understood the ruse.

Eisner's book will not appeal to everyone, for it assumes considerable knowledge of chemistry, entomology and biology. Anyone seeking common names among the thickets of Latin binomens will search in vain, as will those in pursuit of elegant, sustained storytelling. Instead, the reader will encounter a catalogue of scientific investigations, leavened here and there with insightful autobiography. The work's chief value lies in its documentation of a pioneering science, for Eisner's team has fundamentally reshaped the field of chemical entomology; it is in many ways a beginning rather than an end—Wilson himself calls it 'an account of a nascent field of biology'.

For Love of Insects is brimful with unsolved mysteries and clues for the young researcher, with leads discovered but not followed up for sheer lack of time. Even basic matters remain unknown. Are blister beetles, for example, the sole source of cantharidin? Many insect species depend upon it—too many perhaps for blister beetles alone to supply—yet thus far no other sources have been identified. Future discoveries promise to be both prolific and spectacular, and judging from the recent growth of investment in biotechnology, they will be of ever-greater importance to the world.

The Heart of the Country

New York Review of Books, JUNE 2004

Under a Wild Sky: John James Audubon and the Making of The Birds of America, William Souder, North Point Press, New York, 2004.

Audubon's Elephant: America's Greatest Naturalist and the Making of The Birds of America, Duff Hart-Davis, Henry Holt, New York, 2004.

Concern filled the air whenever John James Audubon's birds were hidden from view. Colleagues, publishers and potential customers alike would mutter warnings that *The Birds of America* could never succeed, for the proposed book was utterly impractical. But when Audubon opened his great portfolio of drawings, a silence would descend on the room. 'The effect was like magic,' said John Wilson, as the images conveyed their viewers to the distant and mysterious land of America. As author Hart-Davis rhapsodises: 'The spectator imagined himself in the forest…birds in motion or at rest, in their glee and their gambols, their loves and their wars, singing or caressing or brooding or preying or tearing one another into pieces.'

The Audubon birds seduced even the commercially astute. When the eyes of the experienced Edinburgh print-maker William Lizars fell upon the peregrine falcon he stood speechless, his arms hanging limply at his sides, before he gathered his wits and exclaimed, 'I will engrave and publish this.' As with many a declaration made in the heat of passion, Lizars was unable to deliver on his promise, for he lacked the resources to maintain the flow of prints that the project demanded.

Duff Hart-Davis, Audubon's most recent biographer, informs us that at a metre tall and over ninety kilograms in weight *The Birds of America* is large enough to crush a coffee table. Such a book is in effect unusable, and in the cold light of morning William Lizars must surely have asked himself who would pay the modern equivalent of $40,000 for such a book, and patiently wait the twelve years it would take to complete? Yet in the end it was Audubon who got his way, for so in love was he with his birds that he had to depict them life-sized or not at all; and so to portray a trumpeter swan or a wild turkey, only 'double elephant'—the largest-sized paper available in the nineteenth century—would do, even if occasionally it was necessary to bend the larger birds into awkward poses.

Over the years it's been the very outlandishness of *The Birds of America* that has proved to be its greatest asset, for so few people could afford the work that only around 170 sets were ever made. One hundred and nineteen remain in existence, and so coveted are they that it's usual for decades to pass before a set is offered for sale. The last copy auctioned—in March 2000—sold to Sheik Hamad Ben-Al Thani of Qatar for more than US$8.8 million. Such is the quality of the work that as its new owner turns the thick, textured linen-stock pages admiring the 435 plates, he will find them as vibrant and sturdy as they were at the time of printing more than 150 years earlier. And the birds. It's their eyes that arrest the viewer, for they look out at you with such knowingness and emotion that it takes your breath away.

PLATE XXI

Audubon's stirring evocation of the dangers of life on the frontier.

Perhaps the most famous of Audubon's images depicts a family of mockingbirds harassing a rattlesnake that is attacking them at their nest. The reptile is open-mouthed as it lunges at a terrified victim, while a second member of the beleaguered family, desperate perhaps to rescue its fellow, pecks at the snake's eye from behind. For all its apparent authenticity this illustration is an invention, for it was widely known even in Audubon's time that rattlesnakes do not habitually climb trees, nor do they often eat mockingbirds. Yet so powerful is this frontier allegory that it begs the viewer to suspend their disbelief. And herein lies the wonder of *The Birds of America*, a work filled with images of nature so intimately observed that they continue to astonish, yet so rendered as to be considered by the literal-minded as palpable fiction.

Audubon's biographers are legion and two new ones join the flock this year. American William Souder's byline informs us that he is an 'avid outdoorsman' and contributor to the *Washington Post*, while the Englishman Duff Hart-Davis is a retired assistant editor of London's *Daily Telegraph* and a commentator on English country life. Hart-Davis's hardcover volume is an illustrated account of Audubon's sojourn in Britain, while Souder's unillustrated paperback is a combined biography of Audubon and his rival Alexander Wilson. Intriguingly, while both agree on the essential facts, each evokes a very different portrait of America's most famous naturalist.

Audubon was born Jean Rabin, the illegitimate son of a French sea captain and a chambermaid in what is today Haiti, and according to Souder he 'showed a curiosity about nature as soon as he could walk'. When he was six his father took him to France where he was accepted into the legitimate family, taking the name Audubon and later the Christian name John. An unremarkable pupil who cared for little except drawing birds, nonetheless at age eleven he was accepted into the naval academy in Rochefort. There the young Audubon became an accomplished musician, dancer and fencer, but he did so poorly at his studies that he was dismissed after three years.

Revolutionary France was a dangerous place for an able young man, and John's father, fearing that he would be pressed into military service, sent his son to America to superintend a farm near Mill Grove, Pennsylvania, which he had purchased before leaving the Caribbean. By the time John junior departed, his only accomplishment was 200 studies of European birds, completed when he should have been studying.

Perhaps fathers have always felt they know what's best for their sons, yet it strikes me as strange that Audubon senior did not regard those 200 drawings as an indication of his son's true vocation. Instead he packed him off to a career in farm management, and the result was predictable. Mill Farm languished, and if you wanted to meet John Audubon you were advised to head into the woods where he spent most of his waking hours in hunting and drawing. Some of his happiest days, he later said, were spent in the company of a pair of wood peewees that nested in a grotto above Perikomen Creek, and which eventually became so trusting that he could hold the dear creatures in his cupped hands.

At five feet eight inches tall (1.7 metres)—he frequently promoted his height by several inches—with long dark hair, bright hazel eyes and an aristocratic face, the young John Audubon was strikingly handsome. This combined with his strong French accent and boyish vitality made him irresistibly likeable. At least young Lucy Bakewell thought so. Her family had migrated from England to an adjacent farm known as Fatland Ford, and she seems to have fallen so deeply in love with her Frenchman that she did not demur when, three days after their marriage on 5 April 1808, John took her from the relative sophistication and security of her life in Pennsylvania to the frontier town of Louisville, Kentucky. There they resided for two years in the Indian Queen Hotel amid enough lack of privacy, squalor and frontier roughness to test the truest of hearts. Worst of all, perhaps, Lucy had nothing to do; but even so, when writing to a cousin in England she spoke only of 'the excellent disposition' of her new husband, and of a mysterious, powerful attraction that 'adds very much to the happiness of married life'.

With an entire continent of birds to explore, business seemed dull stuff to John Audubon, who soon moved his growing family a further 300 kilometres down the Ohio to the tiny settlement of Henderson, and thence on to Louisiana. As one business venture after another failed and Audubon became mired ever deeper in debt, he took to deserting Lucy and his two young sons for long periods, during which he travelled in search of birds. It was only when Lucy came to the disappointing realisation that it was she who must financially support the family that her love began to fade—yet she never let on to an outsider that her husband was anything but a paragon of virtue.

Souder finds it curious that in letters Audubon addressed Lucy as 'my friend', and sees his use of 'thee' and 'thou' as merely quaint. Hart-Davis clears away the mystery by pointing out that Audubon learned his English among Pennsylvanian Quakers. Despite this lapse, Souder's account of Audubon's marriage is by far the superior of the two, providing a tender and insightful record of their love in all its vicissitudes. While they were together John Audubon's failure as a provider hardly seems to have mattered, for even after he had been gone for years at a stretch, jailed for debt, and living off his wife's income, the couple could still be blissfully happy in each other's company. Souder tells how, when they settled at Beech Woods, Louisiana, following many privations, 'the Audubons would ride together to a small lake where, while Lucy swam naked, Audubon lolled on the beach admiring her'. When they were separated, however, a great fear and doubting caught at John Audubon's heart, a condition that reached its climax while he was in England trying to get *The Birds of America* published and fully subscribed. With his fortunes changing by the day, there were times when Audubon seemed to be on the brink of madness. He agonised about asking Lucy to join him, but he never confessed to how lost he was without her, nor could he bring himself to command her to leave her employment as a schoolteacher. Tragically, she seems to have read his diffidence as indifference and, with letters taking months to get from hand to hand, a gulf opened between the pair that was seemingly as wide and salt-filled as the Atlantic Ocean. But when, after an absence of three years, Audubon arrived with the dawn at Lucy's house in Louisiana, unannounced and with tears streaming down his cheeks, the gulf closed in an instant.

Audubon's character has proved an endless source of fascination, for he lived by a morality all his own. He was, to begin with, an outrageous liar, and Souder catches him out with some whoppers such as that his father was an admiral, that he studied under the great French artist David, and that he had hunted with Daniel Boone. Indeed, Audubon was characterised by a contemporary as rivalling Baron Munchausen in the lying stakes, and his writings lambasted as 'a tissue of the grossest falsehoods ever attempted to be palmed upon the credulity of mankind'. In fact Audubon seems to have lied freely about everything except his birds and his beloved Lucy; it is as if they were the only real things in the world to him. And his enemies hated him for it.

The English naturalist Charles Waterton, incensed at some of Audubon's misrepresentations, went as far as to write to his enemy George Ord in an attempt to dig up muck on Audubon's personal life. To his credit Ord wrote back, 'He is a well-meaning sort of man, though a great liar.'

Hart-Davis finds less mendacity in Audubon's character, perhaps because he researched matters less thoroughly. Both biographers agree, however, that there was not a streak of meanness or vindictiveness in the man, and that he preferred to ignore his detractors rather than enter into public slanging matches with them. His guiding principle in such circumstances seems to have been derived from his Quaker friends. 'To have enemies is no uncommon thing nowadays,' he was wont to say, but 'To deserve them we must ever and anon guard against ourselves'.

The young Audubon is attractive and innovative—a highly accomplished frontiersman whose unsophisticated world view was shaped largely by the wild woods of the New World. His was a life of direct experience, where rattlesnakes were a terrible threat to animal and human families alike; and so they should be depicted, even if in doing so he was unfaithful to the habits of serpents.

The world that shaped the young Audubon just 200 years ago is, from a contemporary perspective, difficult to conceive of, for wild woods are gone forever. Then, bear, elk and cougars abounded, and even wolf and bison could still be found in Kentucky. It was a land blanketed by thick forests of oak, walnut, hickory, chestnut and ash, where tremendous stands of cedar and cypress grew in the swamps. All vegetable life, however, was dwarfed by the mighty sycamores, the kings of the eastern forest, whose smooth, pale bark-covered trunks could reach six metres in diameter and whose canopies, bedecked with wild vines, reduced the blaze of day to a twilight gloom. And those groves were all alive with birds—including some extraordinary creatures that the world will never see again.

Two species in particular seem characteristic of that vibrant young America—the Carolina parakeet and the passenger pigeon. They were the most abundant birds of Audubon's time, yet not a single one of either species survives today. If you want to imagine the Carolina parakeets, says Souder, 'think of a roiling, deep green ocean falling out of the sky'. All too often that ocean would descend upon crops, and Audubon tells us what would happen then:

> The gun is kept at work; eight or ten, or even twenty, are killed at every discharge. The living birds, as if conscious of the death of their companions, sweep over their bodies, screaming as loud as ever, but still return to the stack to be shot at, until so few remain alive, that the farmer does not consider it worth his while to spend more of his ammunition.

Such scenes had, by 1914, utterly destroyed North America's only native parrot. There was one bird that surpassed the parakeet in abundance. Souder writes:

> In the fall of 1813, while on his way back from Henderson to Louisville, Audubon saw a low smudge in the sky, at first like a dark cloud, pulsing and growing larger. Presently he heard a rumble, and in the same moment the smudge became a surging mass of dark points in the sky. It was a flock of passenger pigeons, flying directly at him.

Although it was midday, the sky darkened as in an eclipse, and as the column of birds thickened, their droppings fell like snow. For three days and nights the vast flock passed overhead, at a steady speed of 95 kilometres per hour (60 mph), undiminished and with no pause. At the last the very air smelled of pigeons, and their droppings had whitened the earth. How many birds were there in that vast flock? Audubon mused:

> Imagine a column of passenger pigeons one mile wide, and assume that this mile-wide flock passes overhead in three hours. If the birds are flying at 60 miles per hour, the whole flock could be visualised as occupying a rectangular area one mile wide and 180 miles long—180 square miles. Now assume a density of 2 birds per square yard…and you can figure the total number of birds at 1.1 billion.

At Audubon's reckoning, the flock that he experienced in the fall of 1813 consisted of an unimaginable 25 billion birds.

When such a flock nested, as extraordinary a scene as was ever found in nature unfolded. 'Here they come', cried the waiting hunters at the sound of the arriving multitudes at one nesting site. The sound of the returning billions reminded Audubon of 'a hard gale at sea', and in the darkness he felt a 'current of air that surprised me':

> Perches gave way under the weight with a crash, and, falling to the ground, destroyed thousands of birds beneath…It was a scene of uproar and confusion. I found it quite useless to speak, or even to shout, to those persons who were nearest me. The reports, even, of the nearest guns, were seldom heard; and I knew of the firing only by seeing the shooters re-loading…The pigeons were picked up and piled in heaps, until each has as many as he could possibly dispose of, when the hogs were let loose to feed on the remainder.

While Audubon mourned the destruction of wild America, it seems that he also contributed considerably to it. Souder tells us that 'a day in which he killed fewer than a hundred birds was a day wasted'. Audubon's love of stalking and shooting is evident in his own writings, a love that Souder evokes in wonderful fashion. 'He remembered what it was like when the stillness of a pallid dawn was split by the whistle of wings cutting through the air, sometimes like a gentle breeze and other times in a prolonged *aaahhhh*, like the sound of tearing silk.' Audubon was an integral part of this world. Most mornings found him in the forest before dawn, stalking, observing and in a naive sort of way, experimenting with his birds.

And it was, perhaps, a kind of frontier literalism that saw Audubon cleave so resolutely to representing all of his birds at life size. Certainly he was neither businessman nor scientist, and his genius lay not in creating scientific illustrations of birds, but in depicting vibrant, living evocations of life on the American frontier. This is not to say that his illustrations are anatomically inaccurate, simply that they are largely experiential, phenomenological, and anthropomorphic; for at times he depicts his subjects as if they had human feelings and motives—and that, of course, is why they continue to enchant us.

Of all creatures, Audubon knew the wild turkey best, and occasionally he felt that he could read the bird's intentions. Souder writes:

> If, for example, he walked briskly through the forest, whistling to himself, he could pass within a few feet of a hen on her nest without making the bird move. But if he attempted to sneak up on a nest, his stealth seemed to alarm the hen.

Anyone familiar with most wild birds will recognise this behaviour, and clearly Audubon is correct: birds, like us, are social animals and they can read our intentions. This is not, however, how professional scientists described bird behaviour in that great systematising age that was the nineteenth century, and it was a clash of cultures—between frontier naturalist and European savant—that would cause him great grief.

Audubon underwent a metamorphosis on crossing the Atlantic to find a means of publishing *The Birds of America*. The city of London, he wrote, was 'like the mouth of an immense monster, guarded by millions of sharp-edged teeth, from which if I escape unhurt it must be called a miracle'. At the centre of this forbidding world sat King George IV. Audubon knew that a royal audience would be highly beneficial, yet he dreaded the meeting, having been told that the king 'has the gout, is peevish, and spends his time playing whist at a shilling a rubber'. But when he did obtain an audience, all went well. 'The King!! My dear book!' Audubon wrote in his diary. 'His Majesty was pleased to call it fine…and my friends all spoke as if a mountain of sovereigns had drummed in an ample purse at once, and for me.'

Audubon did escape from the 'immense monster', though the experience of living in London made him into another man, for the publishing of *The Birds of America* saw Audubon banished for nigh on a decade from his beloved American woods, during which time he was forced to learn a new set of skills.

Subscribers complained of poor quality colouring and issues had to be replaced frequently. The Earl of Kinnoul was a particularly crotchety customer. Upon subscribing, he told Audubon to his face that he thought his work a swindle, and as the project neared completion, he cancelled his subscription after finding pieces of beef (the remains of a worker's lunch) wedged between the plates. And then there were the skinflints like the first Baron Rothschild, who declined to subscribe yet instructed Audubon to send him the book anyway. After having enjoyed the pictures for a year he was sent a bill for £100, at which allegedly he cried, 'What! A hundred pounds for birds. Why, Sir, I will give you five pounds, and not a farthing more!'

As Audubon spent more time in London supervising production, he was forced to rely ever more heavily on the field work of others to procure specimens and observations of species not yet depicted. Divorced from the possibility of seeing his subjects in the flesh, his drawings, which had earlier conveyed such life and emotion, took on something of the stilted look so common in scientific illustrations of the age. It was as if, along with shedding his long hair and frontier clothes, Audubon had shed his native genius and his woodsman's innocence as well. This change is also apparent in his written text: the earlier volumes brim with hair-raising stories of life on the American frontier (including an account of a rattlesnake that kills three members of one family), while the last is burdened with dry discussions of avian anatomy. In the end Audubon even went ahead with a cut-down (octavo-sized) edition of his book.

The Birds of America brought Audubon modest financial success, sufficient for him to purchase a sixteen-hectare property at what is now Washington Heights in Upper Manhattan. With a delightful river frontage, the Audubons built a big, square double-storey house with ample porches front and back that commanded magnificent views of the Hudson River. Audubon did not long enjoy the tranquillity of retirement, however, for once his book was completed he seemed to age quickly. Perhaps the arsenic he used to preserve bird skins had affected him, or perhaps it was the toxins in his paints; whatever the cause, Audubon soon began to lose himself. Two years before his death Lucy wrote to a friend, 'Alas, I have only the material part of my old friend, all mind being gone.' And on 27 January 1851, the prematurely aged sixty-five-year-old slipped quietly from the world.

One of Audubon's greatest friends in Britain was the elderly Northumbrian naturalist Thomas Bewick. As the pair sat drinking hot brandy toddies, Audubon would tell tales of his America and every now and again Bewick would start and say, 'Oh that I were young again! I would go to America too. Hey! What a country it will be!' At which Audubon gently corrected him—and perhaps many a modern reader might too—with 'Hey! What a country it already is, Mr Bewick!'

The Priest and the Hobbit

The Times Literary Supplement, NOVEMBER 2004

Not so very long ago, in a faraway corner of the western Pacific Ocean, there was an enchanted isle, and it was a home to hobbits. Its hills and caves were the haunts of ferocious dragons and enormous rats, and through its forests roamed elephants no larger than ponies. This magical place did not know man, for no human had ever trod its hills. Instead it was a realm of diminutive, almost-human beings whose heads would not have reached your waists. They may have been small, but they were very brave, for they fought the dragons and drove the giant rats from their lairs.

You could be forgiven for thinking that this all sounds like a fantasy, and until a spectacular discovery in 2004 it was. The mystical-sounding place is the island of Flores in eastern Indonesia, and the hobbit is now officially known as *Homo floresiensis*. Her existence was announced to the world in October in the prestigious science journal *Nature*, and the discovery of her skeleton is a finding without parallel, in fact it is so astonishing as to stretch credulity.

The island of Flores lies east of Java and Bali, in the middle of a long chain of islands known as Nusa Tenggara that stretches, with only short gaps, from Java almost all the way to New Guinea. At the western end of the archipelago, between Bali and Lombok, runs Wallace's line, a hypothetical boundary first recognised by the nineteenth-century zoologist Alfred Russel Wallace as the place where the faunas of Asia and Australia abut. Bali supports (or at least once did), a rich Asian fauna of monkeys, wild cattle, deer, elephants and tigers. Lombok, however, has a very different and much poorer fauna, including peculiarly Australian species such as honeyeaters and cockatoos.

Today the only native mammals on Flores are rats. Their ancestors must have reached the island long ago, perhaps on rafts of vegetation washed out to sea during floods. In the absence of competitors the rats have made Flores their own, diversifying spectacularly. One of the most imposing is *Pappagomys amandavillei*. The best part of a metre long, it is a monstrous relative of the house rat, and it even smells like one. Fossils attest to the fact that many of the islands of Nusa Tenggara once swarmed with similar, giant rats, but today *Pappagomys* is the only survivor, the other islands having lost their giant rats thousands of years ago.

Another remarkable Floresian survivor is the Komodo dragon. This giant monitor lizard—almost three metres long and over 100 kilograms in weight—is the world's largest. Once it was also found throughout Nusa Tenggara, but today it survives only in eastern Flores and on nearby Komodo Island, east of Flores.

Until Dutch archaeologist Father Theodore Verhoeven began to investigate Flores' past, rats and dragons were thought to be the only large land animals ever to have inhabited the island. Then, in 1965, Verhoeven excavated a large pit in a cave known as Liang Bua, which is located in a mountain area of eastern Flores. He was intrigued to discover the remains of a kind of elephant known as a *Stegodon*. Although *Stegodons* are entirely extinct today, they were once common throughout south-east Asia, and the Floresian one was rather special, for it was an island dwarf, a descendant of normal-sized elephants that had drifted to the island and which, in adapting to the limited resources available there, had shrunk to the size of ponies.

Father Verhoeven's pioneering investigations indicated that, of the great diversity of species inhabiting south-east Asia, just two types of land mammals—rats and elephants—had made the sea-crossings required to reach Flores. It may seem odd that only the largest and smallest of Asia's mammals were successful, but this pattern is common in the world's islands, many of which once supported rats and elephants that had reached them from adjacent mainlands. It may also seem odd that, having arrived, these very large and very small creatures began to converge in size—the rats growing larger and the elephants shrinking. But again this pattern is widespread and is due to selection for the appropriate body size to exploit an island's limited resources. On Flores the process was so advanced that we can guess that it had been in progress for a million years or more.

Both the elephants and rats presumably fell prey to the island's Komodo dragons. The ancestral homeland of the Komodos is Australia, and until 50,000 years ago an enormous Komodo relative that may have reached five metres in length lived there. In the absence of predators such as tigers, dwarfed descendants of this monster spread throughout most of Nusa Tenggara, becoming established on myriad islands from Australia to its eastern limit of Komodo Island.

Father Verhoeven made one further discovery in Liang Bua that saw archaeologists return to the cave again and again. Along with the elephant teeth, he unearthed an assortment of stone tools, indicating that toolmakers must have reached the island. But who were they?

Between 1978 and 1989 R.P. Soejono, an Indonesian archaeologist, excavated ten more pits at Liang Bua but discovered nothing substantial to identify the toolmaker. Then, in 2001 a team of Australians led by Dr Mike Morwood joined Soejono. They expanded four of his excavations, including the only one lying adjacent to the eastern wall of the cave. It was here, in early 2004, at a depth of nearly six metres, that the toolmaker herself was finally found.

She was unearthed in the final fortnight of the dig. The Australians had already left and the Indonesians were working alone. When they found the skeleton it was as soft as tissue paper, and the delicate work of uncovering, drying and hardening it was painstaking. When she was finally clear of the earth, however, it was evident that the skeleton was female and surprisingly complete—lacking only the arms—providing ample proof of the appearance of its owner.

In life she would have weighed around sixteen kilograms and stood just ninety-five centimetres tall. She was entirely upright in her stance, but her forehead was low and the brain below was no larger than that of a chimp, which is not entirely a fair comparison as her body is so tiny compared with that of chimps. A thick ridge of bone protected her eyes, and she had no chin, all of which made it abundantly clear that she was not human.

Indeed, her skeleton bore unmistakable similarities to that of *Homo ergaster*, an ancient ancestor of ours that flourished in Africa around 1.8 million years ago. Ergaster was the first hominid to leave Africa, and as evidenced by the famous Java Man fossils, had reached south-east Asia at least a million years ago. What we did not know before the finds at Liang Bua was that ergaster had joined those elite migrators the elephants and rats, and had reached Flores.

Sufficient finds have been made at Liang Bua to allow for the reconstruction of parts of the hobbits' lifestyle. They made a number of stone tools, among them wicked-looking stone points that may have been hafted on a stick. An abundance of newborn pygmy stegodon teeth in the cave suggests that the hobbits hunted newborn elephants, perhaps using spears. Abundant bones also indicate that they hunted the giant rats, which from nose to tail tip were almost as long as the hobbits were tall. Whatever else their use, I'm sure that the hobbits' spears were employed to keep Komodo dragons at bay, for these fearsome ambush predators weighed ten times as much as the hobbits, and surely would have eaten them whenever they could.

There is no evidence that our lady hobbit was laid to rest with any ceremony. Instead her body appears to have been abandoned on the cave floor, perhaps in a pool. Although there is charcoal in the cave sediments, there is no evidence of the systematic use of fire, so perhaps the hobbits enjoyed their baby elephant steaks raw. And the hobbits are such distant relatives of ours that it would be surprising if they talked, though surely they had some efficient means of communication.

So how did the hobbits meet their end? Perhaps the most astonishing thing about the discovery is how recently the hobbits lived. Until at least 18,000 years ago Flores was well populated with hobbits, and they may have persisted until even more recently. Modern humans began to spread through Nusa Tenggara around 50,000 years ago and, as they moved from Java towards Australia, Flores lay right in their path. The ancestors of Australia's Aborigines must have met hobbits. They may have overlapped, at least regionally, for 30,000 years; yet there is no evidence of modern humans at Liang Bua. Perhaps people found the mountains of Flores, with their tiny hominids and Komodo dragons, just too spooky and moved on. Whatever the case, a profound mystery exists here, for if modern humans did not kill off the hobbits, then what did?

The discovery of the Floresian hobbit suddenly clarifies a great deal in biology that was, up until now, mysterious. Genetic studies of head lice, for example, indicate that humans host two species that split more than a million years ago. One of the species evolved on our ancestors, while the other, which is found only in the Americas, must have evolved on a *Homo ergaster* or *Homo erectus*-like creature. The astonishing thing is that this louse species appears to have jumped onto human heads around 30,000 years ago. With the exception of the hobbit, *Homo ergaster* was by then long gone, so perhaps the lice date the time of first contact between us and the hobbit.

The hobbit helps explain why Flores alone in the great constellation of islands of Nusa Tenggara kept its giant rats and Komodo dragon. On Flores, and Flores only, the rats and dragons had a million years to adapt to the presence of a human-like predator. Presumably, unlike their more naive relatives on other islands, they learned just enough from the experience to avoid extinction when fully modern humans arrived.

The hobbit also teaches us about ourselves. On reflection, the fact that over a million years ago *Homo ergaster* joined those few elite mammals that could cross water makes humanity's spread around the globe during the past 50,000 years somehow less surprising. And the hobbit reminds us that we are like any other species in that, when isolated on islands, evolution will fit our bodies to the opportunities the size of our 'world' offers. Thus the hobbit tells us that we are not unique; nor were we, until 18,000 years ago, alone.

When a Scorpion Meets a Scorpion

New York Review of Books, MARCH 2006

Life in the Undergrowth, David Attenborough, Princeton University Press, Princeton, 2006.

The Smaller Majority: The Hidden World of the Animals That Dominate the Tropics, Piotr Naskrecki, Belknap Press, Cambridge, 2005.

Locust: The Devastating Rise and Mysterious Disappearance of the Insect That Shaped the American Frontier, Jeffrey A. Lockwood, Basic Books, New York, 2005.

The invention of the microscope revealed wonders to the world, and permitted Jonathan Swift to quip:

> So, naturalists observe, a flea
> Hath smaller fleas that on him prey
> And these have smaller still to bite 'em
> And so proceed ad infinitum.

By the late twentieth century, fascination with the minuscule had begun to pall, and now it takes an exceptional book to reawaken our interest. Thankfully, in David Attenborough's *Life in the Undergrowth*, Piotr Naskrecki's *The Smaller Majority*, and Jeffrey Lockwood's *Locust* we find three exceptional works that do just that.

Life in the Undergrowth is Attenborough's tribute to the terrestrial invertebrates. They are, he says, a group of creatures that make life possible for us—whether as scavengers, aerators of soil, or agents of pollination, to name only three of their functions—but because they are small we largely ignore them. As he succinctly puts it, 'We are greatly prejudiced by our size.'

This is the latest in a series of projects combining television and print in a unique manner that has become Sir David's métier. His investigations encompass disciplines as diverse as palaeontology, botany, zoology and ethnography; and each is similar in scope to a doctoral dissertation. While most of us consider Attenborough principally as a television presenter, he is also one of the greatest ecologists, synthesisers of evolutionary science, and teachers of our age.

In each of his projects Attenborough adopts multiple roles including instigator, researcher, scriptwriter, presenter, and finally author of a book that knits everything together. Because of the highly sophisticated recording equipment and laboratories at his disposal, and because he and his team spend long months in the field, fundamental discoveries have been made during the course of this work. *Life in the Undergrowth* is no exception, with Attenborough's sound recordist discovering that certain caterpillars create sounds that charm ants into caring for them.

The land-dwelling invertebrates are so diverse that they make up most of the species on earth. This makes producing an overview of them particularly challenging. Attenborough adopts an evolutionary approach, and as he tells his tale he picks out species that take a particular adaptation or behaviour to an extreme. In doing this he captures the general direction of the group's evolution, as well as its breadth of diversity, without drowning us in detail.

Life in the Undergrowth commences with the descendants of the first creatures to clamber out of the water and onto land—the scorpions and their relatives. They made the transition some 400 million years ago, long before plants or our ancestors left the oceans. If you have never thought of scorpions as remarkable, Attenborough advises that you try to pick one up, perhaps with a pair of very long forceps. Whichever method you use it will not be easy, for scorpions possess advance warning systems that sense where you are and what you are doing. Their six pairs of eyes are strategically positioned so as to leave no blind spot, and although lacking sharp focus they are capable of detecting the tiniest variations in brightness—and thus movement. Yet they cannot be dazzled because each one has its own built-in 'sunglasses', composed of pigment granules that cover the lens as light increases.

Before it sees you a scorpion will either have 'heard' you through the minute hairs on its claws, or through a slit-shaped organ on the upper part of each leg—so sensitive is this to vibration that it can pinpoint the footfall of a beetle a metre away. Or perhaps it will have detected you with its pectines. These unique, comb-like organs on its belly are packed with nerve endings and are probably capable of smelling or tasting minute traces of chemical compounds in the ground over which the scorpion passes.

When a male scorpion meets a female scorpion, his mind is very much on the ground under his feet. You can tell this from his pectines, which scan the earth while he shakes his body back and forth. He then approaches the female and stings her on the soft flesh in the joints of a pincer. This seems to relax her, allowing him to grasp her claw in claw, bring her face to face, and begin a scorpion waltz. In the laboratory, scorpion pairs have waltzed for two days. But in nature half an hour or so seems to suffice, with the dance terminating when the male locates a really choice piece of ground (the long laboratory waltz may occur because the male cannot find the right type of ground). Soil texture is important in scorpion sex because instead of a penis males have a detachable spike which must be firmly implanted in the ground if insemination is to occur. Once the spike is in place the male manoeuvres his partner so that her genitals are atop it. As the spike bends under her weight two tiny valves open, through which the sperm is released.

It's difficult for human beings to see scorpions at night, but it's easy for scorpions to see each other. That's because scorpions produce bright green fluorescent light, which may be clearly visible to them but only visible to the human eye with the help of ultraviolet lamps. Its superb adaptations have been honed by 400 million years of evolutionary experience during which countless billions of individual scorpions with blind spots, less sensitive pectines, or poor fluorescence have been weeded out, until finally we are left with the seemingly perfect, yet utterly alien, creatures here described.

If you imagine that worms are any less intriguing than scorpions Attenborough has surprises for you. The largest worms on earth inhabit an area around thirty square kilometres in Gippsland, southern Australia. It's difficult to establish just how long these creatures are, for they keep changing their shape from (relatively) short and squat to long spaghetti-like strands. Attenborough settles on a metre; but their changeable form is hardly their most surprising attribute, for the giant Gippsland earthworm is more often heard than seen. As these subterranean creatures move about in their tunnels they produce sounds like water going down a plughole, or more occasionally like a toilet being flushed. The town of Poowong in west Gippsland supposedly derives its name from an Aboriginal word describing the sound of the worms as they shift about: *Pwwwong!*

Every year or so the giant Gippsland earthworm deposits a case containing a fertilised egg in the wall of its burrow. It's about the shape and size of a cocktail sausage, and if you hold it up to the light, inside you will see a single young worm. By the time it hatches twelve months later it will be twenty centimetres long—larger than a normal earthworm. Such slow reproduction indicates that the worms are long-lived and may be as old as you or me.

Biologists were recently asked to relocate a colony of giant Gippsland earthworms that lay in the path of a new highway. Each worm had to be painstakingly excavated and released into a new burrow. To their surprise the researchers discovered that the worms had different personalities: some were placid, others agitated at the intrusion; one was actually described as 'aggressive'. No one seems to know why.

Attenborough raises an analogous question of insect personalities when he discusses the bolas spider:

> We had in front of us a line of bottles, each of which supported a spray of leafy twigs in which crouched a small bolas spider. These tiny creatures catch moths by whirling a filament of silk with a sticky blob at the end, whenever one came near them. Kevin Fleay, the cameraman, had been working with them for nearly a week and he introduced them to me individually. This one, he told me, was very shy. The slightest vibration made her draw up her legs and stay motionless no matter how near a moth came. That one reacted in the same way if the light was too bright. A third didn't seem to mind how much light was shone on her but on the other hand she was unpredictable. Sometimes she would hunt and sometimes not. But the one at the end of

the line, no matter how much she had eaten, or how much light shone on her, would whirl her bolas whenever a moth came anywhere near and usually caught her prey. These tiny creatures half the size of my fingernail each had individual characters.

The fact that invertebrates have characters seemingly similar in their fundamentals to those possessed by ourselves is a theme to which Attenborough returns repeatedly, and as he does so the gulf between the least and greatest of living things diminishes. But *Life in the Undergrowth* offers another revelation that seems to close that gap further. At a time when our rat-sized ancestors were still cowering in the shadows of the dinosaurs it is probable that certain insects had already created cities, farms and skyscrapers, and today their descendants have become highly sophisticated indeed.

Among the most thought-provoking of such creatures are the ranchers. These ants tend herds of sap-sucking aphids, tiny pear-shaped insects, which they milk for a sugary substance that makes good ant food. Just like human farmers, the ants ensure that their herds get the best possible forage. They do this by driving their aphids to parts of the plant that are rich in sap, and when the aphids produce young (miniature versions of the adults), the ants carry them to fresh pastures. Ant shepherds drive off aphid predators such as ladybirds, and in bad weather build shelters of leaf particles and soil to protect their livestock. They have even been observed marking their herds with a substance specific to one ant colony; it resembles our branding of livestock, Attenborough says. But most astonishingly, the ants have discovered how to interfere with the reproduction of their herds so as to maximise production:

just as we castrate calves, so the ants feed their aphids a fluid that prevents them from reaching sexual maturity.

Other ants and some termites have also become farmers, creating intricate underground factory farms, within which they maintain conditions that promote the growth of nutritious fungi. The Bible commands us to look to the ant, but few would expect to find industries of such complexity and sophistication.

The greatest of earth's architects and builders are the termites. These distant relatives of the cockroach build cities whose spires tower far higher above their inhabitants' heads, relative to their size, than do our tallest skyscrapers. Some species in northern Australia build razor-backed structures that point north, maximising the thermal comfort of those within. And in many species of termites the water provisioning, highway construction, and air-conditioning of their great edifices rival in sophistication anything built by humanity.

With its superb synthesis of the majority of living species, *Life in the Undergrowth* is a high point in David Attenborough's career, but it is also an elegant restatement of what he has spent a lifetime trying to teach: we are simply one species among a multitude, all of which are worthy of our interest and respect.

Piotr Naskrecki has travelled the world with his camera, seeking out rare and little-known creatures, and *The Smaller Majority* contains some of the most beautiful wildlife photographs I have ever seen. He does not restrict himself to terrestrial invertebrates, but includes some smaller vertebrates such as lizards and amphibians. Some of his most dramatic photographs are of caecilians, which look like giant earthworms but are actually related to frogs and salamanders. A double-page spread is devoted to anatomical close-ups, revealing that caecilians have a tentacle where you might think the eye should be, while their anus is at the end of the body, demonstrating that, although caecilians are extraordinarily long and slender, they have no tail.

Naskrecki's own specialty is the study of grasshoppers, to which he devotes a dozen or so pages. Some particularly vivid species are found in Australia, as is a locust troublesome to farmers. He writes:

> During a recent locust outbreak in Australia, the government launched a campaign aiming to introduce these insects into local cuisines. To help break the popular reluctance to eat locusts the Australian media started to refer to them as 'sky prawns'.

The idea of Australians eating their way clear of a locust plague, or even tossing a 'sky prawn' on the barbecue, seems remarkable to an Australian such as myself. Like their American counterparts, Australian bushmen love telling tall stories, and I suspect that Naskrecki, as the locust-obsessed visitor, was judged fair game. In fact 'sky prawns' are yet to be seen in the restaurants of Sydney and Adelaide, or even the outback.

In my search for the origins of the 'sky prawn' story I turned to Jeffrey Lockwood's excellent book *Locust*, where I discovered that people of many cultures relish the insects. Among the greatest consumers were the Goshute Indians of western Utah. One anthropologist estimated that a Goshute could harvest ninety kilograms of sun-dried grasshoppers in an hour—which would yield the equivalent calories of 500 large pizzas. In a striking inversion of the 'sky prawn' story, the Goshute, when they were first given prawns to eat, called them 'sea crickets'.

The sea cricket is a mere diversion in Lockwood's book, whose central theme is the tale of the American locust and its impact upon the shaping of the West. As the American frontier rolled westward, a continent of superlatives was revealed to the world: trees taller, older and grander than any seen before; billion-strong flocks of passenger pigeons whose droppings whitened the ground like snow; and buffalo herds that took days to pass and whose lowing was heard hours before the creatures came into view. Although some of those wonders are now just memories, they still help define the frontier. Yet the most abundant creature that ever roamed the West is not even a memory. The Rocky Mountain locust is both gone and forgotten. Its disappearance is, according to Lockwood, 'the quintessential ecological mystery of the North American continent—a century-old homicide on a continental scale'.

Locusts are simply grasshoppers with peculiar habits. There are ten species worldwide, and they are characterised by their roving swarms, which can appear out of nowhere and can devastate crops over a considerable area. Each continent has its own locusts, and each species has evolved independently from less troublesome grasshopper relatives. The Rocky Mountain locust— the sole species recorded from North America—was the most numerous and destructive of them all. Some idea of its abundance can be gained from the size of a swarm that visited Nebraska in 1875. Known as Albert's Swarm (named for the Weather Service pioneer who documented it), it is estimated to have consisted of 3.5 trillion insects. That's 600 for every person living on earth today.

Some sense of what that visitation was like was conveyed by Laura Ingalls Wilder in *On the Banks of Plum Creek* from the *Little House on the Prairie* series. Before the swarm arrived, she sensed that:

The light was queer. It was not like the changed light before a storm. The air did not press down as it did before a storm. Laura was frightened, she did not know why…A cloud was over the sun. It was not like any cloud they had ever seen before. It was a cloud of something like snowflakes, but they were larger than snowflakes, and thin and glittering. Light shone through each flickering particle…The cloud was hailing grasshoppers. The cloud was grasshoppers. Their bodies hid the sun and made darkness.

The next morning Laura found that the prairie grass had been mowed down and the trees stripped of their fruit and leaves. In fact the locusts seemed to have eaten almost anything, from green paint to window blinds and dead bats and live birds—even other locusts. A favourite food was the wooden handles of tools that had absorbed the salty sweat of the pioneers. In the wake of such swarms came starvation.

Throughout the 1870s, military posts across the American frontier dispatched reports on the devastation left by the locust swarms. Each tells only a local story, but when they are put together the extent of the destruction becomes clear. One poignant account from Missouri's St Clair County reads:

We have seen within the past week families which had not a meal of victuals in their house. In one case a family of six died within six days of each other from the want of food to keep body and soul together. From present indications, the future four months will make many graves, marked with a simple piece of wood with the inscription 'Starved to death' painted on it.

Because locust plagues loom large in the Old Testament as a form of divine retribution, some settlers were discomfited morally as well as physically by the swarms. But others saw in them an opportunity to boost their religious convictions.

Around the Great Salt Lake, the pickled bodies of locusts that had drowned piled nearly two metres high along the shoreline. According to the Mormon farmer and railroad grader Milando Pratt, the rotting bodies put forth a 'great stench . . . and cast the aroma of this slowly melting putrid wall upon the windward breezes to be wafted earthward toward our suffering camp'. Starving and beset by stinks, the Mormon settlers must have been tempted to read the plague as a divine order to move on. Their leaders, however, took a different view, for the locust visitation fitted in with their interpretation of the Sabbath.

According to Mormon theologians there are varying Sabbath cycles: a Sabbath one day in seven, and a Sabbath year, known as a jubilee, one year in seven. During the jubilee year the earth should be allowed to rest, with no farming to take place; instead the observant should subsist from a surplus garnered and stored during the preceding six years. Lockwood writes:

> As bad luck or divine providence would have it, the locusts began to arrive the year that the Mormon farmers failed to observe a Sabbath, and the insects bred prolifically and continued their devastations into the following year.

A prominent church official, Heber C. Kimball, put matters succinctly:

> How many times have you been told to store up your wheat against the hard times that are coming upon the nations of

the earth? It only requires a few grasshoppers to make the earth rest, they can soon clear it. This is the seventh year, did you ever think of it?

Respite came from an unexpected quarter. The flag of Salt Lake City bears a seagull. It may seem odd that this predominantly coastal bird should figure as an emblem of an inland city, but seagulls reputedly arrived en masse in the wake of the locusts and thinned their ranks considerably.

With seagulls in short supply over the rest of the West, other pioneers resorted to desperate methods including horse-drawn flamethrowers, gigantic locust-crushers and coal-tar-coated hopper-dozers. All proved useless. Then, in the closing decades of the nineteenth century, the locust swarms stopped coming—and, astonishingly, hardly anybody noticed. This was partly because other grasshoppers became abundant around the same time, and partly because people kept expecting another big plague.

The last time anybody saw a Rocky Mountain locust alive was in 1902, and it was only years later that it began to dawn on people that there would never be another swarm—the reason being the most abundant insect ever recorded was extinct.

Just ten years after that final sighting, an entomologist working in Russia made a truly remarkable discovery. Boris Petrovich Uvarov was studying locust outbreaks around the Caspian Sea when he saw something he thought inexplicable—a grasshopper transformed itself into a locust. It was, a colleague wrote, as if he was seeing evolution unfolding before his eyes. Yet what he had discovered was no evolutionary change but something very different, which came to be known as 'the theory of phases'.

The grasshopper, *Locusta danica*, is a bright green solitary creature that causes no harm to farmers. If their density increases, however, the next generation becomes black and red, long-winged, and prone to travel long distances. Uvarov discovered that the smell of grasshopper faeces and the frequent disturbance of the tiny hairs on the grasshopper's hind legs caused by crowding were the key cues leading to transformation. And he discovered that the changes were entirely reversible: when the numbers dropped, the next generation would develop into solitary, green grasshoppers.

This remarkable discovery raised the possibility that the Rocky Mountain locust may not be extinct after all: perhaps it, too, had phases, and its solitary phase was still lurking somewhere in the West, awaiting the conditions needed to spark its transformation. The theory had many powerful adherents, and some American entomologists even claimed that they had, in the laboratory, forced grasshoppers to transform themselves into Rocky Mountain locusts.

In the late 1950s, a study of male genitalia provided a definitive answer to the riddle. Grasshopper phalluses are precise tools: each species has its own shape, and each will fit only into a female of the same species. A study of the seventeen Rocky Mountain locusts preserved in museum collections revealed that their phalluses were unique. Thus they were not a phase of another species.

While many might read a moral tale in the locust's extinction, entomologists took a more objective view. Some thought that the spread of alfalfa, which disagrees with the creature's digestion, might be the cause; others felt that the demise of the buffalo was somehow involved. Jeffrey Lockwood, however, has his own ideas.

Lockwood figures that the outbreaks had to come from somewhere and that if the cradle of the swarm could be identified, then so would the cause of the creature's extinction. The swarms, he established, originated in the high valleys of the Rocky Mountains. The species probably required just 7500 square kilometres as its nursery, and may actually have used far less. At around the time the locust vanished, the high valleys were being settled. Grazing, irrigating and cropping, it seems, transformed the vital nurseries in ways that made them inhospitable to locusts. Thus a few farmers banished from the land a creature that once rivalled or even exceeded the passenger pigeon in its abundance, and which had threatened farming across a vast region.

At the end of his fascinating book Lockwood takes us to Yellowstone National Park, whose fertile valleys were set aside as a reserve in 1872. The park acted as a last refuge for the buffalo, and Lockwood wonders whether the locust might have survived there also. He writes that among the first grasshoppers he collected there was a female with spectacularly long wings. Of course the females of locust species are difficult to identify, for they lack phalluses. More recently he captured several similar individuals. 'I think I know who they were,' he confides, 'so I released them back into the field. Because I did not remove them from the park, their identities and location need not be reported to the authorities.' Perhaps echoes of the frontier will once again be seen in America.

What Is a Tree?

New York Review of Books, FEBRUARY 2007

The Tree: A Natural History of What Trees Are, How They Live, and Why They Matter, Colin Tudge, Crown Publishers, New York, 2006.

The Plant-Book: A Portable Dictionary of the Vascular Plants 2nd edition, D. J. Mabberley, Cambridge University Press, Cambridge, 1997.

Animal, mineral or vegetable? Whenever our parents bundled us into the car for a long journey my sisters and I kept ourselves occupied with that guessing game. At its heart is the puzzle of how things should be classified, the more ambiguous the better. My inventive youngest sister came up with 'a cow's moo'. Through its astonishing revelations about what is related to what in the plant world, Colin Tudge's *The Tree* reawakens the pleasure of those childish games. But *The Tree* is a far deeper book than this might suggest, for its author has a remarkable ability to ask fundamental questions about trees and their world—questions that, much to our detriment, most of us stopped asking as we grew up.

Humans are innate classifiers, and our earliest efforts were doubtless classifications of convenience: edible and inedible, for example. Despite this predilection, our workaday world is filled with appalling classifications. Consider the forester's venerable division of 'softwoods' for the conifers (including the remarkably tough paraná pine of South America) and 'hardwoods' for the broad-leaved trees (which include the very soft balsa).

And yet we recognise a good classification at once. Perhaps it comes from our sense that the natural world has a true orderliness. Birds, for example, are instantly recognisable as such, as are mammals and frogs; and so with smaller groups like kingfishers, hawks and doves. In pre-Darwinian Europe natural philosophers hoped that by comprehending the 'true classification' of nature they might glimpse the mind of the Creator. Yet in the absence of divine revelation, how could they hope to discern the one and only 'true' classification from less perfect models?

In the mid-eighteenth century the Swedish botanist Carl Linnaeus provided natural philosophers with a hierarchical scheme that classified living things into kingdoms (of which he had just two—plants and animals), classes, orders, genera and species. It is these final two categories that provide the scientific name. Linnaeus, for example, classified himself and other humans *Homo sapiens* (though at first he dubbed us the rather less appropriate *Homo diurnis*—daytime man).

The first part of the double-barrelled name is the generic part. It is shared with a group of similar species, and so acts rather like a surname in a family. The second—the species name—is unique in the genus to that individual species, and so acts like a Christian name.

Linnaeus's scheme was brilliant in its simplicity, and it is the basis of the universal scientific classification used by all taxonomists (classifiers of living things) today. When it came to higher levels (the classes and orders) of plants, Linnaeus turned to vegetable sex. And this scheme, undertaken by botanists down the centuries, really has, to borrow from Andrew Marvell, grown 'vaster than empires, and more slow'. Linnaeus's highest plant categories—the classes—were arranged according to the nature of the plant's male genitals (stamens), while his next level down—the orders—was based on the female genitals (pistils). This 'male on top' approach had some unfortunate consequences: the castor bean tree (a flowering plant), for example, ended up in the same class as the pines (non-flowering plants), and his scheme did not account for the 'plants' that had no obvious sex organs at all, such as algae and fungi.

All of this, however, might have passed as a minor flaw had the Swede shared the prudery of his age. Instead he was quite the opposite. We still have a genus of creepers called by him *Clitorea* (the beautiful blue flowers of one species bear a remarkable resemblance to female human genitalia), and botanical classification is besieged by copious 'phallus' something-or-others (though here the resemblances are I think more imaginative). In Linnaeus's day botany was considered a fit occupation for young ladies, and such provocatively named plants caused professors throughout Europe to obfuscate, or—as Linnaeus's contemporary Johann Siegesbeck did—condemn the entire Linnaean scheme as 'loathsome harlotry'.

The scheme's misfortunes only increased when it was introduced to the English. The man who undertook the translation was Erasmus Darwin (the grandfather of Charles), a ponderous, pockmarked and ungainly man whose principal interests were plants, poetry, sex, and ingenious mechanical devices. Darwin was a wild romantic and, despite his Johnsonian appearance and stammering speech, women loved him. To court his second wife (who was married when they first met), Darwin landscaped an entire valley, damming streams and planting bowers of exotic trees and meadows of flowers. It evidently worked: from his two marriages (and a governess in between) he fathered twelve children.

Darwin revelled in sex in all its manifestations from marital to masturbatory—and perhaps homosexuality as well (he certainly had many homosexual friends, whom he never condemned). Indeed, he believed that sex was health-giving—it cured hypochondria, for example. One wonders, incidentally, whether this had anything to do with the first Mrs Darwin being sickly, overly fond of the bottle and inclined to smoke opium.

Because of his interest in poetry, it seemed entirely natural to Darwin to translate Linnaeus's dense scientific work into rhyming couplets and create a romantic epic. *The Loves of the Plants* was published in 1789 by the radical publisher Joseph Johnson. One of the most unusual scientific tracts ever written, its botanical classification is enlivened with alarmingly anthropocentric descriptions of the goings-on of male and female genitals in their 'nuptial bed', as Darwin refers to the calyx of the flower. Because some flowers have many male parts (some of which can be sterile— and thus liable to be characterised as 'beardless youths') and they share the nuptial bed with just one female part, some of Darwin's 'scenes' resemble the interior of a sultan's bedroom or a Roman orgy more than they do a violet or pansy.

Erasmus Darwin was working at the dawn of the modern era of classification, and throughout the late eighteenth and first half of the nineteenth centuries interest in botany grew apace. It was during this period that many of the world's great natural history museums and herbaria were founded, their collections forming a vast system that allowed the classification of the world to progress ever more expeditiously. And yet still no one could demonstrate that their particular classification was nearer the 'true classification' than anyone else's. Erasmus's grandson Charles provided the answer to that age-old riddle. Evolution by natural selection helped explain the orderliness of nature and, more importantly, it provided the mechanism that had given us the family tree of life. Yet for a century after the Darwinian revolution, most taxonomists continued with their task of classifying the world without fully absorbing the message evolution held for them.

If two organisms looked similar, many taxonomists would say that they must be related. It took a German entomologist, Willi Hennig, working in the second half of the twentieth century, to change that. He saw that only some similarities tell us who is most closely related to whom. To illustrate the nature of Hennig's breakthrough, imagine a family whose members have always had black hair. But then a child with red hair is born, and the mother gives birth to more redheads. These offspring are more closely related to their black-haired cousins than they are to more distant black-haired relatives. Yet anyone using black hair to understand relationships might misclassify all black-haired individuals as close relatives, and the redheads as more distant. Red hair, however, providing it breeds true, would be an accurate indicator of relatedness, at least within the redhead family. Hennig's work gave rise to a new scientific method called cladistics, and it is this method that underpins Tudge's book.

Scientific classification had come a long way between Linnaeus and Hennig, yet despite the great advances, before the 1980s many botanical classifications bore little resemblance to the true evolutionary relationship of plants. One final discovery was required before such classifications could be improved—the deciphering and use of DNA.

Is the mushroom animal, mineral or vegetable? Most non-scientists would place it in the classification of convenience—perhaps with the cauliflower in the vegetable tribe. Indeed, traditional classifications place the fungi alongside the plants. Yet modern evolutionary studies using DNA reveal that mushrooms are more closely related to human beings than to the cauliflower. Given just the three choices the child's game allows, the mushroom is an animal.

It's not that DNA provides some sort of divine revelation about who is related to whom, for it too is prone to convergence in evolution and errors of interpretation. But as botanists combine the results of DNA studies with more traditional methods such as the study of wood structure, and seed and leaf type, ever more robust classifications (ones that are increasingly difficult to find fault with) are emerging, and they reveal just how far astray our classifications of convenience can be. Who, for example, would ever have guessed that plane trees and members of the protea family, such as South Africa's proteas and Australia's banksias, are close relatives? Even more mind-stretching is the newly published finding that the mighty teak is intimately related to herbs such as mint, oregano and basil. Even as I recount it, I'm astonished that botanists now believe cucumbers are close relatives of oaks and beeches—far closer, indeed, than oaks are to plane trees.

This new knowledge, along with an ever-improving fossil record, reveals that the evolution of trees has been more epic than Erasmus, Darwin or Linnaeus could ever have imagined. As Tudge puts it:

It is a wonderful thing to contemplate a living tree, or a fossil one, or any other creature. It is even more moving when we add the fourth dimension, of time, and see in our mind's eye how the ancestors of the tree that grows in the field next door first saw the light in some remote corner of the globe millions or hundreds of millions of years in the past, and floated on its respective bit of continent as the continent itself circumnavigated the globe, and skirted around the glaciers of the ice age, and perhaps sweated it out in some primeval, long-gone swamp, with alligators around its feet and the world's first hawks and kingfishers scouting from its branches.

As rich as the new discoveries are, *The Tree* is about far more than plant classification, and it begins with a question: 'And what, pray, are trees, that anyone should presume to write a book about them?' As you might have already guessed, one of the most challenging lessons of *The Tree* is that the entire concept of 'tree' as a classificatory category has no evolutionary reality whatever, for the things we call trees have arisen multiple times from humbler vegetation, and trees have repeatedly been transformed into vines, shrubs and herbs. Some tree species can in fact exist as either shrubs or trees. As Tudge says, 'Nature was not designed to make life easy for biologists.'

Rather than becoming bogged down in elaborate evolutionary explanation, Tudge uses a child's definition of a tree as 'a big plant with a stick up the middle', and the 'stick up the middle', it turns out, is one of the most fascinating and useful objects in nature. Some wood can be made as sharp as steel and cannot be worked except with tools of tungsten and diamond. Others, such as the Japanese cedar, can be buried in the earth until they become deep green in colour, and are then regarded as a kind of semi-precious stone.

The key ingredient in wood is lignin, a chemical compound that binds together wood's cellulose fibres. Plants without it, which are called herbs, use water pressure to stay upright. Real wood only exists where the lignin is laid down in an intricate and meticulous manner; and wood is, according to Tudge:

> One of the wonders of the universe, remarkably complex, minutely structured, lovely to look upon, and infinitely various. If humanity had only one kind of timber to draw upon it could think itself blessed, but in practice we have many thousands—a tree for every job, and for every decorative caprice.

Tudge's documentation of the specialist uses of timber opens up a world of craftsmanship and acute observation that is unknown to most of us. Why, one wonders, is the katsura tree of east Asia especially suitable for the manufacture of pencils and Japanese shoes? And who discovered that the lignum vitae of Central America makes splendid rollers and wheels in pulleys because the wood is self-lubricating; or that abura wood is excellent for battery boxes because it resists acid? There is something about the timber of the coachwood of New South Wales that suits it to the manufacture of gunstocks and musical instruments, while tropical American snakewood makes marvellous violin bows and umbrella handles. Snakewood, however, would not do for xylophones, and for that musical instrument one must seek out the wood of a *Dalbergia* tree. Presumably someone knows why the wood of the African ekki tree was used to support the tracks of the Paris metro. In view of the present sad state of Africa's rainforests, one wonders where replacement timbers will come from should the existing ones wear out.

Familiar trees sometimes have mysterious uses too. Who for example would have guessed that elm is favoured in the manufacture of 'buttock-moulded seats', or that basswood was the best timber for the fronts of pulpits? And why is it that the jacaranda is preferred when making pianos—but only in Egypt?

Tudge has seen cogs made of hornbeam at work in a century-old brewery near his home, where they perform better than cogs of iron; such sights perhaps inspired him to write:

> The intricate knowledge that our forebears had of each kind of plant and its caprices and possibilities never ceases to astonish me. [It is] knowledge now largely lost, or at least confined to academic tracts of whimsical accounts like this one. Maybe when the fossil fuels run out and heavy industry has run its course, such wonders may be rediscovered.

Of course trees have mysteries far deeper than the functional qualities of the material comprising their 'stick up the middle'. Despite his considerable botanical knowledge, Tudge cannot explain why the Indian rain tree goes out of its way to encourage epiphytes—plants that grow on other plants—when most trees seek to discourage them.

Some indigenous peoples possess enormous botanical knowledge. Tudge writes of Brazilian Indians known as *mateiros* whose expert knowledge of tree species and their uses outstrips that of the wisest professor. Not all indigenous knowledge of trees, however, may be correct. Tudge is unable to confirm whether the asoka tree (a close relative of the Indian rain tree) does in fact blossom more vigorously if kicked by a young woman, as reputed in Indian folklore. Interestingly, in the botanical world scientific facts can be even more fascinating than folklore. Who would have imagined that alder trees accumulate gold in their tissues, or that their near relative the birch accumulates heavy metals in its leaves and so can be used to clean up toxic mine sites?

After leading us through such wonderful diversions Tudge asks again, this time from a functional point of view, what is a tree? His answer, which pertains to all life, is profound. Living tissue, he says, 'is constantly replacing itself, even when it seems to stay the same. It is not a thing but a performance.'

The performance that is a tree is in fact an interaction between the four elements recognised by the pre-Socratic Greeks: air, fire, earth and water. Air is the principal ingredient, for trees are quite literally made of air, or at least the carbon dioxide (CO_2) it contains. For this gas, combined with the hydrogen wrested from water (H_2O) by photosynthesis, is what makes those great trunks, arching boughs and leafy canopies. (Photosynthesis occurs when the green pigment chlorophyll assists in combining carbon dioxide, water and light, thus transforming the sun's energy into a chemical form.) Next time you look at a tree, think that it was, not so long ago, CO_2 wafting about in our atmosphere. It's a thought that has great import for our battle to control global warming. For all our ingenuity, humanity has never devised a machine that can so efficiently and elegantly convert greenhouse gases into the most wondrous natural sculptures known.

There are 'around' 60,000 species of trees and still counting, which prompts Tudge to ask, 'How on earth can anyone—the most astute of hunters and gatherers, or the most learned of professors— keep tabs on 350,000 or so species of plants, including around 60,000 trees?'

The answer, which proves to be a salvation, comes in the form D. J. Mabberley's wondrous *Plant-Book*. From Aaron's rod to the obscure *Zyzyxia*, it lists them all in alphabetical order, and with such wit, elegance and compression as to be breathtaking. I suspect that it may well be the source of many of the more intriguing facts enumerated by Tudge.

The Plant-Book is, being all encompassing and indispensable, the botanical equivalent of Johnson's *Dictionary*. In the acknowledgments Mabberley informs us that 'the first edition was typed with the author's right index finger on a Brother electric typewriter'. The undertaking of this herculean effort clearly required fortification, and Mabberley records his 'appreciation of the work of Philip Glass, Malcolm McLaren, Franz Schubert (1797–1828) and Carl Maria von Weber (1786–1826), which has kept me sane during some of the more tedious episodes'.

A part of just one of the hundreds of thousands of entries that comprise this work must suffice to testify to its excellence:

> *Cannabis* . . . more northerly cult. (in China for 4500 yrs, obligatory crop in Eliz. times in GB, where illegal since 1951) for fibre (hemp used for ropes, fibre-board, paper etc. since 4000 BC esp. in N & NE China where form. only fibre available, prob. used in first paper (AD 105) there) & subsp. *indica* (Lam.) . . . more southerly cult. principally for psychotropic drugs (marijuana, marihuana (Mex.), pot (US, where allegedly the biggest cash crop worth $32 billion), dagga (S Afr.), kif (Morocco)), cannabis resin, which exudes from the glandular hairs & is used like opium (effects described 2736 BC by Chinese Emperor Shen Neng). In India, 3 common forms: ganja (dried unripe infrs), charras

or churras (resin knocked off twigs, bark etc.) & bhang (largely mature lvs of wild pl). Smoked ('weed') with or without tobacco ('skunk') in cigarettes ('joints') or taken as an intoxicating liquid formed from it (hashish; Arabic for 'hashishtaker' = root word of 'assassin'), in food or drink (e.g. in comm. beers in the Netherlands) it has a stimulating & pleasantly exciting effect, relief from muscular sclerosis, cerebral palsy & glaucoma, though addictive & in excess can cause delirium & 'moral weakness and depravity' (Uphof). Seeds the source of hemp seed oil used in varnishes, food, soap, lip balm & fuel in Nazi tanks etc. & used as birdseed & to attract fishes.

Such are the uses of a single species; whose only near relative is the hops vine that gives us good beer.

It is absolutely clear to me after reading *The Plant-Book* and *The Tree* that the extinction of even a single tree species, out of the 60,000 known, would be an immense tragedy for humanity and the natural world.

Getting to Know Them

New York Review of Books, APRIL 2010

The Social Behavior of Older Animals, Anne Innis Dagg, Johns Hopkins University Press, Baltimore, 2008.

Elephants on the Edge: What Animals Teach Us About Humanity, G.A. Bradshaw, Yale University Press, Hartford, 2010.

Animals Make Us Human: Creating the Best Life for Animals, Temple Grandin, Catherine Johnson, Mariner, 2010.

The Hidden Life of Deer: Lessons from the Natural World, Elizabeth Marshall Thomas, Harper, New York, 2009.

Not so very long ago we humans thought of ourselves as a separate creation—the pinnacle of God's work—that had been granted dominion over nature. But then along came Darwin, and we discovered that we are related, through descent, to other animals. Despite this blow to our dignity we long maintained a polite fiction that we're special enough to merit classification in our own scientific family—the Hominidae. In our minds at least, we thus maintained a comfortable distance from the apes. But the analysis of DNA put an end to that, with the demonstration that only 2 percent of our genetic code differs from that of the chimpanzees. Now we and chimps must share a twig in the family tree, and the Hominidae has been expanded to encompass the other "great apes"—chimps, gorillas, and orangutans.

That being said, we clearly differ from the other great apes in many ways, a fact elucidated in Anne Innis Dagg's *The Social Behavior of Older Animals*. It's a highly unusual work in that it treats an age group of organisms that has received little previous attention. It is also a commendably broad study—covering a diversity of species from parrots to primates. Humans and chimps, it turns out, value age in sexual partners very differently. In our species youth is prized, but among chimps the reverse is the case. Importantly, female chimpanzees (unlike female humans) do not experience menopause, and thus can remain fertile into old age.

Flo was one of the most sexually attractive female chimps in a troop studied by Jane Goodall. By the time Flo was forty, her teeth were worn down to the gums and her time as the dominant female in the troop was over, but she still managed to drive the boys crazy, attracting a string of suitors and mating fifty times in a single day. Researchers, wondering whether Flo was an anomaly, carried out an eight-year study of chimpanzee sex. In what seems to be something of an understatement of their results, they concluded that chimpanzee males may not find the wrinkled skin, ragged ears, irregular bald patches, and elongated nipples of their aged females as alluring as human men find the full lips and smooth complexions of young women, but clearly they are not reacting negatively. . . .

There is great variety in the ways older animals differ from younger ones—in both physical and behavioral manner. Older chimps may go bald, and leopards suffer faded spots, but not all creatures bear such badges of seniority. The plumage of geriatric swallows, for example, is indistinguishable from birds in their prime. But old creatures, regardless of species, tend to be less agile than young ones, and more likely to suffer from arthritis, diabetes, cancer, heart disease, and mental confusion. All of this means that they're unlikely to be top of the pack, and the way they cope with this is intriguing.

Sherlock was a male baboon who, at the age of twenty-four, was about ninety in human terms. While still keen on sex, elders like Sherlock often don't have the status required to assert themselves against other males. So they often befriend individual females instead. Remarkably, such friendships are not about sex alone. They often involve nursing females, who, though rightly nervous of most males (who occasionally kill infant baboons), in a remarkable sign of trust will even leave their babies in the care of their older male friends while they forage.

When the end comes for older animals, they do not always go unmourned. Some species, such as elephants and chimpanzees, show unmistakable signs of grief and mourning at the death of a member of their group, and even gray whales have been observed behaving as if paying their last respects to the dead. Astonishingly, careful disposal of the body is not beyond some, for gorillas have been observed to bury their dead, while elephants have been known to raid a shed filled with the body parts of slaughtered elephants, removing the feet and ears (which were destined to be turned into umbrella stands) and burying them.

In many ways, elephants represent the great "other"—enormous, highly social, and intelligent creatures whose ways on occasion eerily echo our own. G.A. Bradshaw's *Elephants on the Edge* is a remarkable study of elephant–human interactions, whose opening premise is that "it is not so much that elephants are *like* us. They *are* us, and we them." This, I fear, the author means literally rather than metaphorically, for she seems to see no difference between the elephant and the human mind. That allows her to attempt psychoanalysis of elephants using methods developed for humans, and to diagnose their "condition" using human criteria. It flows from her premise that elephants should be endowed with all the basic human rights, and that we can expect them to respect our rights in turn. Unfortunately, the implications of Bradshaw's extraordinary opening premise are not fully explored in her book. Instead, it's essentially a catalog of human abuse of pachyderms, which jumps in an instant from the treatment of elephants in circuses to the experiences of Holocaust survivors.

Very few people would accept Bradshaw's premise uncritically, so it's important that we explore the nature of the relationship between humans and elephants. Taking an evolutionary perspective reveals many similarities, but differences as well. Every now and again evolution throws up a new kind of creature that goes on to colonize most of the world. The landmass of Eurasia, being the largest of the continents, has produced the largest number of these species, including the family that includes sheep, goats, and cattle. But North America too has given the world its champions, including the dog, camel, and horse families—arguably man's best friends. Africa, while larger than North America, has paradoxically few such champions. Only two are of any note—the families Hominidae and Elephantidae—yet between them elephants and humans have colonized the habitable surface of the earth. Indeed they are arguably the most successful mammal families ever to have evolved.

In times past the elephants were more successful than people. Dozens of species—from the pony-sized dwarfs that once grazed on the island of Crete to the woolly mammoth and the mastodons of North and South America—colonized the whole habitable world (with the exception of Australia). But then humans spread and climates changed, so today there remain just two species—the African and Asian (though some argue that the pink-tusked, pygmy elephant of the Congo is a third type)—and today all are under siege from a growing human population. Elephants are more truly African than we are, being members of an ancient group known as the Afrotheria, whose ancestors lived in Africa at the time of the dinosaurs. The hominids, in contrast, are only newly African, our ancestors having arrived on the continent from Eurasia a mere ten million years ago.

These disparate histories mean that the last common ancestor of the elephants and ourselves was a rat-sized creature that lived over 100 million years ago. Yet undeniably we share much in common, perhaps because some of our ancestors were shaped at the same evolutionary forge—the productive, crowded, and intensely competitive world of the African savannah. It's this world, in part, that endowed both elephants and humans with exceptional intelligence, and a dependence on complex societies for their well-being. But for all their sagacity, elephants have been losing the battle for survival for the last 50,000 years—since humans started leaving Africa. As humans have encroached upon their world, one after another species has gone extinct, and Bradshaw argues that, as we endanger the last living species, they have become prey to psychological stresses that they are manifesting in startling ways.

About two hours' drive outside Johannesburg lies the small nature reserve of Pilanesberg National Park, which is plagued by strange goings-on among its elephants. Rangers working there have observed young males harassing older females for sex, and tourists filmed the astonishing spectacle of an elephant copulating with a rhinoceros. Then dead rhinos started to turn up, all gored to death by elephant tusks. Bradshaw thinks that these phenomena have their roots in a "complex post-traumatic stress disorder" suffered by the elephants. The stress, she believes, was inflicted by human interactions with elephants—and she thinks that the aberrant elephant psychology at Pilanesberg is only an indication of something much larger.

These are important claims, and in order to assess them properly we need to know more about Pilanesberg's elephant population. Prior to its proclamation as a national park, elephants had been long extinct in the Pilanesberg area, and in an attempt to build up the region's biodiversity, park managers accepted two former circus elephants (both female) and a number of juvenile males that were orphaned during elephant culling operations elsewhere in South Africa. The rhino-raping and killing males, it turns out, originated in Kruger National Park. At the time they were captured, only small elephants could be transported, so no adult male was present at Pilanesberg when they arrived. Among elephants, males and females lead largely separate lives, the females belonging to herds led by a matriarch, and from which males are ejected at puberty. They then join all-male groups, and presumably learn from mature males the recipe for a successful life.

In her search to explain the bizarre behavior of the young males, Bradshaw focuses almost entirely on the trauma they suffered when their families were shot during culling. "Elephant attacks on rhinoceroses . . . reflect the violence that this otherwise peaceful species has experienced," she says. But surely the situation is far more complex than that. What about the circus-raised females? Did they have much experience of elephant sex, and know how to handle young males? Bradshaw tells us nothing of their reproductive histories, nor their interactions with the males other than that they rebuffed "behavior not only unbecoming of a young bull but highly irregular." Such modesty might be fitting in a Victorian novel, but as we seek to understand the Pilanesberg situation we need facts.

Then there's the matter of the rhinos. Frustratingly, Bradshaw tells us nothing of the histories of Pilanesberg's rhino population, and too little of their fate. It's reasonable to assume that the rhinos, like the elephants, came from elsewhere; but had they any prior experience of elephants? If they had never interacted with elephants before, may they not have been vulnerable to bullying by the larger creatures? And what of the sex? Was it only female rhinos that were sexually penetrated and then pierced with tusks, or was interspecies sodomy practiced as well? Pretty much all we know is that forty-nine white rhinos died at Pilanesberg between 1992 and 1996 from such attacks—and that is far too little, in my view, to accept uncritically Bradshaw's diagnosis of "complex post-traumatic stress disorder."

For all its faults, *Elephants on the Edge* deals with a fascinating and little-understood subject, which makes it doubly disappointing to find it so devoid of facts and overstuffed with opinion. Sadly, it seems to be as much about its author's view of human nature as it is about elephants; but even more disappointingly, it has almost nothing useful to say about how humans and elephants might continue to coexist. Bradshaw talks of creating enormous wild areas for the use of elephants—areas large enough for them to migrate in search of food and water. But in an Africa whose human population is growing exponentially, that is a fantasy. It's clear that the millennia-long contest between elephants and humans will only accelerate in the future, and that the elephants can survive only through our good graces, and on our terms. This means that elephant populations will need to be managed. As they overpopulate parks, we can either watch them precipitate collapse of the ecosystem, then starve to death, or we can cull them. In this context, it's hardly helpful to talk, as Bradshaw does, of a "humane self" and an "Auschwitz self" in conflict as we try to manage elephant populations.

If the largest of wild creatures present profound moral and physical challenges to us, so too do the domesticated species with which we share our lives. Temple Grandin is a professor at Colorado State University who has devoted much of her career to the humane treatment and slaughter of the cattle, sheep, and pigs that feed us. She is also autistic, a disability that she argues allows her a special empathy with nonhuman creatures. Her latest book, *Animals Make Us Human*, is an amazing tour de force of animal–human relationships, with chapters on our companion animals, as well as on livestock, wildlife, and zoos.

Most of us would prefer not to know where the meat on our plates comes from. And indeed when we consider slaughterhouses where animals mean only money, such knowledge is enough to turn one off meat for life. Grandin comes at the problem from a very different perspective from most, asking simply, "What does an animal need to be happy?" Even creatures raised for meat, she believes, have the right to a happy life—and they can have it if certain "freedoms" are granted them. Among these are freedom from hunger and thirst, discomfort, pain, injury, and disease; and freedom to express normal behavior and to live free from fear and distress. Yet as she points out, it's far from obvious how such freedoms might be granted, for each species has its own requirements, and conditions that are paradise for one may be purgatory for another.

If we are to grant these freedoms, Grandin argues that we need to understand how animals think, and most of the book is taken up with chapters on the inner lives of our companion animals—from dogs to cows to chickens to wildlife we interact with, and animals in zoos. In each instance Grandin displays an exceptional understanding of beings that, to most of us, remain enduring mysteries. It's hard to know which animals Grandin has the greatest fondness for, but cattle must be high on the list, for she has long experience of them, and has arguably done more than anyone to improve their lot.

Cattle, Grandin argues, aren't tame animals as are dogs or cats, and therefore freedom from fear is a big issue for them. As she puts it, "A central welfare issue for beef cattle is poor stockmanship. People screaming and yelling at cattle, hitting or punching them, shocking them with electric prods—all of these things terrify cattle." In arguing against such practices, she poses a series of immensely practical alternatives, such as positive reinforcement with food treats to move cattle into trucks or chutes. Well-cared-for cattle will "actually SEEK handling procedures," she asserts, and such cattle can remain relaxed, unstressed, and happy all of their lives—right up to the moment of slaughter.

Unfortunately this is not, for reasons both mundane and infuriating, how most cattle live. "Even when plants [i.e., slaughterhouses] know they're losing money by shocking and yelling at the animals, they still do it," she says. "In one slaughter plant I documented $500 to $1,000 savings per day after I had trained employees to handle cattle quietly, but when I left, workers quickly went back to their old rough ways." She feels that the greatest obstacle to the humane treatment of cattle is that "to be a good stockperson you have to recognize that an animal is a conscious being that has feelings, and some people don't want to think of animals that way." She also admits that handling untamed, untrained cattle is frustrating . . . and frustration is a mild form of rage. . . . That's why it's easy for people to blow up at farm animals (or at small children). Getting angry at frustrating situations is natural.

There is also a direct relationship between the way a business treats its employees and the way workers treat the animals in their care. Making sure that workers don't get exhausted by working long shifts, and giving them rewards for measurable outcomes, such as less bruising, injuries, and noise, can all ensure a better life for the creatures that feed us.

Cats are a big part of my life, so I read Grandin's chapter on felines with unusual concentration. I was a little dismayed, therefore, to discover that "animal behaviorists and ethologists don't know as much about cats and their emotions as we do about other domestic animals." I thought I knew my cats pretty well, but Grandin surprised me by having much of great interest to say about these superbly sensual, mysterious creatures. One bare fact that had hitherto escaped me is that there are two basic cat personalities—bold and shy—which are associated with coat color. Black cats, it turns out, are usually laid-back, while tortoiseshells are the typical "scaredy cats." I live with a black and a tortoiseshell cat (known respectively as the Captain and Bernadette), who could be models for this: the Captain is as solid as a rock, his aura of calm spreading far and wide, while Bernadette has been known to take fright at her own tail. Both, incidentally, had identical upbringings from kittenhood.

It turns out that coat color in cats may be associated with genetic changes that confer a defense against feline AIDS, and that in turn are linked to behavioral traits. In cities, where cat populations are high, the spread of feline AIDS (which is contracted through scratches and bites) is greatly facilitated. Black cats tend to predominate in such environments. Orange toms, found in certain studies to be more aggressive than black cats, die early because they spend too much time fighting (thereby exposing themselves to feline AIDS), while the laid-back black toms just lounge about, waiting for their turn to mate. There is so much in *Animals Make Us Human* that is thoughtful and deeply insightful that anyone who eats meat, or has a pet, would be well advised to read it.

Not all of the creatures we encounter are as readily studied as our pets, and in *The Hidden Life of Deer* Elizabeth Marshall Thomas takes us on an intimate journey into the lives of some of the more obscure. Despite the fact that deer are among the largest animals anyone is likely to see around their homes, they are so secretive that we know very little of them. Thomas, who lives in southern New Hampshire, began feeding the deer near her home in 2007, when a failure of the acorn crop led her to put out corn for the many wild creatures facing a lean time. Despite the admonitions of experts, she continued feeding the deer, and eventually came to be able to identify both individuals and deer families, the most frequently seen of which she named the Deltas. These she follows through the full cycle of the year, learning as much as she can about their travails and triumphs. But what strikes the reader so forcibly is the individual nature of deer lives—from those of the privileged deer with high social status to those lower down the totem pole whose life is one long struggle.

The Hidden Life of Deer is a wonderfully careful and honest account of one person's attempt to get to know the wildlife living around her. Not all goes smoothly, however, as food put out for one species is likely to attract another. Here's what happened to Thomas:

The full moon was so bright I thought I'd be able to see animals in the field if any were present. Hoping to catch a glimpse of the Deltas, I went to the kitchen door, a glass door, and cupped my hands beside my eyes to take a look. Surprisingly, I saw nothing at all—just total blackness. This seemed impossible. I looked out a nearby window and saw the whole moonlit scene of the fields and woods, every leaf, every grass blade. I tried again at the glass door, and again saw nothing. As I looked harder and longer, as my eyes got used to the solid black wall, I wondered if an unknown person for an unknown reason had draped a black blanket over our door. But then the blackness began to seem somewhat fuzzy, and I realized I was looking into fur.

You might think that finding yourself just a fraction of an inch from a bear in the middle of the night would be a terrifying experience, especially when, standing upright, your eyes only come up to the level of his ribs. Thomas, however, turned on the porch light, looked into the eyes of the creature just a foot away (which then ambled off), and proclaimed to herself that she'd "just had the greatest experience of my life." The bear, it turns out, was known to Thomas. Indeed she had saved its life. When it was young it had been hit by a truck near her house, severely damaging its right hind leg. The police had arrived to put the creature out of its misery, but Thomas had argued that it should be given a chance:

I told the men they shouldn't shoot him. The men said that the bear was suffering. They also said he was dangerous. He had to be shot, they insisted. I said I wouldn't let them. They told me to go home. I said, "I am home." They told me to go back to the house. I said I couldn't. The officer wondered aloud if I might have been drinking. . . . The officer had not yet taken out his pistol, but he started to cross the road. So before things could go any further, I scrambled up the bank to the bushes and the bear and told the officer to stay where he was. The men looked at each other. The officer said, "It's not your bear."

I said, "No, but it's my land, it's posted, and you'll need a search warrant to walk on it."

I must admit that at this point I began to fall in love (in an un-chimpanzee like way) with this feisty older lady.

Despite such humane actions, Thomas is not averse to hunting, but she believes that the practice needs to be well regulated, and that hunters need to be disciplined and expert. In search of knowledge about hunters, she accompanies her neighbor Don, who has Native American ancestry and hunts with a muzzle loader. He's such an expert hunter that for him the hunting season often lasts less than an hour. "Gaia put the will to hunt deep into our psyches—there's nothing like it," she concludes as she follows Don, stepping carefully, "eyes wide, ears open, hardly breathing . . . an experience of the utmost intensity."

Through the eyes of this extraordinary woman, a reader slowly loses view of "the wild" and instead begins to see individual creatures. It's as if we're granted access to an extended family that includes deer, bears, turkeys, and all the wild things of New England. *The Hidden Life of Deer* is a glorious achievement, giving new meaning to what it is both to be human and to be alive on this planet of wonders.

A Heroine in Defense of Nature

New York Review of Books, NOVEMBER 2012

On a Farther Shore: The Life and Legacy of Rachel Carson, William Souder, Crown, New York, 2012.

Late in the summer of 1962 President John F. Kennedy held a press conference that Rachel Carson's most recent biographer, William Souder, claims brought "something new" into the world. Amid weighty discussions of Supreme Court justices, Soviet intentions at the UN, and news of increased Soviet shipping to Cuba, the president fielded a rather unusual question about pesticide use and whether government agencies would look into it. He replied:

Yes, and I know that they already are. I think, particularly, of course, since Miss Carson's book. . . .

A few weeks later, as the Cuban missile crisis unfolded, *Silent Spring* began its climb to the top of the *New York Times* best-seller list. The long fight to control the use of pesticides had begun. There was a significant victory in 1972, when DDT, which had been found to pollute the atmosphere and soil while entering the food chain and helping to cause death by cancer, diabetes, and other diseases, was banned in the US. Other less dangerous pesticides continue to be used in great quantities in the US, often for the benefit of lawns and flower gardens. Significant health concerns, especially in children, result from such uses, prompting the province of Ontario, Canada, to ban these pesticides in 2009. In 2012 a review in British Columbia recommended tighter restrictions on their use, while a ban is under discussion in Manitoba. In developing countries the use of pesticides continues largely unregulated; around a million human victims still suffer acute poisoning annually.

September 2012 marks the fiftieth anniversary of the publication of *Silent Spring* (in his August press conference Kennedy was referring to advance extracts of the book published in *The New Yorker*). It's a fitting moment to review Carson's achievements, and Souder's new biography provides an excellent starting point. He argues that *Silent Spring* marks the birth of the "bitterly divisive" concept of environmentalism. Before it, environmental politics was characterized, he says, by the "gentle, optimistic proposition called 'conservation,'" which concerns the wise use of resources and has broad appeal across the political spectrum. Environmentalism, in contrast, can be politically polarizing because it involves a clash with vested interests. The president's remarks at his 1962 press conference are especially important for Souder because he believes they initiated a conflict within the US government, between those who sided with pesticide manufacturers such as Ciba and those concerned about the destructive uses of widespread aerial spraying of dangerous chemicals.

Arguably, the greatest casualty of this conflict was Rachel Carson herself. She would be falsely labeled a Communist by her enemies, and investigated by the FBI. The chemical industry and its allies spread lies about her—such as that her research was tainted, and that she wished to ban pesticides entirely—that would persist long after her untimely death in 1964. In fact, she advocated sensible uses of pesticides that would protect crops but not destroy animal life and poison the environment. Sadly, I still meet people whose assessment of *Silent Spring* and its author is influenced by these accounts, despite the fact that they're half a century old and entirely discredited.

Rachel Carson was the most unlikely of revolutionaries. A fifty-five-year-old spinster who lived in Silver Spring, Maryland, with her cat and adopted grandnephew at the time of *Silent Spring's* publication, she was not someone who habitually rocked the boat. Before her book became popular, she worked for years as a writer of government publications for the Fish and Wildlife Service of the Department of the Interior. In fact *Silent Spring* marked a sharp departure from her earlier books, which were best-selling, lyrical feats of nature writing—homages to the oceans and the seashore. Carson was, however, a meticulous researcher and careful writer, and despite the fact that she was not an expert on pesticides and their effects, *Silent Spring* contains few errors. Moreover, the timing of its publication was such that it reinforced fears that humanity's leaders were recklessly gambling with the fate of the earth.

When *Silent Spring* was published I was just seven years old and living in Australia, so my firsthand sense of the danger of the times is limited. But I'll never forget how my mother cried as she listened to the radio and heard of the assassination of President Kennedy in 1963. She saw him, I'm certain, as someone who was keeping her and her family safe in a world that seemed to be going mad. And it was not just the missile crisis. A series of nuclear tests was being conducted in Australia and other countries, and some scientists warned of the dangers. Most of the tests involved hydrogen bombs—the most devastating weapon ever invented—which were being exploded in the atmosphere with unpredictable and often terrifying results.

The very first of these devices was tested by the US on November 1, 1952, on the island of Elugelab in Micronesia. The resulting fireball was more than three miles wide, and it developed into a mushroom cloud twenty miles high and one hundred miles across. When the atmosphere cleared, observers saw a crater 160 feet deep and a mile across where a verdant tropical island had once stood. More powerful devices were soon wreaking destruction far in excess of expectations. In 1954 one such bomb, detonated in the Marshall Islands, produced an explosion two and a half times greater than predicted—the result of a lithium isotope that was thought to be inert but that amplified the reaction so much that the weapon was a thousand times more powerful than the one dropped on Hiroshima. President Eisenhower said that the scientists were "surprised and astonished" at the result, and were now rethinking the precautions needed for future tests.

The mass testing of nuclear weapons in the early 1960s had been unexpected. A moratorium on atmospheric nuclear testing had been agreed on in 1958, but in the summer of 1961 the Soviets abruptly recommenced their program. The US then resumed testing, and by 1962 a nuclear weapon was being exploded somewhere in the world every few days. By August 1963, when the moratorium was again put into effect, over fifty nuclear devices had been detonated in the atmosphere in a little over twelve months. The scale of the tests, and the extent of radioactive fallout they generated, were unprecedented. Soon, high levels of radioactivity were turning up in food, particularly the fish and milk that were being consumed by children across the US.

The earlier round of testing should have warned everyone of the grave dangers involved, for almost as soon as nuclear testing had begun, disturbing phenomena had been observed far from the test sites. In the early 1950s the Eastman Kodak Company in Rochester, New York, started seeing streaks and blips on its unexposed X-ray film. It turned out that the radiation that was spoiling the film was emanating from its cardboard packaging, which had been made in Iowa and Indiana. The manufacturers drew their water supply from rivers flowing out of the Midwest, which were hundreds of miles downwind of the Trinity nuclear test site in Nevada; yet they still carried sufficient radiation to contaminate the cardboard.

Evidence of widespread radioactive contamination was becoming public at about the same time that people were becoming aware of what a nuclear war might entail. At first the US government acted as if it could protect its citizens in the event of such a conflict. But in 1957 Sputnik raised the possibility that an attack on the US might eventually come from space, and by the 1960s the Soviet and American nuclear arsenals could be deployed, en masse, on long-range missiles. As Souder puts it:

Armageddon . . . could now be envisioned as two great shadows rising from the earth simultaneously and passing each other in opposite directions . . . curving toward the end of all things in a white-hot hell of thermonuclear doom.

These changes made America's civilian defenses appear puny indeed. As early as the late 1950s the nation's leaders were giving up on protecting civilians in the event of nuclear war. "You can't have this kind of war," President Eisenhower said. "There just aren't enough bulldozers to scrape the bodies off the streets." For American schoolchildren, this must have been a truly terrifying time, for they were regularly being drilled for the end of the world. Souder writes:

If a teacher suddenly yelled "Flash!" every kid over the age of five knew that meant to "duck and cover" by whirling to the floor and crouching beneath his or her desk, arms wrapped tightly around heads to wait patiently for the shock wave to arrive. There were also panic-inducing policies concerning who was to go where in the event there was a warning of an imminent attack. For many kids, this meant that if you lived close enough to school to run home in less than fifteen minutes you could do so—and presumably then at least die with Mom and Dad. Those who lived farther away were to stay put and let death visit them at school.

As the result of work done by farsighted citizens half a century ago, we're now in a position to assess the long-term effects of radioactive fallout on human health. In 1958 a group called the Greater St. Louis Citizens Committee for Nuclear Information began collecting baby teeth from children living in the area. A study completed more than half a century later, in 2010, showed that men who had died of cancer in middle age had more than twice the amount of the radioactive isotope strontium 90 in their baby teeth as those who were still alive. As with so many environmental toxins, the effects of radiation on human health plays out over decades.

Carson recognized an "exact and inescapable" parallel between radioactive fallout and pesticide poisoning, and there can be little doubt that the public was primed to hear her message because of its concerns about nuclear weapons. Indeed, Americans were already becoming aware that pesticides had the power to poison humans and their food chain in a manner similar to radiation. In 1959, a widespread scare over the use of cranberries erupted just days before Thanksgiving, the result of spraying them with a cancer-causing pesticide. Cranberries were withdrawn from sale.

Then, in 1961 devastating news of another chemical catastrophe was beginning to emerge from the UK. Thalidomide had been prescribed to alleviate morning sickness, and women who took it during a critical sixteen-day period of their pregnancy gave birth to children with devastating deformities of the limbs. The US had been spared the scourge by the dogged persistence of a lone scientist at the FDA, who had managed to stall Thalidomide's approval until the drug's full effects were discovered. The horrors of Thalidomide surely added to the unease many felt at the ever-growing application of new chemicals.

Rachel Carson had been born into a poor family in Pennsylvania in 1907, and it was only as a result of winning a $100 scholarship in a statewide competition that she received an education, attending the Pennsylvania College for Women. She had always been interested in biology and writing, and it was at PCW that she was given the opportunity to develop her skills. Her greatest influence there was her biology teacher, Professor Mary Skinker. "I have always wanted to write," Carson confided to a friend "but I don't have much imagination. Biology has given me something to write about."

It was while at college that Carson went on her first and seemingly only date with a young man, Bob Frye, who took her to the annual PCW prom. He didn't rate a mention in a letter Carson wrote to a friend about the event, but she had plenty to say, Souder adds, about Mary Skinker, whom Carson described as "a perfect knockout." An ethereal beauty, Skinker seems to have been a source of fascination for the girls at PCW, and Carson become infatuated with her. Such hero worship of a beautiful and elegant teacher by her female students is hardly unusual, and Souder, in my view, places excessive sexual emphasis on this episode of Carson's life.

Carson was devastated when Skinker announced that she'd be leaving PCW to complete her doctoral studies at the Marine Biological Laboratory at Woods Hole, Massachusetts. Missing her mentor, Carson happened to read Tennyson's "Locksley Hall," her eyes alighting on the line "For the mighty wind arises, roaring seaward, and I go." She decided then and there that she would follow Skinker to Woods Hole and devote her life to studies of the sea. After graduating from PCW she enrolled at Johns Hopkins, and with Skinker's help obtained a scholarship to study for two months at Woods Hole.

The experience was a mixed one, for although Carson loved studying marine life, she discovered that she wasn't suited to laboratory work. Her M.Sc. thesis was delivered a year late, in June 1932, after which she obtained her job at the US Bureau of Fisheries. This gave her the freedom to write articles and book reviews for magazines such as *The Atlantic*. By 1938 Carson had begun writing a book on the oceans. The project was well timed, for, as William Beebe descended into the ocean depths in his bathyscaphe, major discoveries were being made, and the public's interest in this strange realm seemed insatiable.

A regrettable error creeps into Souder's narrative when he discusses Carson's work on the ocean. He refers to the "abysmal" depths, in quotation marks, though just who he is quoting is unclear. The eternally dark, freezing, and highly pressurized waters Beebe explored may indeed seem abysmal to us, but they are in fact known as the abyssal depths; nor are soundings of the deep ocean commonly referred to as "abysmal soundings." These are not the biography's only faults: parts of it are disordered to the point of distraction. In particular, Souder should have told us more about the extent of the pesticide problem in America in the 1960s. But overall, he has produced a serviceable and timely biography.

When published in 1941 Carson's first book, *Under the Sea-Wind*, was hailed as "beautiful and unusual," the great Beebe himself saying that he "enjoyed every word." Yet sales did not reach 1,700 copies. The experience left Carson feeling that her publisher had not done enough to promote the book; she became a demanding author who in future would look into every aspect of a publisher's handling of her work. With the publication of her second book, *The Sea Around Us*, in 1950, this approach paid off. A poetical description of the oceans and the life they contain, it was an astonishing achievement that began with the formation of the earth and continued right through to the present age. *The New Yorker* had agreed to publish ten chapters in advance, and other chapters were taken by other magazines. When released, the book met near-universal acclaim and would set new records for the number of consecutive weeks it was listed at the top of the *New York Times* best-seller list. Its success gave *Under the Sea-Wind* new life, and by April 1952 Carson had two of the best-selling nonfiction books in America.

Her success sometimes put Carson in an awkward position. People expected her to be an intrepid underwater explorer, while in fact she had learned most of what she knew about the sea from books and other writings. But the financial success her writing brought would change her life. Previously, she had lived with her mother, and money worries were never far away. In 1953, however, she used her royalties to purchase a property on Southport Island, Maine, a wild, windswept place with only 250 residents.

There, in June 1953, she would meet Dorothy Freeman, who, with her husband, Stan, raced their yacht *Draftee* off the island every summer weekend. They were huge fans of *The Sea Around Us*, and when they heard that Carson was building a house on the island, Dorothy wrote her a welcoming letter. The trio struck it off right away and a few weeks later Carson led them on a late afternoon walk to catch the low tide. When they used a microscope to examined samples they had collected, Dorothy said that a "wonderful, beautiful, and unbelieveable . . . new world" had opened to her.

Dorothy Freeman left us a poignant picture of Rachel Carson at the height of her success. As Souder tells it:

Carson seemed "tiny" and often wore a wistful expression. It was hard to believe that so much knowledge resided in such an unimposing person. Dorothy sensed something sad in Carson, who seemed overwhelmed by her sudden prominence.

Carson's relationship with Dorothy Freeman was destined to heal some of that sadness. Each summer the Freemans and Carson would meet on Southport Island and spend their time in seaside rambles and other activities. In 1953 Carson would write to Dorothy:

And, as you must know in your heart, there is such a simple answer for all the "whys" that are sprinkled through your letters: . . . Why did I come to the Head that last night? Why? Because I love you! Now I could go on and tell you some of the reasons why I do, but that would take quite a while, and I think the simple fact covers everything.

While Carson's relationship with Dorothy was expressed passionately on paper, it was otherwise kept quiet. Carson would address her envelopes to "Mrs. Stanley Freeman," but in the letter itself referred to Dorothy as "Darling." Both worried that the "craziness" between them might be revealed, and so began writing two kinds of letters. One contained news and views that could be read by others, while the other, which was usually folded inside the general letter, was intensely personal.

The time that Rachel and Dorothy could spend together was limited, and their relationship seems not to have been physically sexual. Souder recounts a meeting between the two after Carson had addressed a group of scientists in Boston:

As Carson was leaving the hall after she finished, she was startled to find Dorothy waiting for her. Carson impulsively kissed her and whispered, "We didn't plan it this way, did we?" They went back to Carson's room at the Sheraton Hotel and sat on the bed for a languorous hour smiling at each other, unsure what came next.

Without doubt their relationship was deep and fulfilling, and it seems a little unfair of Souder to say that they didn't know "what came next." Perhaps there was no "next" for them: perhaps they were perfectly contented with things as they were. After all, the term "lovers" is one of infinite possibility.

Carson had longed her entire adult life to devote herself to writing. But now that she could afford to do so, she discovered that she was in a kind of prison. She had decided that her next book would be a sort of beachcomber's guide. Writing and rewriting, she became ever more dissatisfied with the project. Finally, in March 1955—a full three years behind schedule—she delivered the manuscript of *The Edge of the Sea* to her publishers. Carson noted that any book she wrote would look like a failure compared with *The Sea Around Us*. But in fact *The Edge of the Sea* achieved considerable success, rising to fourth place on the *New York Times* best-seller list.

Even as she wrote about the sea, the issue of pesticides seems never to have been far from Carson's mind. Nonetheless, she had difficulty in framing the work she wished to write, and was perhaps a little intimidated by the scale of the research involved. She told her publisher, Paul Brooks, that those who criticized the use of pesticides without fully understanding the science did more harm than good, and assured him that whatever she wrote would have the weight of evidence behind it. As the draft chapters began to arrive, Brooks realized just what this meant. A vast amount of hidden research supported the words the public would see.

As the writing went on, Carson's health began to deteriorate. Early in 1960 she suffered from a duodenal ulcer and pneumonia, followed by acute sinusitis. The discovery of two lumps in her left breast later that year seems not to have overly disturbed her; but when she awoke from surgery she was told that one of the tumors had been malignant, and a radical mastectomy had been performed. Perhaps anticipating a brief hospital stay, she had left her seven-year-old grandnephew, whom she cared for, at home. Proclaiming herself cured, she talked her way out of the hospital a week later, and got on with her life. Around a year later Carson discovered secondary tumors on her sternum and embarked on a course of radiation therapy. She would never be entirely well again.

Carson had settled on *Man Against the Earth* as the provisional title for her new book. It was Brooks who came up with *Silent Spring*—though initially as a title for the chapter on impacts of pesticides on birds, rather than for the whole work. Was there ever a more resonating book title? The possibility of a "silent spring" strikes so acutely at our sense of life, beauty, and nature's renewal that it chills us as deeply as a perpetual winter. And it frames beautifully the parable that opens the book—of small-town America, so secure and rich in wildlife, which is unaccountably devastated by a "rain of death."

The success of *Silent Spring* provoked an almost instant backlash from the chemical industry, and in the cold war environment of the time some of the worst smears that could be thrown, as Souder writes, were accusations of communism or socialism:

Subversive, antibusiness, Communist sympathizer, health nut, pacifist, and, of course, the coded insult "spinster." The attack . . . came from the chemical companies, agricultural interests, and the allies of both in government—the self-protective enclaves within what President Eisenhower had called the "military-industrial complex." Their fierce opposition to *Silent Spring* put Rachel Carson and everything she believed about the environment firmly on the left end of the political spectrum. And so two things— environmentalism and its adherents—were defined once and forever.

In fact Carson's position was more subtle and realistic than her critics allowed. Chemical control of insects was warranted in some cases, she wrote, especially for prevention of diseases, and all the more so "in time of natural disaster or of war or in situations of extreme poverty and deprivation. Then control of some sort becomes necessary."

Toward the end of 1962 Rachel Carson wrote to Dorothy Freeman that she felt that she never had any choice but to write *Silent Spring*, quoting Lincoln that "to sin by silence when they should protest makes cowards of men." She also told of indescribably heavy exhaustion, as if she'd come to the end of a long and difficult road. On April 14, 1964 Carson died, aged fifty-six.

Souder claims that today Rachel Carson is unknown to people under fifty, and certainly she is no longer the household name she was half a century ago. But she continues to be well known— indeed revered—by those interested in environmental protection, and *Silent Spring* remains in print. But in a world where humanity continues to struggle with industrial toxins, her legacy is far larger than that. It goes, I believe, to the heart of our relationship with nature.

After recently rereading *Silent Spring*, I discussed Carson with an Indian friend, who put a question to me: "What is more orderly, a jungle or a garden?" After a moment's thought the answer became obvious. Of course it is the jungle, where the invisible laws of ecology dictate the relative abundance of plants and animals, and where they occur. The very shape and position of every leaf abides by those eternal rules. Yet gardens, or cornfields, with their beguilingly simple symmetries, seem to most of us more ordered, and in the pursuit of that order we have spread environmental devastation far and wide, until they enter our own food chain. It was Carson who informed us of the cost of that false sense of order, just as she pointed to a future in which humans might fulfil their needs more wisely, by using their chemical ingenuity to support nature, not destroy it.

PART THREE

Climate
2006–2007

Lies about Power

Bulletin, DECEMBER 2006

Over the past few months the debate about climate change has moved to a higher level. Everyone now accepts the need to shift to a low emissions economy, and various interests are lobbying hard to promote their particular technology and to disparage competitors. So it's not surprising that some bald-faced lies are being told about our country's energy options. This is particularly unfortunate because climate change is now proceeding more rapidly than anyone thought possible, which means that some extremely difficult decisions will have to be made in the near future. Because such decisions may require economic sacrifices, it's best to have as clear a vision as possible of the energy options before us.

Let's look at three assumptions that underpin the Australian government's response to the climate crisis. They are that renewable sources of energy such as wind and solar cannot provide base-load electricity and thus have only a limited role to play; that funding and developing new technologies without imposing carbon taxes or trading schemes can avert catastrophic climate change; and that current funding of 'clean coal' (IGCC with geosequestration) initiatives is sufficient to develop the technology in time to avert climate chaos.

Prime Minister John Howard has stated repeatedly in recent weeks that renewable sources of energy, such as wind and solar, cannot provide base-load electricity; that is, electricity which is available twenty-four hours per day, seven days per week. Base load stands in contrast to 'peaking power', which is additional electricity required at times of high demand, such as on a hot summer afternoon when air conditioners are used. In Australia, our base load is principally provided by coal, while peaking load is provided by a variety of energy sources, including gas, wind and solar.

Howard's argument rests upon the observation that the wind doesn't always blow, nor the sun always shine, so power generation from wind and solar isn't continuous. But this is flawed thinking, and to see why let's start with wind. The technology used to generate electricity from wind has improved markedly in recent years, allowing modern wind turbines to control their voltage and react supportively with other electricity sources, which makes it easier for them to be integrated into the power grid. World-wide, wind turbines now provide 65,000 megawatts of power, with Germany alone having a little under 20,000 megawatts (the equivalent of twenty coal-fired power plants). Countries like Germany have considerable experience in funnelling wind power into their electricity grids, and they are using it to contribute to base-load electricity generation.

The reason that wind can contribute to base load is that while the wind may not blow constantly in any one place, it is usually blowing somewhere. Therefore, if wind farms are distributed widely enough, and are interconnected via the electricity grid, they can supply electricity continuously.

Part of the battle that wind power faces in realising its potential here is that Australia's electricity grid was developed to carry power generated by large, centralised coal-fired power plants. All too often, the large power lines that are the arteries of the grid are nowhere near the best wind provinces, making it difficult to feed significant wind power into the grid. And the way that coal-fired power plants operate makes the Australian electricity grid even more hostile to renewables such as wind. Forecasting generally allows several hours notice as to when the wind will blow, which in theory allows energy providers to shut off or fire up alternative sources of electricity. But coal-fired power plants take longer than this to switch on and off. South Australia's Playford plant, for example, requires two days to fire up and shut down. Because of this, it is in fact rarely shut down in favour of gas (South Australia also has Pelican Point, a gas-powered plant capable of providing base load) or wind. It's as if the old coal plant's very inefficiency protects it from competition from less polluting sources.

Some argue that wind is uneconomic because it requires a back-up power supply when the wind is not blowing, whereas coal does not. But in fact all sources of electricity require a back-up, which is known as 'fast reserve'. That's because all plants—including coal-fired ones—periodically 'trip out', and if the electricity grid is to remain stable there must be a back-up for this instantaneous loss of power.

Australia is a windy place. Indeed our country possesses some of the best wind resources in the world. In South Australia wind power is already contributing 8 per cent of the state's electricity, and if all projects currently on the books go ahead, in a few years it will be supplying 23 per cent. If the federal government were to get the carbon dioxide polluters to pay for their pollution, I suspect that wind could quickly supply up to 20 per cent of the nation's electricity, including significant base load. But this will not occur while coal is given primacy as our means of electricity generation.

Now let's turn to solar technologies to see if they can provide base-load power. Here the situation may seem hopeless, for no solar technology can provide power at night. Yet one of the oldest forms of solar power—solar hot water—can make an important contribution to base-load power generation. Keeping the nation's electric hot water systems running consumes a huge amount of base-load electricity. Indeed, in many Australian houses the hot water system consumes one-third to one-half of the household electricity! Now, imagine if governments banned the sale of electric hot water systems, and subsidised solar hot water—the amount of base-load electricity saved would be enormous, and households would save a great deal of money. All of this means that while existing solar energy options may not be able to generate base load in their own right, they can certainly replace the need for it on a very substantial scale.

One other important contribution to the base load debate is efficiency. Using electricity more efficiently is easy. Just think of replacing those old Edison light bulbs with compact fluoros, which are up to five times more efficient. Such reductions cut the requirement for base-load electricity enormously: indeed they are by far the easiest and most cost-effective way to tackle the problem posed by growing electricity demand.

Why is Australia a global dumping ground for inefficient electrical goods? And why, if they are so worried about increasing demand for base-load electricity, have Australian governments done nothing (or next to nothing) to increase our energy efficiency by mandating stringent efficiency targets for electrical goods?

It's important here also to realise that Howard's argument about base-load power is at best a half-truth. Australia's immediate requirement is for more peaking power, to service our ever-growing love affair with air conditioners. It's a lack of peaking load that threatens our cities with brownouts over summer. Solar panels, of course, provide peaking load in a very appropriate and cost-effective manner, which is why energy providers in places like South Australia are not opposing the feed-in law currently being canvassed by the Rann government. Many countries worldwide have similar laws, which mandate that electricity companies buy electricity from people who own solar panels. After all, it is far cheaper for the companies to do that than building new power plants that only operate for a few weeks each year.

The Howard government's disparagement of renewable energy is part of a pattern that includes championing of nuclear power. Nuclear power may well be part of our future energy mix, but in promoting this technology above others, John Howard is behaving more like the CEO of a company than a prime minister. After all, in a free-market democracy such as ours, it is the role of government to set up a fair and effective framework within which the market operates. And it should be the market that determines which industry or technology thrives and which does not. There is of course a role for government in fostering start-up technologies (such as clean coal, or as Denmark has done with wind), but governments that openly favour and tout one established industry or technology above others are compromising the market's ability to identify solutions to the climate crisis, and potentially damaging both our environment and free enterprise.

Let us now turn to 'clean coal', or IGCC with geosequestration as it is more properly known. The development of this technology has been a key plank—indeed *the* key plank—in Australia's response to the climate crisis. It is also a key initiative of the AP6—the alliance that was set up in early 2006 and widely touted as a rival to Kyoto. The main issue here is time, for we are in a race against time to stabilise our climate, and an undue emphasis on technologies that will not mature for some years or decades may cause us to lose that race. Naturally the rate at which new technologies can be developed is partly determined by how much is invested in their development.

It is widely accepted that we have as little as a decade left in which to act to stabilise our climate. This does not mean we have to create an entirely new energy economy in this time, but that we must have set a dramatically new trajectory, and have achieved substantial emissions reductions. In this context, it's important to recognise that clean coal power plants do not yet exist *anywhere* in the world. By placing our trust in them we are gambling our future on an unknown quantity.

Given the Australian and US governments' great trumpeting of clean coal and other low emissions technologies, you might expect that they have invested mightily in them. Sadly this is not the case. The amount spent by the US federal government on all energy research and development in 2005 was just US$3 billion, down from $7.7 billion in 1979. At the same time, spending on military research and development had reached $75 billion by 2005, up 260 per cent (inflation adjusted) on its 1979 level. The situation in Australia is little better.

In the 1990s the Howard government abolished the federally funded authority responsible for researching and developing renewable energy technologies, and as a result our country lost many researchers, including at least four leading experts in solar energy who took their technologies overseas. As of October 2006, the amount being invested by Australia in the development of new energy technologies is peanuts compared to what is required: half a billion dollars (a sum announced two years ago which only began to be allocated this year) and a mere $100 million to support clean coal initiatives through the AP6. Taking the long view, it's pretty clear that the Howard government's destruction of our energy R&D in the 1990s stymied our country on the eve of our battle to stabilise the climate, and has hardly begun to catch up in terms of funding.

As far as IGCC and geosequestration goes, the emerging facts reflect the US and Australia's poor record of funding. America's hopes are all focused on a project called Futuregen, which is a 285 megawatt IGCC and geosequestration power plant that was supposed to open in 2012. But delays, including indecision on its location, suggest it will not open on time. This means that there is now a good chance that the world's first clean coal power plant will be built in Germany.

The German power company UWE is well advanced in its planning for a 450 megawatt IGCC and geosequestration plant. Reflective of the costs of this new technology, the plant will only produce 360 megawatts of usable electricity, because much of the energy it produces is required to run the complex plant itself. This plant results from a €2 billion investment by UWE, and is on schedule to open in 2014.

As important as clean coal technology may prove in decades to come, this woefully slow progress is manifestly an inadequate response given that we have just a decade to set a new trajectory and achieve steep emissions reductions. For the Howard government to be discussing the inadequacies of renewable energy in terms of base load at times like this is madness. What we clearly need is for industry and government to be investing billions in deploying existing technologies as well as developing new ones. And this will only happen if carbon taxes and trading schemes are put in place.

With all these facts in hand, I think that the future for the coal industry is bleak. What will happen, for example, if in twelve to twenty-four months' time the rate of melt of the Arctic and Greenland ice continues at the rate we saw in 2005–06, or if it were to accelerate? Then the world will face an imminent crisis, and will have to implement tough measures that will have adverse impacts on coal. It's plausible, in such circumstances, that calls will increase for the closure of the most polluting coal-fired power plants long before they've repaid their investors. This may seem far-fetched, but consider that we'll be making choices about whether to abandon cities such as Amsterdam and Shanghai, or to walk away from a few billion dollars worth of stranded assets in old coal-fired power plants. These decisions will be made in an environment where people will well remember the disinformation that allowed the problem to become so critical in the first place.

Given this possibility, is it wise for Australians to be investing in new coal infrastructure, such as Queensland's Kogan Creek power plant, or new port facilities for exporting coal? To future generations, these investments may appear like the half-carved statues, abandoned before they were completed, which are found in quarries all over Easter Island. To avoid littering our landscape with such monuments to overweening pride and ignorance, Australians will need a new energy policy, or perhaps even a new government. And to keep our economy thriving, we will certainly need new technologies and industries to replace the declining role of coal. What, one wonders, is the Howard government doing to woo back all of those brilliant innovators it forced overseas in the 1990s?

Australian of the Year 2007

ACCEPTANCE SPEECH, JANUARY 2007

There is no greater honour for an Australian, I believe, than being nominated Australian of the Year. I'd like to thank everyone who thought me worthy of this great honour. But it comes with a deep obligation, for it speaks eloquently of the desire Australians have to address climate change.

We are, on a per capita basis, the worst greenhouse gas polluters in the world, and that's intolerable. I don't think any of us want our children asking in future why we didn't give our utmost when it was still possible to influence the course of events.

The best thing I can do for my country in this role is to continue to challenge, and work with, all Australians—and particularly our governments—to stabilise our climate. And, Prime Minister, I need to add that I will be passionately critical of delays or policies, by anyone, that I think wrong-headed.

Really, there is only one set of accounts that matters here— the one held in our atmosphere, for the amount of polluting

greenhouse gas it contains will profoundly affect our future. And it's on lowering the level of these gases that my sights are set. This is possible, but only if we all work together.

Thank you.

Saving Water and Energy

Age, FEBRUARY 2007

What is the best way to save water? You might be surprised to learn that turning off the light can help. It takes enormous quantities of water to generate Australia's electricity. That's because we're so dependent upon old-fashioned coal-fired power stations. For every megawatt of power they generate, they use two tonnes of water (and produce one to one and a half tonnes of CO_2 and lesser amounts of greenhouse gases such as methane and nitrous oxide).

So great is the power demand of a city such as Sydney that a fifth of that city's water needs is consumed by electricity generation. That water is used in steam generation and cooling. Nuclear power uses lots of water too. Those ominous, steaming towers that most of us associate with nuclear power plants are in fact cooling towers, and it is water vapour, not radiation, that they emit. Coal-fired power stations often have a lake of warm water nearby. That's the residue of water left from cooling the plant. In colder areas like Victoria's Gippsland, these warm ponds steam eerily in winter. Interestingly, legends of the bunyip abound in the same regions.

There are of course technologies that can generate electricity using less water than conventional coal, or no water at all. The newest two of Queensland's coal-fired power plants are air-cooled, so while they still generate greenhouse gases, they don't use precious water. Modern gas-fired power plants use just one tonne of water for each megawatt of electricity generated, and far less CO_2 than coal, so switching to them is a great step forward. But wind, solar and hydropower don't use *any* water at all, and none of these technologies generates greenhouse gases in the production of electricity. Some kinds of geothermal energy (such as that found in central Australia) also use no water, and generate no greenhouse gases. Hastening the uptake of any of these technologies can thus help address the water crisis.

There's no need to install solar panels to help save water (though that helps significantly). Buying a green energy option can do a great deal, and it's cheaper. It takes around one megawatt of power to provide electricity to 600 homes—by either switching to green power, or by saving electricity, there's lots you can do to save water.

All around Australia our water crisis is growing so desperate that the managers of the old-fashioned coal-fired clunkers are facing enormous problems in sourcing water. In New South Wales the dam levels have fallen so low that the remaining water has become too salty to be used to cool the power plants, so managers have to invest in a form of desalination. And everywhere coal-fired power plants are trying to source recycled water for cooling. This sounds like a great idea, but recycled water is valuable stuff, and will become increasingly valuable in the future. Should we really allow it to be used in such prodigious quantities to keep the old clunkers going?

The rising price of water, and the need to resort to technologies such as desalination, will surely drive up the price of the electricity generated using this technology, thereby making renewable forms of energy more competitive. This means that the old-fashioned coal-fired power plants are beginning to be caught in a pincer movement, which must inevitably hasten their decommissioning. Given the enormous problems Australia faces in managing water, and in combating climate change, it may be best to address the issue of their decommissioning now, rather than wait until the ever-drier heavens force the issue.

Tropical Forests

Age, APRIL 2007

Many people dismiss the idea that planting trees can play a role in combating climate change. It seems just too simple—even a little naive—and to some it implies that the industrial polluters will be let off the hook. Industry must play its part—by setting targets for emissions reductions and with carbon trading—but new scientific evidence indicates that tree planting also has an important role to play in combating climate change.

To better comprehend the power that tree planting has in controlling climate change, it's important to remember that trees are built out of CO_2. Many people think that trees somehow 'grow' from the soil at their base. In reality they grow from the air, drawing CO_2 out of the atmosphere to make bark, wood and leaves. Trees are in fact the most efficient 'machines' we have to draw CO_2 out of the atmosphere. Not all trees, however, have an equal capacity to cool our earth.

A recent study of the projected impacts of tree planting worldwide used computer models to determine where forests should be planted to maximise cooling. The study concluded that it is the tropical rainforests that have the greatest potential to cool our planet. That's because they grow very rapidly (thus drawing the maximum amount of CO_2 out of the air), and they transpire lots of moisture, thereby adding a further cooling effect. It is for these reasons that people interested in combating climate change are looking increasingly towards the tropical regions of our world for a solution to the climate crisis. Incidentally, planting trees in cooler regions was shown to be a bad idea. This is because a dark green tree canopy, which would replace winter snow, would reflect less sunlight back into space, thereby heating our planet. This effect is so strong that even when the CO_2 drawn out of the atmosphere by the trees is taken into account, the overall impact is greater warming in the medium term.

How much CO_2 could be drawn out of the atmosphere by replanting the tropical rainforests? Anyone who has travelled to the tropics will have seen the extensive grasslands and degraded forests that now exist there. These areas were once covered in verdant forest, which has been destroyed by human activity, and now the land lies under-utilised or abandoned. These broad acreages, however, are increasingly being eyed off by developers, who are keen to dispossess the villagers and plant crops such as oil palm and soybeans.

It is very difficult to say precisely how much carbon could be sequestered if the tropical forests and other habitats re-grew, but some estimates are as high as 200 gigatonnes of carbon. (Carbon, rather than CO_2, is typically what is measured in such studies.) This is about as much additional carbon as has been emitted by humans since 1800 (the beginning of the Industrial Revolution). We can think of this pollution as the burden that we in the developed world have placed on the atmosphere as a consequence of our prosperity. If we wish to stabilise the climate something must be done to reduce this pollution.

Anyone seeking to sequester carbon in tropical forests would need to work closely with the people who live there. Tropical farmers are some of the poorest people on the planet. Can we trade fairly with such people? I believe that we can. Imagine a world in which every primary school in the tropics has its own computer, and a solar panel to power it. The computer could download satellite images of the land controlled by the village, with an analysis of how the forest cover is increasing, and how much they will earn as a result. One of the most exciting aspects of this proposal is that it allows a direct cash (or cash-in-kind) transfer to the village, bypassing corrupt officials.

A trade in carbon is likely to be fairer than other kinds of trade because the crop (the growing forest) never leaves the hands of the farmers. They would control it in perpetuity. We would be purchasing our climate stability by growing those forests, and it takes tropical forests a century to mature. Thus, to be effective, the scheme would have to bring peace, stability and prosperity to the growers, otherwise the growing forests would be imperilled.

How much would such a scheme cost? The Stern report suggests the costs might be around $5 per tonne, while pilot programs (focusing on the regeneration of water catchments in the Philippines) are currently costing around $2 per tonne. This is cheap by any standard; nonetheless the problem is now so large that the developed world would need to start spending $10–15 billion per year to encourage reforestation on the necessary scale.

The re-growing of forests would have many additional benefits for those living in the tropics. The villagers will doubtless come to see their forests as a kind of carbon bank, from which they could withdraw as needed. They may, for example, fell trees to build a school, church or other building, and this should be permitted, but with a consequence: the payment for carbon sequestration would lower as a result. And of course the villagers would plant trees that benefit them—perhaps fruit and nut trees, or those that could feed livestock, providing a second benefit. Growing forests, and thus using the land, would also strengthen traditional land title, providing an added deterrent to the loggers and oil-palm planters.

The $200 million global forests initiative recently announced by the federal government could be used to kick-start such a scheme, and the APEC meeting, in Sydney in September, could be used to expand it to other countries. It is important to realise, however, that the initiative described above will be entirely wasted unless we greatly reduce our emissions of greenhouse gases.

In addition to a forests initiative we will need national emissions reduction targets, a carbon trading scheme, *and* we will need to ratify the Kyoto Protocol. The great damage we are doing by failing to ratify is becoming increasingly evident, with developing countries such as China and India increasingly citing our non-ratification as a justification for their own growing pollution.

Efforts aimed at growing tropical forests are an important tool in combating climate change, though they represent a one-off chance to reduce greenhouse gas pollution. So if we keep on emitting carbon pollution we will end up wasting this opportunity to purchase future climate security.

A New Adventure

On the 26 September 2005, after five years of research and writing, *The Weather Makers* was launched by Sigrid Thornton at the Australian Museum. This was to signal an entirely new career direction for me, but because the scientific evidence indicated that humanity had just a decade to avoid a dangerous climatic tipping point, I felt compelled to act sooner rather than later. It was a huge leap of faith.

By launch day only part of the work needed to create a successful book has been done, and a month-long national book tour lay ahead, including visits to larger regional centres. In Byron Bay nearly 1000 people gathered at the local high school, many of whom were already deeply committed to combating climate change. More unexpected, and gratifying, were the capacity crowds in Alice Springs and Darwin. While climate change was a long way from being a page-one issue in Australia in 2005, a discernible groundswell of concern was building.

Earlier that year I had committed to making a five-part documentary series about life along Australia's largest river system—the Murray–Darling. After a decade of scant rainfall, water levels were critically low, and in *Two Men in a Tinnie*, John Doyle and I wanted to show Australians, in an entertaining way, how serious the situation had become.

Circling over Roma in central Queensland as we began the series, John and I saw a devastated landscape. In a rush to beat Queensland's new land-clearing laws, bulldozers had flattened almost all remaining trees. Most of the land had been dry rainforest—a mixture of vines, bottle trees and other bush and tree species that survive in seasonally dry environments where there is protection from fire. The dry rainforest is one of Australia's most endangered ecosystems.

South-central Queensland, where the Darling originates, seems to be a wild frontier of water extraction. The Maranoa and Culgoa rivers were not flowing, and for many miles there was not even enough water to launch the boat. Everyone blames everyone else upstream for the lack of water. This appropriation of water and the drying climate mean that the floods that used to bring life to the river floodplain no longer arrive in the south.

John Doyle has an immensely popular radio and TV persona— Rampaging Roy Slaven—that became a passport to anywhere we wanted to go. Big Bob Buchan, the mayor of St George, sought him out and embraced him with the same enthusiasm as the Aboriginal elder sitting in front of the Brewarrina pub did. 'Hey, Roy! Brother, how ya going!' he shouted as we walked by. And John gave him the same warm welcome he gave the mayor.

There were eight of us on the shoot—all men. I admit to preferring the company of women, so the thought of spending two months in an all-male camp didn't initially appeal. After only a couple of weeks the fart jokes were already starting to get thick, as was the odour in the swag and boat. Things got really tough when we struck the Bogan flea. Just south of Bourke we inadvertently camped in a big patch. I had met the flea before, out along the Cooper, so suggested moving. It was late, though, and no one else seemed worried. 'John,' I said, pointing to a small, grey and innocent-looking burr. 'This is a Bogan flea, and if you get just one in any article of your clothing, you'll have to burn the lot!'

Despite my warning disaster befell when, during the hours of darkness, John felt the call of nature and wandered into a monstrously dense patch of the flea. His feet, hands and his underpants all picked up a dose, and next morning he was suspiciously restless in our tinnie, the *Bismarck*. John wouldn't discuss the matter, but I divined the cause and, mindful of the 1000 bumpy kilometres before us, urged the burning of the contaminated undies. But John claimed a shortage and refused to give them up for cremation. 'Well, mate, I hope you've got a scrotum of iron,' I replied grimly, hoping to prompt a last-minute surrender. It was only days later, downstream of Wentworth where the Darling joins the Murray River, that John's restlessness subsided.

Michael Heyward at Text Publishing had sold publishing rights to *The Weather Makers* in dozens of overseas territories, and my first foreign tour kicked off with an extraordinary event— speaking in London at St Paul's Cathedral, with Sir David Attenborough. I'm not normally nervous about public speaking, but this occasion really had me on edge and, as people poured in and the rector predicted an audience of around 2000, I must have shown it. Perhaps to calm my nerves, he offered to give me a brief tour of this haven of spirituality.

Directly below the podium I was to speak from is Nelson's tomb, while all around are striking memorials to the great and the good of London dating as far back as the seventeenth century. As we moved towards our seats we passed the epitaph of Christopher Wren, the architect who designed the cathedral. Carved into a simple stone block are the words: *Reader, if you seek his memorial look around you.*

Suddenly I'm hit with the full force of what I'm about to do, and the terrible responsibility we all bear in relation to climate change. Future generations will find our memorial all around them, too, either in a clean blue sky left to them by caring ancestors or an atmosphere so choked by greenhouse gases the Earth's climate system is thrown into chaos.

Sir David was running late. I had to speak first, and was so overwhelmed with emotion that it was hard to form the words. I bumbled on, talking about the Great Aerial Ocean, how easily polluted it is and how vital it is to all life when, to my great relief, Sir David appeared at my side. As he began to speak about the glories of the natural world, a tidal wave of love the likes of which I've never before experienced emanated from the audience. Most of the people there have been watching David since television first beamed into their homes—in some instances over sixty years ago. They've raised families and grown old alongside him and, in his unique, modest way, he has enriched their lives by revealing the wonders of nature. He is a hero to them all, but that night I'm sure that no one thought him a greater hero, or owed him a greater debt of gratitude than myself.

Britain has done more than any nation except perhaps Germany to reduce its emissions of greenhouse gases, yet almost all of this has been achieved through changed regulations to industry. While the public as a whole is aware of climate change, people have not been asked to take action themselves. The extent of work remaining to be done came home forcibly when I visited some amateur potters who had a large electric-fired kiln in their basement. I asked about its impact on their power bill, and they merrily replied, 'Oh, we don't need to worry about that. We're pensioners and our electricity bill is capped!'

A week later I was in the US, where climate change awareness seemed confined to cities on the east and west coasts. The book tour took me right across the country, and my days consisted of early starts for radio interviews—most involving talkback, a useful way to gauge the local mood—followed by a dash to the airport to a new city, print and television interviews, an evening talk and dinner. Away from the coasts the talkback was agony. Inevitably there was at least one caller per show who believed that the issue of climate change was fraudulent, and who would then loudly tell me that I was a fraud too. One TV station in Pittsburgh even refused to have me as a guest because the producer was a climate change sceptic. I concluded that the money that big oil and big coal have spent on deceiving people about climate change has certainly been effective here.

But hope can be found in the most surprising places. In Washington, researchers working for a junior senator approached me and I spent a few hours talking with them. I told them to stay in contact if I could help further. Only months later did I hear the senator's name again: Barack Obama. And I was heartened to learn that interest in the topic is bi-partisan—both Tom Daschle, a left-leaning Democrat, and James Woolsey, ex-Director of the CIA whose politics is proudly right wing, listened with interest and sought further information.

In Canada *The Weather Makers* had rocketed to the top of the bestseller lists. Canadians are avid readers, and serious books can influence the course of politics here. Just prior to my arrival in early 2006 a new government had been elected. Prime Minister Stephen Harper is a conservative from the oil-rich province of Alberta, and has been consistently scathing in his rebuttal of climate change, and of the Kyoto Protocol. At the time my tour started, Canada was chairing Kyoto's Council of Parties for some crucial meetings and the Harper government seemed hell-bent on destroying the entire process. Everywhere I spoke the audiences were huge—typically around 1000—and they showed deep embarrassment at Harper's approach to Kyoto.

As I toured British Columbia, Ontario and Manitoba, it became clear that local politics and reading books were not the only things influencing Canadians' attitude towards climate change; there was evidence of it happening all around them. In Toronto the Minister of Forests lamented the immense tracts being killed by the spruce bark beetle. The creature is breeding prolifically in this unusual warmer weather, causing the largest case of forest die-back ever documented. I was told the lumber men just can't fell the dead trees fast enough, then was asked what can be done. I could only reply that there may be no short-term fix, and that an effective global emissions program is needed for long-term control. And in Winnipeg a senior public servant told me that the number of pedestrians suing the city after falling over has skyrocketed. With the warmer conditions, the snow on the footpaths now melts and refreezes repeatedly over winter, creating treacherous ice.

In the far north the winter that had just passed was so brief and mild that the ice roads did not form properly. These roads traverse frozen lakes and rivers, and they provide the only land-based access to many remote communities. The length of time that they are safely navigable dictates what volume of goods can be transported, so they are critical for getting bulk supplies and equipment to towns and mines alike. While I was there, concern was expressed that some mines would be forced to curtail their activities, and that remote Inuit townships would face food and fuel shortages. The trucks supplying Inuit communities are often driven by young volunteers, and in 2006 two trucks and their drivers had simply vanished. Presumably the vehicles broke through thin ice as they crossed a poorly frozen lake or river. Commenting on the issue, one Inuit woman said that 'climate change was now killing our young men'.

I could see striking similarities with the Harper government and Australia's Howard government. But on returning home in May 2006, I found climate change had not yet become a priority issue—in fact, I felt as if I'd come back to Sleepy Hollow. A mood of scepticism still permeated much of the Australian media, and with the government denying there was a problem and the opposition giving it a low profile, an increasingly concerned public lacked the means to be heard nationally. As a result most action was local, with community groups, councils and state governments implementing initiatives. Even so, Australia's emissions were growing rapidly.

I had little time to reflect on what was happening at home before I was off on another three-week tour of the US. From Sarasota to Miami, right across Florida, the hurricane damage was widespread and deep. And so the modest audiences I attracted there puzzled me. The large number of retirees in Florida might have had something to do with it. Perhaps they think they won't be around to see the worst of climate change.

Things were very different in New Orleans. The driver who met me at the airport took me through the most severely affected districts of the city, but even months after the hurricane I could see that little had been done to clean up the devastation. Downtown, large buildings were still barely functioning hulks and a distinct whiff of decay remained in the air. I was late getting to one interview because most of the entrances to the skyscraper remained barricaded. The homeless used the lower levels, which reeked, and it was an eerie trip up to the studio from where I could look out over the ruined city. Yet even here I encountered callers who denied vehemently that climate change was real.

While in the US I received a phone call from Sir Richard Branson's office. He'd read *The Weather Makers* and wanted me to go to Necker Island, in the British Virgin Islands, to address the Virgin Group of companies on climate change. I thought this was important, and that Branson was committed to doing something about the issue. This was borne out a few weeks later when I heard he had decided to funnel all profits from his air and rail businesses towards fighting climate change and into developing non-polluting fuels.

After another brief respite at home I travelled to Europe, with a first stop in Helsinki, Finland. Although they value their forests and privileged lifestyle, the Finns as a whole seemed to know or care little about climate change, which is in stark contrast to Scandinavia. Sweden, for example, has declared that it will replace its oil exports with biofuels derived from its forests and croplands by 2025. But, despite their great forests, the Finns seemed hardly interested in such 'alternative' projects and are instead building new nuclear power plants to generate electricity. I reasoned that the debate is in its infancy here, and it's still largely the intellectual elites who understand the issue.

Denmark provided another surprise. This country of just 5 million has been disproportionately influential in the development of renewable energy technology, principally through fostering the modern wind-energy business. Today the wind industry employs more people than does the fishing industry. Remarkably, though, despite such a strong start with renewable energy, the general awareness of the scale and dangers of climate change appeared sketchy.

In the Netherlands, where the dangers of a rising ocean are understood at a deep, visceral level, the public sentiment, surprisingly, seemed to be characterised by a world-weariness. In the past the Dutch government had been very proactive on the issue, but by mid-2006 it was as if people just didn't want to hear about it. I asked Geert Mak, a Dutch historian, why this was so. 'Have a look at the Dutch newspapers for the 1930s,' he replied. 'In 1933 they were full of articles about the mortal danger of Nazism, but by 1938 they were all but silent on the topic. For us Dutch, sometimes threats become so great that the only way we cope is by turning away.' And sitting in an Amsterdam cafe, which was several metres below sea level, I could empathise with this singularly Dutch means of coping with a world that invites disaster.

Germany arguably leads the world in carbon emission reductions, and *The Weather Makers* had found a wide audience there. I got the sense that this economic giant is the engine driving much of the European response. My book had won the 2006 Corine O_2 Prize for Non-fiction and I travelled to Munich for the ceremony, which bizarrely turned out to be an hour-long live-to-air TV program. In the audience were activists from the town of Schoenau in the Black Forest, who had purchased their local electricity company and turned it green. I had written about them in *The Weather Makers*, so it was gratifying to meet and celebrate with them on this special occasion.

In France, Spain and Italy in 2006, climate change was an emerging issue. Spain, especially, has a proactive government, evident in the progress being made with solar power and biofuel programs. In Madrid I met one of Europe's leading experts in the production of ethanol from cellulose. This is different from the technology that turns corn into ethanol in the US, and is less harmful to the environment because it uses crop waste. It will eventually produce transport fuels from a wide variety of waste materials, and will not (as corn ethanol can) compromise global food security. I was heartened to learn that progress here had been so rapid and that commercial production may be just a few years off.

My daughter Emma came with me on this trip, and when my duties were finished we visited Venice. The side streets, canals and smaller plazas charmed me in a way no other place I've seen before has and, to my surprise, were relatively free of tourists. We discovered, however, that this unique and precious city is subject to flooding more than 200 times per year. Much is being done to protect it from encroaching waters but ultimately, unless climate change is addressed, the rising Adriatic must win the battle.

Around September 2006, while I was still in Europe, a huge shift in public sentiment towards climate change occurred. It was as clear a manifestation as one could wish for of the telekinetic nature of our global human society, for news from Australia, the US and even China confirmed that the shift was instantaneous, decisive, deep-rooted and from all quarters. The few political leaders who were still denying the existence of climate change—such as President George Bush and prime ministers John Howard and Stephen

Harper—seemed to have been caught off guard, and appeared dangerously isolated from public opinion.

I've tried to understand why this shift occurred when it did, and admit to being mystified. A number of factors doubtless influenced it, among them Al Gore's *An Inconvenient Truth* and Sir Nicholas Stern's report on the economics of climate change. But there had been movies and reports and books before. The fact that humanity—across many cultures, regions and languages—was receptive to the message at this particular time cannot be easily explained. Perhaps the situation is analogous to a stock market crash. Observers there can identify the underlying conditions that make a crash possible or even likely, but no one, except through good luck, is able to name the hour and day that a crash will occur.

I left Europe to return home via Africa. A mate had started an ecotourism venture in Kenya and had asked me to come along on a fourteen-day safari. I agreed, both because I wanted to help him with his conservation effort, and because I was keen to talk to the people living in northern Kenya, a land afflicted by drought. We saw lion, giraffe, elephant, and rarer creatures such as Grevy's zebra, which I was particularly taken with. It is the largest and most elegantly striped of all zebras, and is a kind of living fossil whose lineage goes back about three million years. A few years ago there were around 5000, but today only 2000 survive, in part because of east Africa's chronic low rainfall—a result of climate change.

At the remote camp of Sarara, north of Nairobi, I asked village elders about the drought. This is the homeland of the Samburu people, traditional cattle grazers who have developed an intricate system of subsistence. There was an air of despair about these dignified old men as they explained that the weather patterns and signs of rain are now so altered that their long experience is no longer useful in advising the youth where to lead the cattle. Apparently American food aid is all that's keeping many in the region from starvation.

That evening I learned of a most remarkable consequence of the drought. The Samburu circumcise their youths in grand ceremonies which are held every seven years or so, when enough cattle and other foods have accumulated to support such celebrations. Circumcision represents a transition to manhood, and until a youth has passed it he can't marry. But it's been fourteen years since a circumcision ceremony has been held here. There are now 40,000 uncircumcised young men, some in their late twenties, waiting their turn. All of the eligible young women, tired of waiting, have married older men (multiple wives are allowed), so there are no wives for the new initiates.

I could never have imagined that climate change would have such an effect on an entire society. But on reflection it makes perfect sense. Cultures such as the Samburu are intimately linked to their environment, so as these pressures increase it becomes more difficult to maintain long-held traditions.

My next trip was to Necker Island in the Caribbean. The place is a tropical paradise and we stayed in a pavilion perched above a reef. One morning my wife Alexandra and I had the chance to stroll one of Necker's more remote beaches. It was pure bliss to feel the warm sea between our toes, and on the sand I found a brightly coloured helmet shell the size of my head. As I bent to pick it up, reflecting on the joys of desert island beaches, I saw beside it a soggy one-hundred-dollar bill. Unsure whether my host likes to play jokes on his guests, I mentioned it to the island manager. He admitted that our splendid shell was an exceptional find, but the bill was less surprising. The Caribbean is a haunt of drug-runners, we were told, and occasionally both money and drugs are swept away by waves and tides. While on Necker, Richard Branson told me about a prize he was soon to propose. The Virgin Earth Challenge prize is worth US$25 million, and will be awarded to a project that can draw at least one gigatonne of carbon per year from the atmosphere.

I left Necker Island for Borneo. Before stepping down as Director of the South Australian Museum, I'd promised to lead a group on a trek up Mount Kinabalu in Sabah, so the plan was for ten days in the jungle. But on arriving I discovered that the great forests of Borneo had been turned into lumber and instead before me, as far as the eye could see, were oil palm plantations.

The local inhabitants along the river Dyak had a lot to say about climate change. Raimie is a thoughtful and intelligent wildlife guide at Sukau Rainforest Lodge and was adamant that the weather in Sabah has changed significantly. The dry season is now much hotter than it used to be, with days above 40° Celsius being common. He has also noticed that the heat arrives earlier in the dry season, and that the season lasts longer. One of the consequences of this shift is a greater prevalence of fire, and Raimie mentioned that a year earlier, in neighbouring Kalimantan, 1000 orang-utans burned to death—a significant proportion of the world's population. Such catastrophes are reported occasionally in the media, but the link with climate change is almost never made.

Back in Australia for Christmas, I discovered I was odds-on favourite to be the 2007 Australian of the Year. Aussies will bet on anything, it seems, though it was a strange feeling to have people back you like a horse in a race. My reckoning was that I'd been too outspoken about climate change to be an acceptable candidate to the powers that be.

To my astonishment, on 25 January I found myself standing on a podium with the prime minister, accepting a large blue glass rectangle on which was inscribed my name and 'Australian of the Year'. It was a hugely humbling moment and with it I felt a deep sense of obligation to my country. I prepared a short speech, and said:

> The best thing I can do for my country in this role is to continue to challenge, and work with, all Australians—and particularly our governments—to stabilise our climate. And, Prime Minister, I need to add that I will be passionately critical of delays or policies, by anyone, that I think wrong-headed.

There was a roar from the crowd. People later told me that the PM looked uncomfortable, but Mr Howard is nothing if not a gentleman and he spoke to me warmly after the event.

Receiving such an award led me to think on how best I could serve my country. It was clear that two things needed to be achieved. I felt that in this election year I should encourage both parties to put forward the best climate change policies they're capable of. To do this, though, Australians needed to understand the issue better, otherwise the policies would mean little. So for me 2007 was to be a year of public education and commentary on climate change policy, a task I resolved to do in as non-political and objective a manner as possible. Climate change is a global problem, too, so in order to do my best by my country I decided that, if the opportunity arose to do something outside Australia, I'd grasp that as well.

In March 2007 I was once again in the US, and Texas figured large on the agenda. The state felt big enough and diverse enough to be its own continent. First stop was Houston, where, on a day with high pollution levels from the local oil refineries, the locals say that they 'can smell the money'. I braced myself for the usual radio talkback sceptics, but they never arrived. Instead I found that things were changing.

Houston mayor Bill White was one of the few politicians brave enough to provide a quote for the US edition of *The Weather Makers*. He was second in charge of the Department of Energy under President Clinton, and he told me he was soon to source one-third of the city's power from wind. And it was his legal practice that put pressure on power company TXU, causing them to abandon plans for eleven coal-fired power plants in Texas.

Yet 'Big Bill' was not my only surprise in the Lone Star State. A man called Michael Zilkha had requested a meeting. His family once owned the largest patch of oil and gas in the Gulf of Mexico, but Zilkha and his father Selim sold up, invested in wind power and made a second fortune. Now they've moved into generating electricity from waste biomass. It hardly sounds as sexy as oil, but when Michael explained their vision to me I could sense a third fortune in the making. The 1.5 megawatt generators he's manufacturing are designed for use in timber mills, and the prototype was nearing completion. Its efficiency is an astonishing 75 per cent, and it runs on *sawdust*! Good news when you consider that there are 150 timber mills in the US, all remote from power whose electricity costs have risen from 2 to 8 per cent in the past couple of years.

An Iranian chauffeur drove me from Houston to Austin and I asked him what it was like to live in Texas. 'Americans keep complaining to me about their crazy president,' he said, 'but they never think about me. I've got two crazy presidents!' Austin is the most cultured city in Texas. It has been running electricity-efficiency programs for nearly thirty years and even though annual gains have been modest, they've now added up to a colossal achievement.

From Austin it was on to Lubbock. This town is located on the Plano Estucado, so called because it's so flat and featureless that the Spanish pioneers lost their way if they didn't put stakes in the ground to guide them. The main street struck me as odd, then I realised why: many of the businesses lining it are funeral parlours. When I mentioned this, my host mumbled something about 'the rapture' and 'transit lounges'. Lubbock is the buckle in America's Bible belt. At the lecture that evening a member of the audience politely asked about a petition, reputedly signed by 17,000 climate scientists, which disagrees with the findings of the Intergovernmental Panel on Climate Change (IPCC). I replied as politely as I could that there weren't that many credible climate scientists in existence, then wondered if the perfidy of the climate change deniers would ever cease.

On the plane from Seattle to Fairbanks, Alaska, were several people with fuzzy orange hair. I assumed it was a new trend. At my hotel there were a few more orange mopheads, and I went to bed baffled. Only in the morning did things become clear. The red noses started coming out at breakfast, and I learned that Fairbanks was host to the international clown convention. Over the next few days the hotel staff joined in the fun and it was impossible to get a straight answer about anything from anyone.

One of the great things about visiting Alaska was that the hotel staff would wake you if the northern lights put on a show. When the phone rang at 1.30 am on my first night I leaped out of bed expecting to hear of some disaster from Australia. I then looked out the window and saw an astonishing greenish, rippling light sweeping the northern horizon like a spotlit curtain. It lasted only a few minutes, but was hauntingly beautiful.

An expert team of researchers at the University of Alaska has been studying how the region's climate is changing, with a special focus on water. Much of Alaska is a polar desert, and Fairbanks itself receives only 25 centimetres of rain per year. Climate modelling now indicates that even if rainfall were to increase there would be less available water, because the soil will be warmer and the evaporation and transpiration of water by plants will have increased. The lead researcher admitted that past modelling had significantly underestimated the impact of these factors on water availability. Alaska's water problem is similar to that in Australia, where stream flow has declined more dramatically than rainfall as warming has tightened its grip.

On my return trip to Washington I addressed a rally calling for action on climate change. I couldn't have imagined anything like this taking place a year earlier. The Foundry United Methodist Church where we spoke is a historically famous venue for social protests, and it was packed to the rafters. Bill McKibben, who has been a climate change campaigner for years, spoke about how in 2006 he led a walk to the Capitol building in Vermont and persuaded the governor to act on the issue. He had started with a handful of supporters, but the group walked for five days, picking up people as they crossed the state, until they were 3000 strong. It wasn't science that changed the governor's mind, McKibben told the audience, but social activism. Listening in the crowd was Rocky Anderson, the mayor of Salt Lake City. He told me he was intending to step down as mayor to develop initiatives on climate policy. With so many passionate and capable people giving the issue everything they've got, I now feel that the US just has to succeed in turning the tide in this issue.

Back in Australia the drought situation had worsened, and public awareness of it and its link to climate change had never been higher. Prime Minister Howard declared himself a 'climate change realist', and established an inquiry into carbon trading. He still, however, refused to set a target for emission reductions, and his carbon trading scheme, if it eventuates, will start around 2012.

As I write, climate change has become a key 2007 election issue. The Labor Party has said that it will ratify the Kyoto Protocol and set a target of 60 per cent for emissions reductions by 2050. And so there appears to be a real choice at the ballot box. Whichever party wins, however, it will be difficult for them to turn things around, for the dinosaur industries and their lobbyists are now entrenched at every level of the bureaucracy.

In February 2007 I attended the inaugural meeting of the Prince Albert II of Monaco Foundation, established to combat climate change and to foster sustainability. I was intrigued by the initiative because Monaco was one of just four nations (the others being Lichtenstein, Australia and the US) that had not ratified the Kyoto Protocol by the time it came into existence in 2005. I asked Prince Albert about this and he explained that his father Prince Rainier had remained unconvinced there was a climate change problem. It was, Prince Albert felt, a generational thing, his father's generation being more sceptical of the issue than younger people.

One of the first things that Prince Albert did when he was able was to ratify the Kyoto treaty, and Lichtenstein soon followed.

He then set up his foundation, to which he personally donated nearly €10m. The prince's actions are a fine example of how a committed leader can influence events, and a sad reflection on how Australia and the US are left standing alone as the Bonnie and Clyde opponents of the Kyoto Protocol.

If there are tides in the affairs of men, looking back over these last two years I feel that I've been carried far from my starting point by a powerful rip. Nothing—not myself, the environment movement, the economy or the world—is the same today as it was just two short years ago. We have now begun to face up to the grave threat presented by climate change, and have become aware we are in a race against time. But there is hope, for we are slowly moving together to reduce the pollution that's causing the problem. By making such efforts to determine the composition of the atmosphere, humanity will, for the first time, be taking responsibility as a species for its impact on Earth. And by doing this we will no longer be one species among many that influences the planet; indeed, we will become the architects of our planet's climate system. This may change us forever, for being planetary engineers will profoundly alter the way we think about our environment and ourselves.

In the first half of 2007 the Danish government invited me to launch a progressive policy called the One Tonne Challenge, which encouraged Danes to reduce their carbon emissions by one tonne per year. After the presentation, I was introduced to Erik Rasmussen, CEO of a think tank called Monday Morning. The Danish government had just won the right to hold the Fifteenth Council of Parties meeting of the Kyoto Protocol. This will be held in Copenhagen in December 2009. Erik and I are aware that, in all probability, this meeting will be of critical importance in deciding the climatic future of humanity.

We talked about how previous meetings had failed, and we realised that if businesses undermine the process or remain neutral, governments were unlikely to do the hard work required. We decided to found an international council of businesses that would strongly urge governments to come to an agreement and allow humanity to avoid dangerous climate change.

The Copenhagen Climate Council was founded on 31 May 2007. As chair of this council, my focus for the next three years will be to ensure that it is as influential as it can possibly be, with practical measures and long-term plans on how best to combat climate change.

Sources & Suggested Further Reading

PART ONE: IN THE FIELD

WHO KILLED KIRLILPI?
'Some Aspects of the Ecology and Physiology of Australian
Xeromorphic Plants', N. C. W. Beadle, *Australian Journal of Science*
30, 1968, pp. 348–55.

'Firestick Farming', R. Jones, *Australian Natural History* 16, 1969,
pp. 224–28.

'How Old Is Zone Fat Lake George?', R. Wright, *Archaeology in
Oceania* 21, 1986, pp. 138–39.

EMPEROR, KING AND LITTLE PIG
'The mammals of the Solomon Islands, based upon the collections
made by Mr C. M. Woodford during his second expedition to
the archipelago', O. Thomas, *Proceedings of the Zoological Society*,
London, 1888, pp. 470–84.

*A naturalist among the head-hunters, being an account of 3 visits to the
Solomon Islands in the years 1886, 1887 and 1888*, C. M. Woodford,
George Philip & Son, London, 1890.

THE FALL AND RISE OF BULMER'S FRUIT BAT
Mammals of New Guinea, Tim Flannery, Robert Brown &
Associates, Carina, Queensland, 1990.

'*Aproteles bulmerae* (Chiroptera: Pteropodidae) of New Guinea Is
Not Extinct', D. Hyndman & J. I. Menzies, *Journal of Mammalogy*
61, 1980, pp. 159–60.

'Fossil and Subfossil Fruit Bats from the Mountains of New
Guinea', J. I. Menzies, *Australian Journal of Zoology* 2, 1975,
pp. 329–36.

IRIAN JAYA'S NEW TREE KANGAROO

Mammals of New Guinea, Tim Flannery, Robert Brown & Associates, Carina, Queensland, 1990.

Pygmies and Papuans, A. F. R. Wollaston, Smith, Edler & Co., London, 1912.

MEN OF THE FOREST

Tree Kangaroos: A Curious Natural History, Tim Flannery, Roger Martin, Peter Schouten and Alexandra Szalay, Reed, Chatswood, 1996.

PART TWO: ON OTHER PEOPLE'S WORDS

GLOW IN THE DARK

Brief Lives, John Aubrey, edited by Oliver Lawson Dick, Secker & Warburg, London, 1949.

'A History of Luminescence from the Earliest Times to 1900', E. N. Harvey, *Memoirs of the American Philosophical Society*, vol. 44 (APS, 1957.

The Chemistry of Phosphorus, John Emsley and Dennis Hall, Wiley, New York, 1976.

THE MNEME-ING OF LIFE

'A Note on the Origin of Memes/Mnemes', J. Laurent, *Journal of Memetics—Evolutionary Models of Information Transmission* 3, 1999.

The Selfish Gene, Richard Dawkins, Oxford University Press, Oxford, 1976.

The Case of the Midwife Toad, Arthur Koestler, Random House, New York, 1971.

The Life of the White Ant, Maurice Maeterlinck, Victor Wolfgang von Hagen and Alfred Sutro, George Allen & Unwin, London, 1927.

In the Australian Bush and on the Coast of the Coral Sea: Being the Experiences and Observations of a Naturalist in Australia, New Guinea and the Moluccas, Richard Semon, MacMillan & Co, London, 1899.

Die mnemischen Empfindungen, Richard Semon, William Engelmann, Leipzig, 1909.

The Mneme, Richard Semon, George Allen & Unwin, London, 1921.

WHO CAME FIRST?
Prehistory of the Americas 2nd edn, Stuart Fiedel, Cambridge University Press, Cambridge, 1993.

'Ambiguities in Direct Dating of Rock Surfaces Using Radiocarbon Measurements', W. Beck, D. J. Donahue, A. J. T. Jull & G. Burr, *Science* 280 (5372) 1998.

Ice Age People of North America: Environments, Origins, and Adaptations, Robson Bonnischen & Karen Turnmire (eds), Centre for the Study of First Americans, 1999. (New edition published by Texas A&M University Press, 2005.)

THE LADY, OR THE TIGER?
The Malay Archipelago, Alfred Russel Wallace, Macmillan & Co., London. (Reprinted Dover Publications, New York, 1962.)

THE HEART OF THE COUNTRY
Wildlife in America, Peter Matthiesen, Penguin, Harmondsworth, 1959.